Man with the Mantle

JAMES MCCONNELL

WHITEWELL METROPOLITAN TABERNACLE BELFAS

Man with the Mantle

JAMES MCCONNELL

Conversations with the Pastor about ministry

"Man with the Mantle" is based on the straight talking conversations with John McCreedy and the dedicated recordings of Trevor Bowron with the Pastor. Some events may not be as others recall them and opinion is their own. Both John and Trevor previously worked as part of the full-time staff at the Whitewell Metropolitan Tabernacle and are still committed members of the church. The concept was adapted and produced by Gayle Hunter, herself a lifelong friend of Whitewell and with the help of many, this labour of love has come to fruition. It was agreed to leave the conversations as candid as possible to allow the flow of read and give honour to whom many know as the greatest Evangelist of this generation - Pastor James McConnell.

Proceeds of this book are being donated to **The Shepherd's Academy** at Whitewell Metropolitan Tabernacle

THE MAN WITH THE MANTLE

Hardback ISBN: 978-0-9927219-5-4

Printed by W&G Baird
Front Cover Image by Norman Hobson
Design by N&EA Brown

Photography Stephen Hamilton, Press Eye, Belfast Telegraph, used by permission
Anniversary Recordings, WTP©2007 ©2015 www.whitewell.church

Published by GHPR Belfast

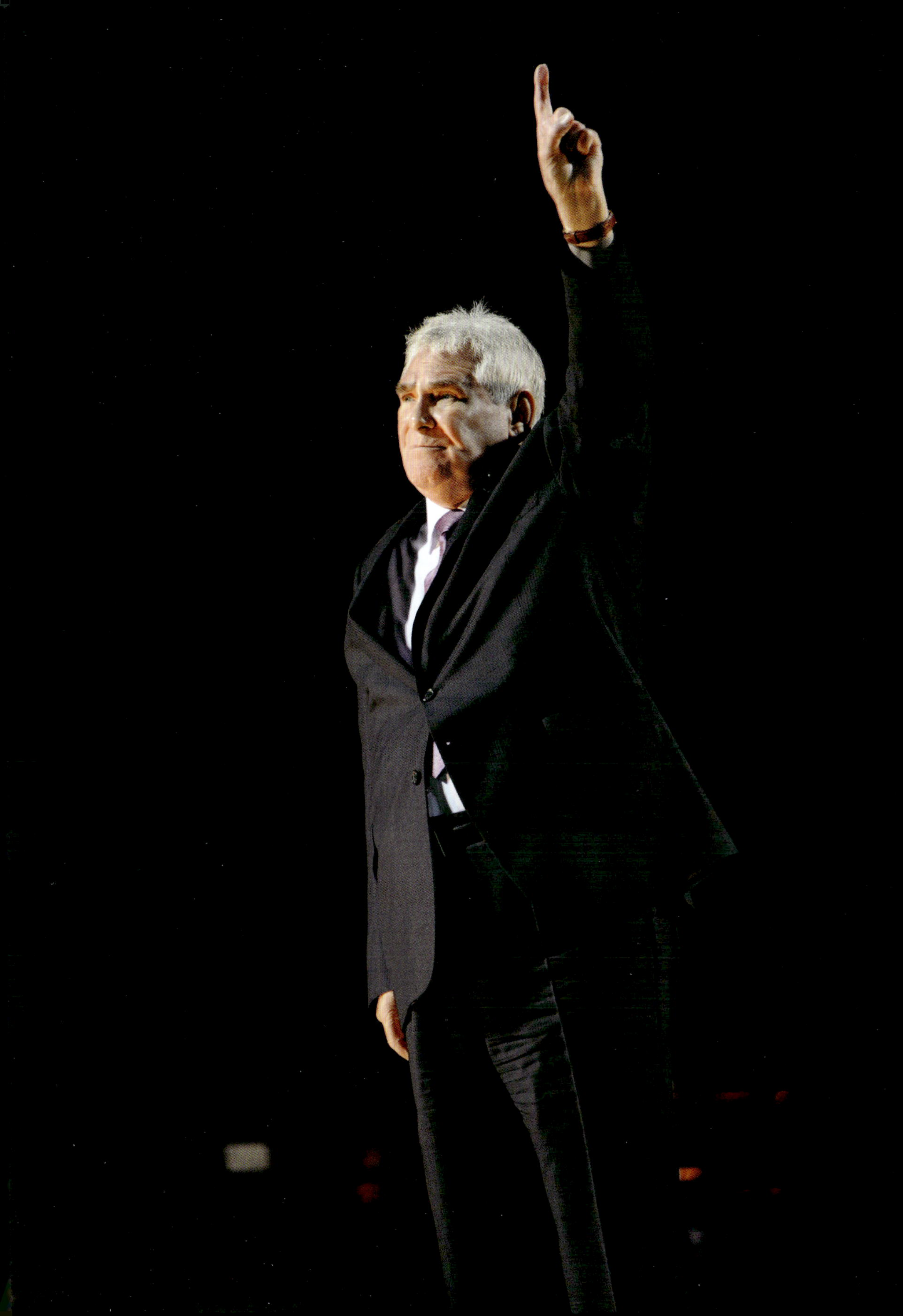

Foreword

RT Kendall

Although my meeting with Pastor James McConnell came late in my life (and his), it was one of those times you describe as "love at first sight."

I always knew I would like him.

It is a pity that I did not meet him during my years at Westminster Chapel but after my retirement. But when we met, noting his mischievous smile, we "hit it off" (as they say) immediately.

An orphan at a young age and raised by his grandfather, James McConnell did not wait long before preaching. He preached his first sermon at the age of 13. But, of course, he would not have known that he would end up preaching worldwide, including many visits to America back then. One of the things we had in common was that we saw ourselves as evangelists.

James McConnell was a legend in his own time. For that reason, I feel unworthy of writing this foreword. However, had the late Bob Gass been alive, also a prodigy in his time, Bob is the man who would have almost certainly written this tribute. When Bob interviewed me on his programme three years ago, I did not know he came to Christ under Pastor McConnell's ministry. Wow! What a testimony to Pastor McConnell's influence!

I remember having lunch with the Pastor for the first time. There were eight or ten around the table. They should not have seated us together! I'm ashamed to say I was almost entirely unaware of all those watching and trying to eavesdrop that would have enjoyed a word with him. I loved his cheeky sense of humour. But more than that, I was impressed by his shrewdness, perception, knowledge, and godly observations. He had promised to come to London during my many visits after that to see me. Both of us vowed we would make a particular time for each other. But sadly, that did not work out.

Nevertheless, I always let him know I was his senior! Although, of course, I was two years older than he, his longevity in Whitewell Metropolitan Tabernacle in Belfast - 1957 to 2014 (over fifty-seven years) - far outdistanced my time in London (only twenty-five years).

One of my faithful members in Westminster - Jonathan David - had a secret ambition for years that James McConnell and I would meet. At last, his dream was fulfilled, and Jonathan always came to hear me preach when I went to Whitewell. He always knew how well we could get on.

How right he was! I pray that when you read what follows in these pages, you will receive a blessing and that this book will be life-changing for you.

That would give Pastor McConnell great honour and delight.

RT Kendall

Senior Minister

Westminster Chapel (1977-2002).

Tribute

to Pastor James McConnell

Although Pastor McConnell would be 29 years my senior, I have grown up with him in many ways, and at the most influential moments of my own life, he was there personally. First, he dedicated me as an infant to the Lord, and it was under his gospel preaching I found the Saviour. Second, he was the vessel God used to speak to me prophetically, calling me to prepare for the ministry. Third, he married Donna and myself, ordained me to the ministry, and dedicated our three sons to the Lord when they were babies. Finally, he asked me to return to Whitewell to be his associate. I have had the privilege of being with him and watching him preach and lead and Pastor in good and bad times.

I am, therefore, immensely thrilled and hugely honoured to have been asked by Pastor McConnell to write this tribute for the book *'Man with The Mantle.'*

Everyone who has any interest in the Christian ministry needs to read this book. Of course, there are other books about Pastor McConnell's life and upbringing, but this book is different because it's about the ministry and how 'to do church.'

It's not about someone just telling us all how to do it. Instead, it's a record of the experiences of a man sent by God who rolled up his sleeves and did it himself.

Suppose you want to know how to plant a church and keep going when the going gets tough. Maybe you desire to know how to preach the Word to the same faces year after year and stay fresh and see them grow into a great church. Suppose you want to know how to win souls and teach the glorious truths of the Bible. This book is a must if you're growing a church and inspiring others to go and plant churches. There are over sixty years of experience to glean from these pages.

Genesis 6:4 tells us, "there were giants on the earth in those days," and indeed, James McConnell was a spiritual giant on Ulster's spiritual landscape for many years. I have had the privilege of walking with this giant, and it is my prayer that as you read this book, God will raise a new generation of giants in this island home of ours. Perhaps even you, dear reader, could be one of those giants.

I pray this book will have as wide a circulation as possible, and many will be inspired by this orphan boy who God clothed with His mantle for ministry.

God bless.

Pastor David A. Purse
Senior Pastor:
Whitwell Metropolitan Tabernacle
Belfast.

Introduction

Anyone who attended the Whitewell Metropolitan Tabernacle during the ministry of Pastor James McConnell will have been familiar with that special moment at the close of the service known as 'the appeal.' Here the Man with the Mantle came into his own. A soul winner of soul winners, James McConnell's passion for winning souls for the kingdom of God, was a rare gift indeed.

Where do you stand with God? Are you saved, Are you saved? You're either saved or you're not saved. If you're hoping your saved you're not saved! The bible says, "whom the son sets free is free indeed."

"Is there another one? Can I see another hand, Is that it then?"

These were all trademark sayings as he searched tirelessly for one more convert to Christ. While people may have sighed, shuffled, and even wanted home, the Pastor desired nothing other than one more conversion.

He began his ministry in the 1950s and had several locations before the opening of the Whitewell Metropolitan Tabernacle in 1994. His preaching attracted large audiences' and sparked a move of God not seen since the 1859 Welsh revival.

It's thought that the Welsh revival produced no fewer than 100,000 converts, a figure synonymous with the beginning of Pastor McConnell's ministry in 1957 until his retirement.

When it comes to 'soul-winning,' James McConnell's name is not out of place alongside evangelical greats like Smith Wigglesworth, William Branham, Dr Billy Graham, and Reinhard Bonnke, to name only a few. Indeed, he became known as The 'Billy Graham' of Northern Ireland.

He was a giant of our times and a man with an incredible passion for ministry.

Pastor McConnell lived a life with passion and drive. Even in his retirement, he remained as passionate as ever about the work of God. He was an outspoken and controversial character. His passion was pure, never afraid to defend his beliefs. The

Pastor was an outspoken and controversial character but always passionately defended his beliefs. While some disagreed with him, they never questioned his pure passion.

"Without passion, success and the ministry of soul-winning is impossible. You can't fake passion; it comes from within." **James McConnell**

Despite undergoing quadruple heart bypass surgery in 2011 – and suffering from prostate cancer, the Belfast-based preacher enjoyed a long and successful career for well over half a century as Senior Pastor of the Whitewell ministry.

James McConnell won countless souls to Christ during his heyday, regularly taught to thousands of people at weekends, and helped establish over 60 churches, including ministries in Europe and Africa. The Pastor enjoyed a long and successful career for well over a century despite undergoing serious heart surgery in 2011 and suffering prostrate cancer.

During this long period, what helped him stand out was that unique Mantle to win souls for Christ. So, what is a man with a mantle according to the scriptures?

A mantle from God is not just protective; it is a beautiful thing because it represents God's anointing.

We read how "Elisha took the Mantle of Elijah that fell from him **2 Kings 2:14** In other words, Elijah transferred his Mantle (the anointing) to Elisha. It also says of Gideon that the Spirit of the Lord came upon him. The Hebrew reads: "And the Spirit of the Lord put Gideon on like an overcoat."

The purpose of Elijah's visit was to save lives, not destroy them and his unusual mantle enabled him to do this. Thus, the name Elijah means Jehovah saves.

Similarly, people often commented on how the Pastor displayed a most unusual mantle - able to remain strong in the face of significant opposition during his ministry and yet help minister to and impact many souls simultaneously.

During a recent visit to Whitewell, Californian-based Pastor Harrison, the son of the well-known evangelist Bayless Conley, once said of Pastor McConnell, "I think Pastor James is the John Wayne of the religious world," that certainly made the Pastor chuckle! It is well known how Pastor McConnell addressed thousands of people from every background carrying the gospel's message to many venues province-wide during his controversial and dynamic calling. Thousands of believers in Northern Ireland and further afield found faith in God through his ministry.

However, the purpose of this book is not to retell Pastor McConnell's life story, of which there are several books. Instead the aim is in some way go towards leaving a legacy that reflects on the spokesman he was and the passion he exuded, making the book an enjoyable read for all

Christian ministers, politicians, government officials, business executives, people of prayer, those with a prophetic gift, people with a vision of any description, budding preachers, students, and most importantly, the youth of the next generation or even sportspeople can all hope to glean something from "Man with the Mantle".

The book is highly positive and uplifting but hard-hitting at times, something we expect from a straight-talking preacher like the Pastor.

Contents

WHITEWELL AN TABERNACLE BELFAST

Passion for Focus

We are what we repeatedly do. Excellence, then,
is not an act; but a habit.
Aristotle

1.

Football or Faith?

I would get up in the morning thinking about preaching and go to bed at night thinking about it. No matter where I went, preaching God's Word and Whitewell is all I considered. You ask how essential focus in the ministry is. Focus is everything and is critical in the church. If a minister isn't focused, then he's wasting his time. He will prove ineffective and build nothing, but if a minister stays focused and anointed, anything is possible. Keeping one's eye on the ball or 'the prize' as the apostle Paul put it is the key to succeeding in the ministry. **James McConnell**

For decades, Pastor James McConnell and the Metropolitan Tabernacle, Belfast, had enjoyed awesome experiences with God the Holy Spirit. Still, a massive testing time was approaching, not least in the Pastor's life - a trial that began with a significant illness.

Approaching 11 am on Sunday, July 17, 2011, and there was still no sign of Pastor James McConnell at his church. Whispering had started.

For almost 60 years, he'd scarcely been away from his ministerial post. His people knew that if the Pastor broke both his legs and arms, he would still find a way to reach his pulpit on Sunday.

Not surprisingly, many of his congregation grew restless and concerned by his striking absence. He'd rarely be later than 10:30 am, let alone not turning up at all. The Pastor loved God's House and, throughout his ministry, had always concerned himself with making sure people found the right seats.

It became an obsession with him!

He would always arrive immaculately dressed and never leave meeting and greeting to others. The call of God and the House of God was his responsibility, and he took it seriously.

On Sunday evenings, he would attend to car park duty, waving at those who arrived for the service and helping to park hundreds of cars, no matter the weather. Even the deacons couldn't keep him from what became a weekly ritual to greet his congregation. He just loved to welcome people and was conditioned to be in God's house early to make sure everything was in order, which brought great reassurance to his flock. The sight of the impeccably dressed Pastor suited and booted with a freshly ironed shirt and tie, rushing around the sanctuary long before the service commenced, became a familiar and comforting one for Whitewell members. The 'Shepherd' of the house was there, and all was well with the world!

On more than one occasion, one section of the vast auditorium seemed to bug the Pastor towards the top right-hand side. A curtain lay slightly open, causing him to race up the church, close it, grunt something under his breath, and then return to the church's middle section to shake hands with his arriving congregation.

"Great to see you" or "alright, wee darling" were just some of his usual greetings to the ladies, while the men were asked how their favourite soccer team performed the day before, or "It's time you got a haircut, son."

He was a straight talker, and the people loved that.

But, sadly, not this Sunday.

His absence was noticeable, and the longer it went on, the more concerned the flock of God became.

Questions like, "Where's the Pastor?" or "Have you seen 'the Bishop'?" were being asked from the pews. People looked at one another with alarm written all over their faces.

The head deacon, Derek McIlveen, usually up to speed on such matters, couldn't on this occasion provide any reassurances. For unknown to him and the rest of the Whitewell people, the 74-year-old Pastor had suffered a major heart attack at his home just before he was due to leave the house to conduct morning worship.

The Pastor was immediately rushed to Antrim Area Hospital and told he'd suffered "considerable damage" to his heart, requiring "quadruple heart bypass surgery" within the following six weeks.

During the most prolonged absence of his ministry, the then associate Pastor, David Purse, took charge, overseeing proceedings.

Of course, the incident threatened to spell the end of the Pastors' long and distinguished career. The writing was on the wall. All reports emerging from the hospital suggested this, and a lesser diagnosis would have finished most people.

But Pastor James McConnell is not most people!

He has a remarkable passion for God's work and his calling. During his former years of service to his congregation, he'd bounced back on numerous occasions from all sorts of setbacks. From betrayal, unfortunate business deals, cruel critics, personal mistakes, and multiple interruptions to the ministry during the period known in Ulster as "The Troubles," the Pastor has remained focused and bounced back from all of it.

And astonishingly, he would bounce back from this scare, too.

Within just a few weeks, he received a standing ovation when he attended his church. And, within a few months, he was resident again in his pulpit doing what he does best, preaching the Word of God and assuming his duties as the Senior Pastor of the Tabernacle. Of course, his ministry return was against every common-sense piece of advice, both from his family and the medical profession. But as far as the Pastor was concerned, if he was well enough to return to church, he was well enough to preach again! And so, remarkably, for many more months, even years afterwards, the Pastor continued to ply his trade at the Tabernacle, preaching copious amounts of Christ-centred sermons to the Whitewell people and further afield.

During this unexpected season of his life, he resembled something of a "new man," belying what he'd previously experienced when prostrate in the hospital close to "death's door." Even the doctor who treated Pastor McConnell viewed his "Lazarus-like recover as "highly remarkable" and "most unusual."

This assessment from an experienced consultant suggests that Pastor James McConnell is a unique individual, not just for his sustainability and bounce back-ability. He is also widely respected for his phenomenal focus on his calling - a principle he has retained from his earliest beginnings. In addition, his sheer focus and passion for ministry led to his determination to recover from an illness that would most likely have ended lesser individuals.

Hardly surprising, however, if one recalls his constant devotion to his profession. Despite receiving many invitations to preach in America years previously and worldwide during his career, he remained attached to his post at Whitewell for over half a century.

Of course, a small corner of North Belfast may not have proved appealing to some preachers, but it was always his number one priority, and he never deviated away from it. Even the lure of Africa, America and other far-flung destinations couldn't persuade the Pastor to leave his local calling. On the contrary, from the day God anointed him, although born in East Belfast, Pastor James McConnell was faithful to his North Belfast patch, and he's adamant it was never a struggle to retain such focus.

A surprising number of famous faces have hailed from the small district of North Belfast where he operated. For example, world-renowned actor and director Kenneth Branagh, broadcaster Eamonn Holmes, Ciaran Hinds from Game of Thrones, Mary McAleese, the eighth President of Ireland, Carl "The Jackal" Frampton, one of the most successful boxers in recent years, well-known BBC Broadcaster, Stephen Nolan, Anna Burns, winner of the Man Booker Prize, and comedian and actor Frank Carson all began their lives in this small pocket of Belfast.

And North Belfast was also the starting point of Pastor James McConnell's ministry - a place he never moved from for the rest of his days.

His only purpose was to preach Christ and lead men and women to God. Indeed, from the age of 13, when he preached his first sermon, James McConnell says he's never had any other desire than to perform God's work in the place of his appointed vocation and to see souls saved. He was born to preach to his fellow countrymen – and, preach to his nation, he has done. James McConnell is, and always has been, a born evangelist and soul winner!

His focus on souls came naturally with the anointing God had given him. So how vital is this sort of single-mindedness in the ministry to ultimately win souls and help change lives?

The Belfast born preacher should know!

His focus became stretched during his early days when choosing between football and his developing faith. But in the end, even the lure of a professional football career couldn't prevent Pastor McConnell from becoming a firebrand preacher of significant standing. He loved football but knew he would have to choose if he was faithful to God and the ministry, so he eventually followed God's lead.

He still recalls how local football scout, the legendary Jackie Milburn, formerly of Irish league club Linfield and Premiership giants Newcastle United, called at his house to try and persuade him to become a full-time professional, only to be informed by his wife Margaret that her husband was a Pastor and he was at the prayer meeting.

Of course, Milburn is remembered not just for his footballing talents but also for spotting the superstar Paul Gascoigne who won England fans' hearts when he burst into tears during the 1990 World Cup finals.

"Give James the victory over the football," prayed the women at the little Bible Pattern church attended by Pastor McConnell during his youth, and the rest is history. From that point on, there was only ever going to be one winner – the preaching of the gospel of Jesus Christ! Thus, a great evangelist was born, imploring the question; if God hadn't answered those prayers, would thousands of souls have been won to Christ over the next 60 plus years? For all we know, Northern Ireland might even have produced another soccer legend!

While a full-time professional soccer career didn't ultimately materialise, there's little doubt James McConnell went on to become a seasoned premiership performer in preaching terms and in his ministry. For just as it takes many attitudes and attributes to make it in top-class sport, church ministry requires unique qualities to succeed, particularly an ability to remain focused on the job at hand.

Before examining the subject of focus in more detail, our starting point in this book it is worth noting how Paul the apostle speaks in Philippians as "not having arrived;" It is a significant and influential observation from the apostle.

"Brethren, I count not myself to have apprehended (arrived) but this one thing I do, forgetting those things which are behind, and reaching forth unto those things which are before I press toward to mark of the high calling of God in Christ Jesus."
Philippians 3:13-14

Paul highlights in this passage how he was looking for a better resurrection and a better home, which, of course, was his ultimate focus – the arrival at his heavenly dwelling place. But he also displayed exceptional focus here on earth, having been transformed from a man who hated, persecuted, and even killed Christians to become one of the greatest preachers of the gospel. From persecuting Jesus and his people, he overcame continual persecution in his ministry to achieve the goal of spreading God's Word.

Paul outlines how Jesus Christ apprehended him (arrested him), or as one former Anglican minister put it: 'The risen Lord came down to the Damascus Road, hid behind a bush, and as Paul passed by, jumped out and grabbed him.' From that point on, Paul had no other desire or goal than to serve the Lord and remain focused on the cause of Christ. **James McConnell**

As he walked through the bushes in East Belfast's Ormeau Park as a little boy, a young, ambitious lad called James McConnell had a similar experience. To this day, he believes God jumped out from behind those bushes, grabbed his life, and used him for His glory and in so many other remarkable ways. He, too, felt a calling, burden and compulsion to carry out the cause of Christ that many of his peers did not. It became a life-lasting transformation!

Preaching is a privilege, not a right. It's a call and a vocation, not a career or occupation. Understanding this is what keeps a man humble and pliable in God's hand. Unfortunately, preaching is frequently opposed, and only the intense and focused will make it in the ministry. Suppose you realise that it is on God and Him alone that a preacher relies on, not oneself or one's ability. In that case, your focus will continue, but start assuming any success or progress is down to you, and the problems will soon appear. Heaven help a person in the pulpit who is content with their own ability or worse, who isn't supposed to be there. **James McConnell**

It's a humble approach that has served him well. Even at the height of his career, the Pastor would regularly rebuke himself before his congregation with the words, "This is not my work, but God's. We should give Him all the glory! Say, praise the Lord! Say it again and again and again! It became his trademark statement.

"Keep your eyes on the stars and your feet on the ground," said Theodore Roosevelt, something which sums up a man with a focus like an apostle Paul and many other dedicated servants of God – even a man like Pastor James McConnell!

Such men have cried tears for God's people and loved God's people more than their own lives. Yes, they could be stern when they had to, but the balance was in the balm and the willingness to keep restoring the broken. They understood their fallibility and significant limitations. The key to every successful ministry is a desire to forgive others as Christ has forgiven us.

Nothing will make one lose focus quicker than pride and loss of reality. The ministry is not about being high up and better than others but remaining down low so you can reach, teach, and bless others. The ministry shouldn't be seen as an opportunity to rise high when the point is to bow low and serve. It is called humility, and humility is the starting position of every minister. **James McConnell**

The great apostle didn't expect or feel entitled to neither be in the ministry nor claim to have achieved great things. Instead, he counted it an honour and a privilege to serve God and His people by stating, "I thank Jesus Christ our Lord, who hath enabled me, for that he considered me faithful, putting me into the ministry." **1 Timothy 1:12**

In the same way, Pastor James McConnell contends he remains indebted to God for counting him faithful, for putting him into a little local hall on the Whitewell Road back in 1957, then blowing upon it and expanding it, ultimately allowing him to see thousands converted to Christ. Here may well be the principal reason why he has shone brightly in the ministry; because right from the start, he understood the call of God and the importance of what it means to be focused!

The Pastor continued to preach long after his retirement, which verified his incredible focus and desire and habit for heavenly things. It's a testimony to his insatiable longing to rescue and restore the souls of humanity and an illustration of how focused he remains on his calling to the ministry.

Though various bouts of illness have hampered him since his retirement, especially before the publication of this book, he never made any secret of the fact he missed tremendously everyday ministry's thrill during his time as the Senior Pastor at Whitewell.

And he regularly confessed how he would give his eyeteeth to be doing again what once came so naturally to him while serving in the ministry full-time. Is such reminiscing surprising, given his care for one flock, one community, one profession, and one thing for over sixty years– the preaching of the gospel of the Lord Jesus Christ? He always said he dreaded retirement because he had only ever known one thing – preaching and ministering at his local church.

With no interest in holidays, hobbies like golf or gardening, or other activities, his biggest problem since retirement has been finding a replacement for full-time ministry. This gives rise to an interesting question. What do we do when "the party is over," so to speak? What, for example, replaces the primary gift and desire in our lives once it has all finished?

While working as a young broadcaster in the early nineties, I recall one of my colleagues looking across the desk at me and surprising me with the question: "What happens when all this has gone?"

More usually a cheerful character, he was in a philosophical mood, referring not only to the end of his busy daily schedule but also to the demise of any popularity to which he'd become accustomed. He was considering what happens in retirement and when the lights have gone out and the stage curtains are pulled over.

In the same way, what happens when God calls time on our routine is something all of us think about at some stage, not just this broadcaster or the Pastor.

Giving everything up and slinking away quietly into the background is a hard ask for any focused and driven individual, no matter their field.

The Pastor was born to preach, pray, and push souls towards God's eternal Kingdom – something he loved to do so. Even his early love for the game of football was no match for what ultimately became a remarkable and highly successful life in the pulpit. Nothing - absolutely nothing - compared to his desire to preach.

It was his sole focus and lifetime duty and all he ever yearned to do.

Brethren, I do not count myself to have apprehended; but one thing I do, forgetting those things which are behind and reaching forward to those things which are ahead, I press toward the mark for the high calling of God in Christ Jesus.

Philippians 3:13

2.

This One Thing

In terms of ministry, God is not just looking for faithfulness; he wants to give us success through vision, focus, and surrender, but this applies in the life of every Christian, of course, not just a requirement for God's ministers. Joshua wrote: *This book of the law shall not depart from thy mouth, but thou shalt meditate therein day and night, that thou mayest observe to do according to all that is written therein: for then thou shalt make thy way prosperous, and then thou shalt have good success. Success, therefore, is not just a modern word, but a God-word! It is a Bible promise.* **James McConnell**

Just as Paul was a man with a one-track mind for the gospel, to be a servant of God, the Pastor staunchly believes a minister, leader, or Christian person must possess this one-track mind to experience success within the ministry.

There was only one thing on the Apostle Paul's mind during his earthly ministry - preaching the Word of God. To the extent he remarked in his letter to the Corinthians, "For I determined not to know anything among you, save Jesus Christ, and him crucified." **2 Corinthians 2:2**

And again, in a letter to the Philippians, he wrote, "Yea doubtless, and I count all things but loss for the excellency of the knowledge of Christ Jesus my Lord: for whom I have suffered the loss of all things, and do count them but dung, that I may win Christ," **Philippians 3:8**

While it is essential not to neglect one's spouse, family, and friends, even daily responsibilities, the Pastor believes this "all or nothing" mentality is what God seeks in His ministers. He describes it as a "surrendered life" to the things of God, without which no ministry will last.

The scripture highlighted by the Pastor suggests that Joshua's success and the success of Paul came through extreme focus, the reading, and the preaching of God's Word. The Pastor has also endeavoured to excel by regularly serving up 'fresh bread' to his congregation. A man with a one-track mind, ministering to his people on Monday evening, Wednesday evening, and Friday evening and twice on a Sunday, not to mention the many other preaching engagements he accepted on what he describes as not "Whitewell nights."

The lure of additional money or more attractive opportunities was never a factor in his life. If anything, it was unthinkable for him to leave his parish to prosper elsewhere, a trend that seems to be on the rise today.

This passion for focusing on his patch appears to be archaic compared with so many ministers currently. While today some Pastors might appear more relaxed about leaving their pulpits and people for weeks and going on the road, this wasn't the practice when the Pastor was in office. Some are touring in America, while others are busy with external commitments and activities and so they don't always spend time focusing on their primary calling - their local flock. It is, of course, sometimes necessary and beneficial for a preacher to accept invitations elsewhere. Still, Pastor McConnell believes continual absence from a church pulpit is a backward step, not just detrimental to the ministry of God's people, but ultimately soul-destroying for ministers and their flock.

If a minister continually leaves his flock, he states that he is not interested in them. He is too big for them and is not interested in their needs. If God calls you to a particular work, stay there, and build something, don't keep leaving, or you will never produce anything worthwhile. More than this, you will lose clout and relationship with your people, and they will look to other more faithful servants for help and counsel, even less talented ones. People are not interested in their Pastor's ability as much as in the heart of their Pastor. Preaching a blinder of a sermon is useless if there is no real heart for the people from the preacher at the end of it. On the other hand, if a congregation has the heart of its Pastor, amazing things will occur in that same ministry. Of course, I do not mean telling the community that their Pastor loves them; instead, the Pastor must demonstrate this love by action. **James McConnell**

In the parable of the talents and the pounds, the Lord Jesus said: "Well done thou good and faithful servant: thou hast been faithful over a few things, I will make you ruler over many things: enter into the joy of thy Lord. **Matthew 25:21**

Of course, the apostle Paul narrowed it down even further, adding those thought-provoking words, "This one thing I do." In other words, Paul said the secret of a focused life is rather than attempting to do a collection of things; all be it with good intentions, preachers and leaders thrive better by concentrating on their primary gift (the one thing they do best), and God will anoint it.

Paul's 'one thing' was preaching God's Word in the place God had called him, but such a focus is becoming less frequent today. A multitude of distractions is causing many sincere preachers to lose their way, especially on social media.

In that legendary epic movie Ben Hur, the Roman Tribune, Messala, who oppressed the people of God, was asked, "How do you fight an idea? He answered: "with another idea."

A successful Christian leader will undoubtedly receive many opportunities to embrace a different idea to the one God first initiated, yet will not lose God's original vision favouring another view or counterfeit alternative.

I have had many counterfeit ideas put my way by the enemy over the years, and most of them involved leaving my primary calling from God. If it appeals to your ego or flesh, it is usually not from God. I remember telling a young Pastor who was continually departing his church to preach in America that he needed to be with his people more. I told him: 'If you want your work to build, you must be there to oversee the project. How can the work grow when you are away for weeks, and is this neglect fair to your people? Although it was a rebuke, the young Pastor not only accepted my advice but rectified the situation, and his church has gone from strength to strength since. He now focuses on making a success of the work God called him to do. **James McConnell**

During his ministry at Whitewell, the Pastor was himself so committed to the work of God; the people used to joke about how he would even attend the "Jumble Sales."

He loved his calling and church, possessing a genuine passion for his vineyard and people. The Pastor would drive each day a few short miles to the church and back again, rarely going anywhere else unless it was to a hospital or private visitation. Such was his lack of interest in anything other than his preaching and congregation; even his family members would pick his suits at the local shopping centre and bring them home for him to try on.

In a similar capacity, the former Arsenal manager, Arsene Wenger, once admitted that he could only drive to and from the Arsenal training ground despite being in London for many years due to his focus on the club. He confessed to rarely venturing outside of a 10-mile radius from he arrived from France in 1996 because, as he put it, "I don't need to."

Wenger would appear on interviews on Match of the Day with the same Arsenal-coloured tie every week. He was a man content with his station and lot in life. He loved his club and life's calling and had a one-track mind! No wonder he went on to produce an unbeaten team in 2003/04 known as the "Invincibles!" not suffering a defeat the entire season.

Here too, was Pastor McConnell, focused and seemingly invincible!

In those days, while other preachers were flying worldwide every week, receiving large financial gifts and praises, the Pastor quietly built a megachurch in his backyard. He would drive the short distance of 4 miles or 11 minutes from his home to the church every day to take care of the church business.

Pastor James McConnell loved the work at Whitewell, and the evidence was his consistent focus. It wasn't only the Pastor who became focused, however. Like many great leaders before him, he taught his team to do likewise. From Pastors, to the other faithful deacons, musicians, and volunteers, the Whitewell ministry was a well-oiled machine full of driven and dedicated individuals.

I recall learning just how focused the Pastor was in those days when I showed up slightly later than usual. I was on my way to a service and had stopped on the M3 motorway to assist a lady whose car had broken down. It was approaching twenty minutes to eight when my phone rang. I thought it was the breakdown company, but instead, it was the Pastor.

"Is everything alright, John? He asked. Yes, why do you ask? I replied.

You're usually at the church by now. I was checking to see if all is okay."

I was stunned. I was just ten minutes later than usual, yet the Pastor had noticed my absence. He missed nothing when he was in the zone. His focus was incredible!

He would telephone the youth Pastor on a Saturday to inform him he was coming to the Saturday youth night, even though everyone knew the Pastor's ID had expired years ago! He would frequently pop his head in at tea gatherings and additional church activities, only to be asked why he was there!

He felt it was "half-hearted" not to want to be at his pulpit or involved with every facet of the work. But, nevertheless, he believed and still does that when a minister has a love and vision for his people, he sticks with his people, even to the detriment of himself.

As for taking holidays, he recalls having only one break in 1958 in the South of Ireland with his wife Margaret, and the next one didn't happen until 20 years later when the church elders demanded he finally took time off.

Is this a good thing?

Is it even a God thing?

Doesn't the Bible tell us that rest is a gift, even a command from God?

Isn't it proper to focus on spending time in God's presence and resting for a while?

Sometimes, but not consistently, the Pastor believed taking a break may be highly effective and recommended, especially in the ministry, but the Pastor wouldn't have done things any other way than in a hands-on capacity. His work ethic was second to none and, while it wouldn't suit everyone, it served him. Not everyone could cope with this schedule, however. God anoints people in different ways, and many ministers end up "burnt out" over the years, trying to copy another's work ethic. The good advice is: never try to run on someone else's treadmill – it could end up killing you!

For example, Pastor McConnell's idea of holidays was when he occasionally took up an invitation to go to another country to preach the Word. Yet, it was always for a short period before quickly returning to preach again to his home flock.

Retired, he flew to California in August 2018 and taught for five days at the Cottonwood Church, where no fewer than 350 people accepted Christ. Later that same year, he held outreaches in Ethiopia, and again over 300 souls came to Christ.

You may take the man out of preaching, even the ministry, but never preaching or the church out of the man! It's all so different from the great clergy member Alexander Whyte, one of Pastor McConnell's boyhood heroes who advocated as much as three months break from the ministry each year. Although the Pastor is a big fan of Whyte, having regularly read his commentaries and even enjoyed and expounded many of them for years, he strongly disagrees with Whyte about holidays.

Alexander Whyte believed a break gave you refreshment and rest, which I think is a lot of nonsense! The more you seek the Lord and preach the Word, the sharper you become. Whyte thought you came back fresh from holidays, but I believe a minister is only original when the anointing of God is on them. It's like the old saying "practice makes perfect," and the more a minister is in the zone, the sharper and more effective he becomes. **James McConnell**

He highlights this by emphasising how some Pastors return from holiday needing another one.

Some Pastors returning from holidays look like death warmed up and would scare you into heaven. All joking aside, I am genuinely concerned about this matter. Many of God's servants today seem more interested in holidays than souls. Years ago, God's servants laboured for the Lord from day to day. While I believe ministers of the gospel should be well rewarded and looked after if they are faithful to their people, if they are not, then the opposite is true. It is fair game to ask why they are receiving large salaries for little effort and contribution. Undoubtedly, we are living in days when shepherds have become less interested in the people and the people less interested in the things of God. I believe it's a generation where many people seek intelligent ministry and even politically correct ministry; I call it tripe ministry! One of the fruits of a loyal servant of God is faithfulness to the Word of God and His flock. A servant of God preaches the words of God, not the words of men, and he labours faithfully in the field God has placed him. **James McConnell**

Straight talking, but then Pastor James McConnell has never been afraid to give his opinion. His outspokenness is legendary at Whitewell and beyond. No one is safe, not even a room full of fellow ministers at a UK-based minister's conference about the ministry's call. For example, the Pastor received an invitation to the platform to provide what the attendees assumed would be a heartening encouragement message. Having listened to their previous discussions for most of the morning session, when he finally arrived at the podium, the Pastor shocked the watching clergy by stating: "some of you would be better getting a job."

It caused many aspiring ministers to slink down into their seats and fast for three weeks afterward, while, of course, the Pastor wasn't on most of the clergy Christmas card lists later that same year either!

As for Pastor McConnell's desire to always be present and focused on what he excelled at - preaching the Word - he recalls how it was both a love for the work and a duty to God and the people which compelled him to remain faithful, and this is what drove him on. Rightly or wrongly, he believed that if he weren't personally present, the work would suffer and decrease.

Again, this approach contrasts today, where there appears to be more emphasis on strategy and delegation. Besides, he was the leader, and that's what he would do.

He always remained concerned about the church at Whitewell, an organisation he's proud to have built from scratch. It's a view that may seem obsessive, even outdated. Still, in being faithful and reliable, the Pastor has become a role model for many of his congregation and young ministers who see him as someone who led his flock by example. People didn't always agree with him, but he won their respect and the respect of those outside his church.

It's commendable remaining interested and determined for a few years, of course, but how about 60 plus years? As RT Kendall eluded to in the foreword of this book, how does one stay so incredibly focused for so long, especially when the tide is often against you? The Pastor contends we don't learn this sort of focus from books or even college courses; instead, it is the calling of God. It's a built-in gift God has placed within all his chosen ministers. But, unfortunately, it is also evidence of something which appears to be in decline - "work ethic."

In our modern Laodicea period, we live in what is a lukewarm generation.

The Bible has already predicted, ours is a society that appears to fit God into its schedule rather than fitting in with God's purpose. Is there a solution to apathy and detachment?

Lots of sincere believers are asking this question today.

If there is a decline in dedication, can our current generation shine and become focused again, in the same way the Pastor has managed to remain resolute for decades?

The answer from the Pastor is encouraging - yes!

Regardless of an apparent "falling away" predicted in Thessalonians' and Timothy, he believes we can solve humanity's selfishness and greed. It is God's unselfish and focused generals who will lead the way.

No matter how bleak it seems, remember Jesus told the Laodicea generation to: 'Buy of me gold tried in the fire, that thou mayest be rich and white raiment that thou mayest be clothed and that the shame of thy nakedness do not appear, and anoint thy eyes with eyesalve, that thou mayest see.' **Revelation 3:18**

I am convinced that here is the key to building a great ministry, even today to "buy gold from God Almighty" and listen and apply the words of Jesus, the secret of all great leaders of focus. Or, as Jesus told his followers, "But seek ye first the kingdom of God, and his righteousness; and all these things shall be added unto you" . In other words, keep doing the one thing God has called you to do, keep focused, and success will become your experience. **James McConnell**

If leaders do not remain focused on the big picture and stay focused on the plan,
everyone else eventually wanders off

Alastair Campbell

3.

The Influence of Focused Spiritual Giants

There are many 'barking dogs' in the ministry, and a Pastor needs to learn how to ignore them. Their bark is often worse than their bite so keep going and pay no attention to them. If God has set you a task, finish it, and move on to the next one. I have failed many times, but God has covered my mistakes, and I thank Him for it. Here is an essential key to a minister or leader staying focused. If a person refuses to forgive others or themselves, if they refuse to get up and go on, if they dwell on things from the past, it will prevent them from carrying out God's purpose for their lives. A leader eventually must come into the presence of God and confess their failures and sins and cry for the blood of Jesus to cleanse them. No matter how great the level of hurt and disappointment, a minister must get up and go on regardless if they wish to survive; there's nothing else to it. Start all over again if you must but keep going forward, and God will help you get there. **James McConnell**

At the height of his ministry, the Pastor never doubted that he was overseeing an end-time, Laodicean work. Instead, he resolutely followed the one-track mind example of the great apostle Paul and other Biblical giants and, in doing so, beat the trend.

This approach worked consistently, but he insists it was also down to the help and guidance of four spiritual giants who significantly influenced his ability to focus: James Forsythe, Gordon Magee, Bill Drost, and the great Elim preacher, George Jeffreys, profoundly impacted the Pastor's ministry.

Every young protégé requires a mentor or mentors, and James McConnell was no exception. Indeed, God gave him focused men and faithful men who were highly gifted in their own right. Men he believes were at the top of their trade with few equals.

Forsythe cared for him as a boy and even taught him how to worship. Although Forsythe would often begin in the wrong key, the presence of God soon followed, and heaven came down. As the years continued, the Pastor appeared to possess the same curious gift. Regularly he began singing in the wrong key, making it a nightmare for his musicians, but when the presence of God followed, no one cared. The anointing of God would flow, and all was forgiven because everything required spiritually had arrived.

Meanwhile, Gordon Magee, who the Pastor considers one of the leading Bible exponents of his generation, taught him how to preach. It was crucial in the shaping of James McConnell, the preacher. He continued, Gordon Magee is still one of the greatest preachers of the scriptures he has ever encountered, including being above many of our modern-day TV evangelists. As the Pastor treated me one day to a tour of his library, he said of Magee: "You would have loved him, John. He was strong but full of grace and a better preacher you couldn't hope to find."

I could see the love and admiration in his eyes for a man who had so strongly shaped his life.

He continued: *If Gordon Magee were alive today, he would still be in the world's top ten preachers. He was genuinely prolific. When I was a boy, I remember saying that I would be a better preacher than you, Gordon, causing him to burst out laughing. But on his death bed, he told me I was a better preacher than him, to which I said, 'no, I'll never be a better preacher than you, Gordon, but I thank God for you and for the impact you've had upon my life. He was an extraordinary man.* **James McConnell**

The Pastor would later dedicate a room at his church to the late Gordon Magee, a unique library and prayer room named the Magee Room, which has been well used by the Whitewell congregation, especially on Friday evenings at their weekend prayer meeting. Heaven came down at some of those meetings, which the Whitewell people still talk about today.

Pastor McConnell admits he spent his early days studying Magee's ministry's mastery, observing how he communicated with his people and the way he delivered his message. Looking back, he willingly admits he patterned his style and ministry on those early sermons. Nevertheless, it is essential to point out that he wasn't trying to be someone else because he has always believed in God's anointing for his own life. While preachers can learn from other preachers, the successful ones have distinctive gifts from God and do not need to imitate their role models indefinitely.

Magee would later pay Pastor McConnell the ultimate compliment describing him as– "The Man with the Mantle." It was approval Magee would not have given out lightly.

But the Pastor maintains another man divinely appeared in his life at just the right time. He recalls how after visiting the renowned preacher Smith Wigglesworth, Bill Drost, an influential evangelist, and a man, the Pastor claims "transformed South America with the gospel," impacted him considerably, and taught him a great lesson about focus, an experience he's never forgotten.

One day, as Drost approached the home of Wigglesworth carrying two daily newspapers, Wigglesworth rebuked him sharply, saying: "Get rid of those papers, young man, they are of the devil!'"

Wigglesworth then laid hands on Drost and told him he would preach in South America and win many souls. Significantly, nothing of great note took place for the first two years, and Drost even considered returning until he sought God one final time. Just as well for something remarkable followed. Sitting beside a riverbank, Drost noticed some leaves catching fire. Immediately, God told him to go back and preach again, and that night, 20 souls gave their hearts to Jesus. The Pastor recalls that Bill Drost had baptised no fewer than 39,000 people within three months of the experience. The following year over 60,000 people crammed into a local football stadium where many of them received salvation.

That powerful Christ encounter and extensive outreach had a massive sway on Pastor McConnell's mindset for ministry. It would appear Drost's experiences were a dress rehearsal for what would materialise later in the Pastor's life.

The young McConnell began to dream of such days himself. Those experiences with Bill Drost formed Pastor McConnell's thinking and reminded him never to give up until God moved. Fast forward decades, and his dream became a reality. Since those early learning days, he's preached in numerous football stadiums and auditoriums throughout his home country of Ireland. These outreaches included seven times at the King's Hall, Belfast, and seven times at the Ulster Hall in Belfast and trips to Dublin in Ireland. In addition, he has ministered at virtually every football stadium in Northern Ireland, including the national stadium at Windsor Park, making him the original Carl Frampton of the preaching world!

Pastor McConnell held over eighty tent missions during his sixty years and preached at various local leisure centres and schools across the province, a list far too vast to include in this chapter. *See Outreach list in Part Nine Passion for Souls*

So, when Drost eventually returned from South America, it became a role reversal time. Instead of Pastor McConnell watching Gordon Magee as a young man, Drost began to study James McConnell. Having witnessed him expertly dividing the Word of truth for several months, he asked: "Is this young man for real?"

Drost monitored the young James for two years and then invited the Pastor and his wife Margaret and Linda and Julie, their two young daughters, to Malaga in Spain. It was only a matter of time before Pastor McConnell accompanied Bill Drost to Colombia. One after the other, men and women flocked to the altar to get saved at those sensational services.

I remember one preaching engagement in Colombia when over 3,000 people came to Christ in one week. The anointing was dripping off Drost, and you would have needed to be there to understand just how amazing he was. We talk about anointed preachers today, but this was a man at the peak of his preaching career. When he spoke, the hairs on the back of your neck stood up. It was a life-changing occurrence. He was like Billy Graham and Reinhard Bonnke all rolled into one, a genuinely fantastic preacher of the gospel. **James McConnell**

The next spiritual giant of foremost influence was George Jeffreys, who Pastor McConnell greatly admired during his youth. However, many familiar with his story may not know that Jeffreys laid hands on the great German evangelist Reinhard Bonnke. Thousands of people came to Christ through Bonnke's ministry following that experience. The 75-year-old evangelist shared at a US conference how he met George Jeffreys, a minister of healing in the UK. At the time, Jeffreys was in his 70s, and Bonnke was a 22-year-old Bible college student. "He prayed for God's blessing for me, and I picked up a mantle," claimed Bonnke. Notice the language of Bonnke – he picked up a mantle!

All great soul-winners are familiar with God's mantle. A man with a mantle is a man with a mission to see 'hell empty and heaven full'. - a quote made famous by the late great Reinhard Bonnke at all his international gospel crusades.

Meanwhile, Jeffrey's progress is significant because, in his early days, Pastor McConnell confesses he felt seriously tempted to follow him even to the extent of joining his gospel campaigns. But, having been to hear his great role model one night in the

Wellington Hall, Belfast, he felt a pair of hands putting his arms into his jacket and hugging him when reaching for his coat. It was Jeffreys encouraging the young James. That began a meaningful relationship between the two as Jeffreys took a genuine interest in the boy preacher, McConnell.

Jeffreys, who filled the Royal Albert Hall in London numerous times with a ministry of signs and wonders, and founded the Elim Pentecostal Church, even began writing from England to the elders of the church young James attended to check on his well being. He had learned he was an orphan, and Jeffreys soon became a steadying influence in his life. Pastor McConnell describes Jeffreys as "a spiritual giant like the great Baptist preacher, Charles Haddon Spurgeon," and says, "He is undoubtedly the forgotten man of the Pentecostal movement."

Notwithstanding, James McConnell managed to resist those powerful desires to follow his boyhood hero, remaining focused instead on what God called him to do in an out-of-the-way part of Belfast. Here again, was the evidence of his great purposefulness and determination to stay committed to the call of God for his own life. After all, on reflection, had James McConnell followed George Jeffreys, God may never have used him to build Whitewell and impact the province of Northern Ireland and further afield in the way he did. Yet, in Almighty God's providence, the countless conversions under his ministry prove that the Pastor made the right decision to stay focused on his calling to a small group of people in North Belfast. That's not to say he didn't consider the idea of "what might have been," but in obedience to the will of God for his life, he continued to move forward and put personal glory aside. This extraordinary focus has proved most useful, especially when "learning from previous mistakes," as he puts it.

Total focus is only possible when a person looks forward and refuses to look back at difficult situations in life, failure, or what might have been. Moving on is the key to focused energy and ministry and staying true to your vision, or at least the vision God has given to you. Saying no to good things to wait faithfully for God's best is always the challenge for any minister and not dwelling on what might have been. Every Pastor or leader passes up opportunities and makes mistakes, but the great ones keep going forward anyway and don't look back. Lot's wife looked around, and it cost her everything. The old saying is true: "There's no use crying over spilled milk!" **James McConnell**

He maintains he never regretted not following Jeffreys, preferring to keep his eyes on his calling. So here is another attribute required of all aspiring ministers – the ability to leave certain things behind. But, of course, such an approach can be easier said than done! And it can also profoundly impact a leader's people.

But, as a British journalist and former political aide to Tony Blair, Alastair Campbell once wrote: "If leaders do not remain focused on the big picture, and stay focused on the plan, everyone else eventually wanders off."

All leaders are tempted to respond to their critics or "cry over spilled milk," as the Pastor puts it, but the truly great ones keep their eye on the prize and press on regardless. When Nehemiah rebuilt Jerusalem's broken walls, he frequently received opportunities to take his eyes off his vision and defend himself from false accusations. Still, he refused to answer any of them. Instead, he proved a man with a purpose, direction, and vision.

Nehemiah refused to come down from his building project or look back. He was too busy fulfilling God's purpose for his life! So instead, he stayed true to the vision. Like Noah, he ignored the critics and finished the work.

In this respect, Pastor McConnell now believes, on numerous occasions, having looked back with at least some regret at opportunities lost. However, he believes if every minister of the gospel accepts their failures and losses and stays true to the vision God has given them, even ignoring the critics and the injustices, and trust God to propel them forward again, they can recover from unfortunate and challenging experiences.

The great Winston Churchill remarked: "You will never reach your destination if you stop and throw stones at every dog that barks." The Pastor likes this quote.

There are many in the ministry, and a Pastor needs to learn how to ignore them. Their bark is often worse than their bite so keep going and pay no attention to them. If God has set you a task, finish it, and move on to the next one. I have failed many times, but God has covered my mistakes, and I thank Him for it. Here is an essential key to a minister or leader staying focused. If a person refuses to forgive others or themselves, if they refuse to get up and go on, if they dwell on things from the past, it will prevent them from carrying out God's purpose for their lives. A leader eventually must come into the presence of God and confess their failures and sins and cry for the blood of Jesus to cleanse them. No matter how great the level of hurt and disappointment, a minister must get up and go on regardless if they wish to survive; there's nothing else to it. Start all over again if you must but keep going forward, and God will help you get there. **James McConnell**

Here is precisely what the apostle taught. He encouraged the believer to "press on" to obtain the prize.

Similarly, like a high-powered sports star during his ministry, the Pastor was driven on by the prospect of a prize and gold medal at the end - a crown of life from Jesus His Saviour. It may seem unusual to mix excellence, passion, and determination in Christian ministry with excellence, passion, and commitment in sport. Still, you require extraordinary passion to be the best in the sport, and to excel in Christian ministry requires similar zeal and determination. Even the great apostle Paul described the Christian life using athletic metaphors. His goal was to: "win the 'race' of the Christian life, not to lose it." **Philippians 3:12-14**

Floyd Mayweather Jnr, the undefeated boxing Super Featherweight champion of the world, a man whose boxing record is second to none, is quoted as saying, "Tough times don't last, but tough people do."

People today blame this thing and that thing, but show me a church, and I'll show you its leader. If the leader is faithful and focused, the church will thrive. Paul gave his young protégée Timothy such advice. Paul says, 'Don't look back, Timothy. Let the wind blow on you and go through with God. Press on and forget your past successes, as well as the failures. Looking back at success is just as toxic as dwelling on defeat. Resting on one's laurels is like sleeping on wreaths. A minister must keep going no matter what. It's the only way to succeed. **James McConnell**

The apostle Paul had a steely determination like this. He endured unimaginable hindrance and pain, which included shipwrecks, stoning, and imprisonment. Yet, he was able to still declare in his letter to the Philippians those great words: "This one thing I do, forgetting those things which are behind and reaching forth unto those things which are before, I press toward the mark the prize of the high calling of God in Christ Jesus." **Philippians 3:13-14**

In a generation where people are easily offended, and widespread political correctness exists, a determination like Paul's is required to succeed. It is essential to continue reaching forth with no shortage of courage and boldness, especially when others seek to derail what God has purposed in his people's lives. Even though the wind is in your face and the tide of public opinion is firmly against you, it's vital to keep pressing on. Keep repeating what God instructed you to do with supreme determination. **James McConnell**

As we close the opening section on Focus, the reader may be intrigued about the most focused person the Pastor has encountered.

Is it a fellow minister, a sports star, a biblical hero, or a TV evangelist?

Following his lifetime of focus, who most impressed him in this respect? Interestingly, it isn't Paul the apostle, James Forsythe, Gordon Magee or Bill Drost, or even his boyhood hero George Jeffreys. Instead, he acknowledges a much superior person.

The person with the most incredible focus ever must be the Lord Jesus Christ. When it comes to His vision, we are all out of our depth. It was fantastic. When the hour and time had come for Jesus to go to the cross, the Bible says, "He steadfastly set his face as a flint to go to Jerusalem." The Greek New Testament reads: 'fixed his face.' Here is the perfect picture of every focused servant of God – a fixing of their faces towards the call of God. Regardless of the waiting punishment and precarious state, He found Himself in, Jesus never lost sight of his cause – the souls of men and women. Without this one-track mind, nothing will work. If your mind is on other things, nothing is achievable. Your people will suffer, and your ministry will die. Your people will lose interest quickly. My advice to all aspiring ministers and people of any vision is to fix your face on Jesus: 'Get focused on His calling and then, only then, start building. Passion for and finding one's focus is the starting point for every Christian minister and anyone with big dreams in their chosen field. **James McConnell**

Passion for Preaching

Study to show thyself approved unto God, a workman that needeth not to be ashamed, rightly dividing the word of truth.

2 Timothy 2:15

4.

Preacher not Politician

The days of watering down the gospel with 'easy religion' must cease and be replaced by the gospel's clear-cut message. However, crucial to point out is that it is not "foolish preaching," which wins people to God, but as Paul said, "the foolishness of preaching," - the idea of men and women coming and sitting and listening to God's servant. Still, it's how they listen and how God speaks that matters. **James McConnell**

Most adolescents are uncertain about what they want to do when they grow up.

Not James McConnell.

He never wanted to become an astronaut, a doctor, a lawyer, a bus driver, a fireman, or a politician; he knew from childhood his calling in life. Indeed, from the tender age of eight, he was convinced God had called him to one profession alone– the preaching of the gospel.

And he has always preached that gospel without fear or favour. James McConnell lived to preach rather than preached to live.

As modernity irrevocably appears to be changing our churches' culture, many Christians seem fearful of a future without sound biblical truth prompting the debate: can God replenish our pulpits with the great preachers of the past?

Pastor McConnell believes God can reproduce similar spiritual giants; albeit, their methods will probably look very different.

In Whitewell's documentary 'How Shall They Hear Without A Preacher,' Pastor McConnell stated: "if preaching were a crime today, thousands would be proved innocent!". It was a reference to the lack of God-inspired preaching in our 21st century pulpits. While methods are changing, preaching content can never change because only through the foolishness of preaching can people find Christ.

From the parklands of Belfast to one of the most listened to preaching pulpits in Europe at one stage, God ordained the steps of an ordinary young man called James McConnell to proclaim His Word. His great friend, and author of the Word for Today, the late Bob Gass, said of him: “Who but God would choose a fisherman named Peter, a tax collector called Matthew, and a doubting saint-like Thomas to transform the first-century Church? Or look behind a hedge and find a Rodney “Gipsy” Smith or go down to a park in Chicago and find an outfielder like Billy Sunday or go to Harland and Wolff Shipyard and find a James McConnell, pick them up, anoint them and use them to touch the world.”

The foolishness of preaching is a remarkable profession, indeed. Still, it takes courage and boldness to not only speak up but speak well for God, especially in a politically correct era like ours.

In this respect, James McConnell never lacked courage. He is considered 'the old school, dyed in the wool' Pentecostal preacher who refuses to cut corners and someone who says it like it is. People are not always comfortable with his delivery, but many prefer it. Long standing member of Whitewell Sammy Wilson MP is no stranger to controversy and outspokenness and a long-standing admirer of Pastor McConnell, having defended him on several occasions throughout his ministry, most notably in 2016, after the Pastor found himself in court answering charges of race hate speech.

Sammy is on record as saying: “I like his straightforward style where he doesn’t mince his words and isn’t afraid to offend. He knows what he wants to say, and he says it. If you look at some of the Old Testament kings, they brought prophets along and berated them until they told them how it was. People like that, especially in Northern Ireland, and so do I. However, even if they don’t like it, I get the impression that it wouldn’t matter to the Pastor. He knows he has an assignment from God, and he’s going to carry it out.”

In an era when technology and other distractions threaten the substance of God’s Word, the Pastor believes there’s a need more than ever for imaginative presentation of the gospel. If this transpires, people will continue to flock to God’s House not just for the singing, worship, and other programmes but also to hear quality ministry. Not even generational change can prevent it.

Nevertheless, to help us face the future, we sometimes need to step back and recall our past.

Years ago, people were conscious of a reverence that quickly reminded them that they'd come into the House of God, a holy and sacred place. Back then, beautiful stained-glass windows and prominent pulpits in many churches spoke of the magnificence and centrality of God. In those days, a sense of reverence seemed to exist that no longer appears evident in this generation. Even the very pews had that "church smell" not found anywhere else, but, of course, today is a very different look and experience, more likely to produce the smell of haze and blind you with lighting, which makes it hard even to find one's seat.

Compare this to years ago when, as you entered Church, all sorts of emotions took hold. Firstly, a fear that the preacher would pinpoint something that wasn't quite right, but a sense of joy emerged because people also realised they would meet with God, a God they would find mercy, love, and forgiveness.

Does this kind of reverence still exist?

In his book, The Holiness of God, the American minister, RC Sproul, wrote: "Ours is a day when men feel a sense of the absence of God. We see no burning bushes, no pillars of fire, no incarnate Christ walking in our midst. Gone are the gothic arches, gone are the stained-glass windows, gone are the sermons which stir the soul to moral anguish. Instead, ours is an upbeat generation with the accent on self-improvement and a broad-minded view of sin."

It hasn't always been like this, of course. For example, the marvellous preaching of both Martin Luther and John Calvin produced a continental reformation. At the same time, in evangelical terms, it was both Thomas Cranmer and Hugh Latimer who led England in the reformation, while Wycliffe's Bible influenced both Tyndale and his contemporary Luther.

Even preaching greats like John Knox, Alexander Whyte, Joseph Parker, and most eminently of all, perhaps, CH Spurgeon all graced our churches' pulpits. The United Kingdom has, without a doubt, been truly blessed for many centuries by numerous renowned biblical orators, and many of these men inspired the Pastor, most notably, CH Spurgeon.

One of these renowned men's outstanding features was their emphasis on God's grace to change men's and women's lives. Today, a resurgent grace revolution is under attack, even referred to as "easy religion" by many legalistic preachers, but an emphasis on the "grace of God" is making a marvellous comeback, regardless.

Alexander Whyte from St George's Free Church Edinburgh was a great personality, and his preaching power greatly influenced many people. A humble man accused of being too liberal – he refused to stop reaching out to people of all cultures with the message of God's grace. He had good times and bad times like most preachers, and I always liked his quote: "I have known what it is to preach to a packed St George's, and I have known what it is to preach to an empty St George's." Joseph Parker was quite a character and a great preacher of the gospel. Still, my all-time favourite must be CH Spurgeon, another immense preacher and a man with an exceptional personality. Parker once chastened Spurgeon for smoking a pipe, and Spurgeon replied, "I will stop smoking the pipe when you stop going to the theatre." They were tough old boys, but I am sure they had great respect for one another deep down. Their common denominator was the grace of God and a message of hope. **James McConnell**

Even in Northern Ireland, preaching giants such as Willie Mullan, the Rev Ian Paisley, the Rev Sam Workman, and James McConnell remind us that passion for preaching was once the norm and not the exception. The Pastor remembers these men well and still holds them in the highest regard because he insists every one of them was a soul winner. They cried tears for their people. Or, as Spurgeon once said, "Winners of souls must first be weepers for souls."

Willie Mullen was a man born for an era that desperately needed to hear the Word of God, and he succeeded in building one of the largest bible classes with over 600 people in attendance. In those days, that was some crowd, and he had an authentic ministry. The Rev Ian Paisley was another man God raised for purpose, plan, and nation. I had good relations with him in the early days, but as the years progressed, our separate callings' and busyness meant we didn't see as much of each other, but I always admired and respected him. I still recall how we shared a room in Scotland, and we fought all day and night about matters of theology. While we were from two different denominations, Ian from the Free Presbyterians and me from a Pentecostal background, we respected one another. He even visited my house regularly in those days, and the first place he headed to was my library. "What book are you reading now, McConnell?" he would ask in that beautiful and unique Paisley accent. I think he was impressed with my library. **James McConnell**

While Paisley was both a renowned politician and a powerful preacher, James McConnell never sought any career other than the ministry. For him, preaching was his only calling. Nothing better illustrates his passion for preaching than the quote: "If God has called you to preach, don't stoop to become Prime Minister."

He has always believed that the preaching of God's Word is the highest calling anyone can receive because the gospel preacher is God's representative who stands between the living and the dead.

The Rev Sam Workman eventually became a close friend of Pastor McConnell's, especially towards the end of his life. Following retirement, he and Elim Superintendent Sandy Wilson started attending the Tabernacle to hear "the Bishop" bring the Word, which greatly encouraged the Pastor during those days.

That was a big compliment to know that two men I viewed as "great servants of God" like Sam and Sandy valued my ministry and teaching. Sam had transformed a congregational church close to Whitewell and done many other great things during his career. At the same time, Sandy, who many are aware was the Father of well-known DUP politician Sammy Wilson, was extremely well respected. So it encouraged me greatly to see them at the services at Whitewell. **James McConnell**

All were great students of God's Word, and significantly, during his early life, James McConnell also accepted and grasped Paul's words to his young servant Timothy, the words - "Give attendance to reading." **1 Timothy 4:13**

Having been taken to Church as a young man by his grandfather, the young James found himself surrounded by preachers, bibles, and pulpits - inevitable then that perhaps he would end up in the ministry, not politics or any other career.

He was born a preacher, not a politician!

Not even the deadly disease of Tuberculosis, which eventually wiped out his parents and sister, leaving him alone, could prevent this.

With only God to rely upon, it was here that the young James McConnell began a life of study of God's Word. Having been used to running the streets, he left school at age 14 and quickly found a job. Then, during his devotional time, he read a life-changing line in the second book of Timothy: "Study to show thyself approved unto God, a workman that needeth not to be ashamed, rightly dividing the Word of truth." **2 Timothy 2:15**

It revolutionised his entire thinking and became a sentence that utterly transformed his young life. Suddenly it occurred to him how he didn't have to study anymore to impress men, something he had been unconsciously trying to do during his youth. He had wanted so desperately to impress men like James Forsythe, Gordon Magee,

Bill Drost and George Jeffreys, but not anymore. So those words "Study thyself approved unto God" resonated with him. He also gained encouragement from watching University Challenge, a highly successful TV programme in the UK, which tested the academic ability of some of the top students in Britain and was hosted by Bamber Gascoigne.

When I watched University Challenge and heard the students saying, "I'm reading mathematics" or "I'm reading geography," a light switched on. From there on, I can honestly say I began to read and study the Word of God. I saw the difference reading had made in the life of those students. They were intelligent people, and so, in the same way, I wanted to learn and grasp everything I could about God's Word. If they could succeed, so could I, all-be-it our subject matter was very different. **James McConnell**

The Pastor recalls when once in a Bible shop with his friend Robert Gass, the man told Robert to look at the shelves and see Christ's life work in men's lives. The Pastor says he overheard those words and understood their significance, and immediately bought every book he could find on the life of Christ. These books are still in his library today and books he has exhausted and benefited from for years. It schooled him on authentic ministry and how to provide it. It's something he has never regretted, nor his flock.

While reading is good, what we read is just as important. Today, Bible study often reveals a lack of emphasis on the life of Christ in favour of many other doctrines and principles from the Word of God. Of course, people should study these things, but a Christian's progress is more evident by not relegating Jesus to the periphery of their teachings. It applies to every would-be successful preacher. The mark of the Pastor's ministry was always his focus on the life of Christ. Every sermon highlighted the magnificence and beauty of Jesus Christ. It would be hard to find any address by the Pastor where Jesus wasn't the central character.

Similarly, when we see Jesus on every page of scripture, something extraordinary happens. From Genesis to Revelation, the hidden charms and truths of Christ begin to enlighten the believer in a way systematic study does not. Suddenly reading our Bibles is no longer a chore or even viewed as a duty; instead, we are alive, vibrant and exciting.

Extensive and, at times, laborious Bible study is not the answer for a broken and bewildered world; a better understanding of the true nature and person of Jesus Christ is what brings transformation and lasting change.

When the Lord is at the centre of everything we do when his power, mercy, and compassion are made evident, the struggle turns to success, while sickness gets replaced by good health, The great preachers of the past all focused on the life and ministry of the Lord Jesus Christ.

It was what Jesus taught his followers. As two disciples walked and talked with Jesus on the road to Emmaus, the Bible records, "And beginning at Moses and all the Prophets, he expounded to them in all the scriptures, the things concerning himself." **Luke 24:27**

Christ's open secret on studying the Bible is how every page in the Bible is about Jesus. Here is His challenge to every would-be preacher and New Testament saint.

Jesus in the Old Testament is concealed, but in the New Testament, He's revealed.

Christ desires that we study the Bible to see Him and all the things in scripture concerning Himself. It's interesting that during this same incident, the two disciples concluded: "Did not our heart burn within us while he talked with us on the road, and while he opened the scriptures to us?" **Luke 24:32**

When Jesus is made evident through the Word of God, our hearts burn and respond.

When people are part of an anointed ministry that unveils Jesus in the scriptures, not only will their hearts revive through the goodness of God, but deliverance and healing will start to flow. When Christ is present and preached, good news also follows. A blessing begins to gush in our lives, finances, relationships, and homes.

To this day, Pastor James McConnell retains an impressive library at his home in Belfast, a testimony to how his devotional reading about Christ has never stopped and even progressed over the years. Christ has been his passion and priority from those early days with his boyhood friend, Bob Gass. Nevertheless, he believes we live in days when few people are reading and studying the life of Jesus as they should, which he equally believes is responsible for producing sub-standard preaching and lack of conversion.

It's sad when ministers know little about the life of Christ and get up and say whatever comes into their heads, but that's not feeding the sheep. Before Paul died, he reminded Timothy not to forget to bring the books and the parchments". Of course, reading is essential if great sermons continue, but hear me, reading about Jesus will propel any would-be and inspiring preacher to another level. Many are buying DVDs and audio

cassettes, and preachers are buying them too, but there's nothing like reading the Word of God and studying the life of the Saviour. It will transform a minister and a ministry.
James McConnell

He should know! Once the Pastor grasped this fact in his spiritual walk and started to explore the hidden treasures of Christ, his ministry exploded. Moreover, it's no exaggeration to say that a mighty door opened to him from that point on, and a prolific preaching giant marched onto the evangelical stage.

I am the voice of one crying out in the wilderness,
'Make straight the way of the Lord,' as the prophet Isaiah said.
John 1:23

5.

A Voice for the Nation

No man can claim success in the pulpit on his own. Everyone needs to stand on the shoulders of someone else, and Charles Spurgeon was one of the shoulders I stood on. He was a spiritual giant and reading about him greatly influenced my life. He had an understanding of the grace of God like few others, and his way with words was masterful."
James McConnell

There have always been seasons when a voice is required to help steer a nation in the right direction, especially when countries experience darkness and even silence from God. World leaders and leading clergymen and women have all been used to help influence their generations at such times.

None, however, have influenced their fellow men more, perhaps, than John the Baptist.

He arrived between the Old Testament and the New Testament, following a long silence from God. But so prolific was John the Baptist's ministry and how God eventually spoke through him; he is known as "The Voice."

Oh, for a voice again to break the silence of heaven in our generation!

Today, preachers often go to where the people are: social media, a big city, or a central conference, which is expected; in John's case, however, the people went to where he was.

The Bible records how they came out to hear him.

They flocked in their droves to get a glimpse of this eccentric Old Testament preacher who had a message about repentance and a message about a Kingdom. The Bible states: "Then Jerusalem and all Judea and all the region about the Jordan were going out to him, **Matthew 3:5**

John's gift to speak to the multitudes is one many preachers today would love to have – for he knew how to point people to Jesus. But, he made it clear he wasn't Jesus himself, and his only assignment was to preach Christ and His forgiveness.

One of the most significant statements ever made by John is found in the gospel of John, where it recalls, "The next day John seeth Jesus coming unto him, and saith, Behold the Lamb of God, which taketh away the sin of the world **John 1:29**

Here the prophet offers the people great hope by pointing them to the only way of Salvation. There is an immediate connection made with Isaiah's prophecy many generations previously, who had talked of a messenger – "A voice of one calling in the wilderness" - which God would send to prepare the way for the coming of the promised Messiah.

This messenger was none other than John the Baptist, who appeared in the desert of Judaea.

John's role was specific; to prepare the people for the Messiah's coming, point people to Christ, and offer them another world. He did this by telling people to repent as the Kingdom of Heaven was near. "I am the voice of one crying out in the wilderness, 'Make straight the way of the Lord,' as the prophet Isaiah said." **John 1:23**

While baptism was a Jewish ritual and people were immersed in water to symbolise cleansing, John's baptism symbolized repentance.

John was a second Elijah. He dressed and acted almost precisely like Elijah. John even ate wild locusts and honey, wore clothes made of camel hair, and had a belt tied around his waist. Many would think him out of the ordinary if he were operating today. Yet John was a forerunner to the Messiah, saying, "I baptise you with water for repentance, but one who is more powerful than I is coming after me; I am not worthy to carry his sandals. He will baptise you with the Holy Spirit and fire."

There was never any ambiguity in the announcements from John. He knew his calling and always made Jesus the central theme of his message and even stated on one occasion for the need to decrease so that Christ might increase. "He must increase, but I must decrease" **John 3:30**

John's ministry appears, therefore, to send two powerful messages for every would-be preacher. Firstly humility is essential in leading people to Christ, while preaching on Jesus is vital to winning souls. Even Jesus Himself said, “And I if I be lifted up from the earth, will draw all men unto me **John 12:32**

Pastor McConnell’s own story is a rag to riches account of how a unique gift to preach about the Lord Jesus, coupled with an insatiable desire to learn about the things of God, would ultimately elevate him beyond many of his peers despite being left as an orphan for most of his youth. God gave him a voice, and his voice became his passport.

James McConnell would turn out to be 'no ordinary teenager' and 'no ordinary voice.' Moreover, he became one of the foremost preachers of the gospel over the last 100 years. John Glass, a former General Superintendent of the Elim church worldwide, and Eric McComb, a former Elim Superintendent in Ireland, admired Pastor McConnell’s preaching ability.

“In the style of preaching that he brings, I don’t know anyone who equals Pastor McConnell. No matter where he has preached, he always preaches with great acceptance, and I’ve never known a time when he has preached the gospel and souls haven’t responded and found Jesus as their Saviour.” John Glass

Former Irish Elim Superintendent, Eric McComb, who, like James McConnell, has been willing to call a spade a spade over the years, has always admired James McConnell’s straightforward presentation. “I listened to the Pastor for the first time in 1973, a tape someone had given me, and his preaching was forthright. You knew there was a heaven, and you knew there was a hell, and you knew there was a saviour from sin whose name was Jesus.”

In preaching terms, James McConnell’s most significant influence on the international stage was undoubtedly the great Baptist minister CH Spurgeon who once famously stated: “no man should preach from a text until it has first leapt at him like a lion; from a thicket.” That’s advice James McConnell has taken and lived by. As a young man, he recalls reading Spurgeon and being encouraged to read Matthew Henry, referred to as “the prince of commentators.”

At the time, James McConnell had no money to buy Matthew Henry’s commentaries, but Spurgeon had informed his students to “sell their beds” and buy the books anyway. So, of course, with hardly a bed to sell at that stage, the young James followed that advice and read Mathew Henry every day alongside Spurgeon, Alexander Whyte, and George Henry Morrison. But it was mainly the remarkable ministry of CH Spurgeon at the Metropolitan Tabernacle in London that inspired

Pastor McConnell to begin his ministry at Whitewell back in Belfast in 1957.

Spurgeon preached to thousands of people at Elephant and Castle during his tenure. He planted over 200 churches in London that he filled with his Pastors and started an orphanage during his 38-year pastorate. It was a remarkable ministry that people talk about to this day. Spurgeon became a great teacher just as Forsythe, Magee, Drost, and Jeffreys had been mentors to James.

The Pastor recalls the story of two Americans who visited London for a holiday. At the time, Joseph Parker was an immense preacher in London in the City Temple. The Americans went to hear Parker in the morning, and when the service concluded, they both said, "What a preacher!"

Later that same day, the Americans returned to hear CH Spurgeon but couldn't get in until two people kindly gave up their positions in the aisle. When the two Americans emerged at the close of the evening service, they said: "What a wonderful Christ!"

Spurgeon was a man who consistently lifted the name of Jesus and preached regularly on the text "Awake to righteousness and sin not."

Considered the first Pastor to build a megachurch in London, he was most respected during his extraordinary life between 1834 and 1892.

Regarded as "the prince of preachers," regardless of which denomination his admirers belonged to, he was revered by many ministers due to his understanding of the life and mission of Jesus Christ and his preaching about the grace of God.

One of his greatest quotes about the grace of God is as follows: "No doctrine is so calculated to preserve a man from sin as the doctrine of the grace of God. Those who have called it 'a licentious doctrine' did not know anything at all about it."

In essence, Spurgeon was saying that only the grace of God has the power to preserve someone from sin, which, of course, is what Jesus and the Apostle Paul revealed in the New Testament.

CH Spurgeon was famous for his wit and sense of humour, and the Pastor certainly learned from his teacher how to keep things light when darkness is present.

People lost count of the many times the Pastor used similar humour and laughter to lighten his congregation. Stories abound of funny situations of how the Pastor seized the moment. Like the evening, he concluded a Monday night prayer meeting by asking if anyone in the congregation would suggest a final chorus. A lady shouted, in a broad Belfast accent "Rain on me." Just then, what sounded like hailstones began belting down on the roof of the church, and the Pastor quickly countered, "I think you mean the song "Reign in Me, Sovereign Lord" but, lady, there's no doubt that is the quickest answer to a prayer I have seen for years, let's sing it." The congregation erupted, and everyone skipped home through the downpour of blessing with a smile on their faces.

Notwithstanding, like Spurgeon, the Pastor was often used as a voice to the nation when hope, not humour, was required. Powerful sermons about how Jesus could save people during dark times became his forte. The similarity in his and CH Spurgeon's ministry was striking.

Despite their noticeable theological differences, when a young James McConnell began his ministry at Whitewell in 1957, in Belfast, Northern Ireland, Spurgeon's Metropolitan Tabernacle at Elephant and Castle London was rebuilt following a great fire and bombing during the war.

However, it would be 1994 before Pastor McConnell would name his church the Metropolitan Tabernacle Belfast, after he too began to attract thousands of people to hear the gospel, requiring him to find a larger sanctuary on the Shore Road in Belfast. History was repeating itself on the other side of the channel and in a very different era.

CH Spurgeon was a Baptist, and I'm a Pentecostal. While we may differ theologically, the Baptists love the water, and the Pentecostals love the fire, so there is plenty of steam when they come together! **James McConnell**

Wittiness aside, the Pastor believes Spurgeon was a spiritual giant God raised for his generation and beyond. He cites his tremendous lectures to his students as one of the finest Christian books written, and even today, people are in awe at what Spurgeon built and achieved for the Lord's work. Yet, it is significant how the Pastor has also accomplished numerous similar feats for God.

Of course, there's a marked difference between Spurgeon's generation and the current one. During CH Spurgeon's ministry, London's population topped just 2 million people, which today has increased to almost 9 million people – a sizable jump. Neither Spurgeon nor his generation had access to the technology we enjoy today. But while there are more souls to reach in this generation in London and elsewhere, due to distractions and a watering down of the gospel, some fear people will not come to know the Lord Jesus Christ in the same way as Spurgeon's era.

Technology is defining our generation, and new ideas are being embraced.

Still, with new laws and constant politically correctness, the church is also currently at a genuine crossroads regarding ministry styles like CH Spurgeon and Pastor James McConnell. As many preachers struggle to fit in with these new demands, it is worth considering how it was not 'newfound things' but 'forthright preaching' which took the ministry of Pastor James McConnell in a little hall on the Whitewell Road in Belfast in 1957 from 10 people to the opulent surroundings of their new megachurch on the Shore Road in 1994.

Since then, thousands of souls have been won to Jesus Christ through Pastor James McConnell's preaching at the Metropolitan Tabernacle in Belfast.

Just as CH Spurgeon, Joseph Parker, Alexander McLaren, and JC Ryle, the former Bishop of Liverpool, even the prolific Billy Graham, and many more left their mark in their generation, so, too, Pastor James McConnell has left his stamp on his age.

And just as CH Spurgeon's preaching inspired the Pastor to pursue a career in the ministry, so, too, the work of James McConnell himself motivated many of his protégés to take a step of faith and begin their ministries. The ambitious project in Ballymena Co Antrim, by the Green Pastures Church, spearheaded by Pastor Jeff Wright, is one such testimony to the teaching and preaching, and motivation found in Pastor James McConnell.

For example, when Jeff initially came to the Tabernacle, he never considered entering the ministry. Still, once he'd been part of the work and exposed to Pastor McConnell's love for Jesus and lost souls, it became infectious. From there on, he was only ever interested in one thing – the preaching of God's Word.

He recalls: "Pastor McConnell's preaching brought me to a place where I would have done anything for God, and that's why when I got the call, I knew I was ready. The Word brought life to me, and that's what this generation is missing - someone who can get experience through the Word.

There's nothing wrong with the Word; it is all about what we bring out of it. James McConnell brought such richness out of the Word it inspired me to get it to others.

I believe it's not a lack of desire people have for the Word; it's more down to the preacher and his inability to bring out the hunger and thirst for what's in the Word. In short, preach about Jesus, and people will respond."

Pastor McConnell's pure passion for preaching about the Saviour and his ability to make God's Word relevant has stretched far and wide, even to the corridors of power at the Northern Ireland government buildings at Stormont.

For example, many a wet wintry evening, the people of Whitewell got down on their knees and called out to God on behalf of their nation, local politicians, and leaders. Following the words of 1 Timothy 2, where Paul encourages the church to pray first for Kings and leaders and those in positions of authority, the ministry at Whitewell has bombarded heaven on numerous occasions for its own spiritual and secular leaders. No surprise then, many local politicians eventually made their way to the Whitewell ministry during those years, noting the Pastor's candid style and concern for the land. While politicians use their voices to help change society's laws, preachers like James McConnell use their voices to change people's very lives. When Pastor McConnell spoke either in his church or elsewhere, people listened. His voice of both warning and comfort during some of the darkest days in the history of Ireland North and South proved invaluable. People have not always agreed with him- indeed, often they may have been downright offended - but they listened at crucial moments to the voice of God through his ministry.

So, how important is a voice in the ministry?

Many preachers today have microphones, but how many have a voice?

When the late, great Billy Graham thought of giving up a college course in preaching, the college president Bob Jones reminded him that God made his voice to stir hearts and draw people to Christ. Jones said: "You have a voice that pulls. God can use that voice of yours, and he can use it mightily." What a timely intervention that became!

Such voices often speak when society doesn't want to hear their message, but God's generals have always been willing to provide such a voice and the necessary spiritual guidance required by a nation.

Like John the Baptist, known and referred to as "The Voice" – a man who cried in the wilderness the message of repentance, God has found a voice for every generation, including this one.

The Pastor's voice has equally been reserved for the pulpit and rarely for politics. But, like John, he knew a genuine distinction needed to be made between politics and preaching or between the religious and political systems.

To this end, it's a matter of history and record how the Pastor faithfully spoke out before the Troubles, during the troubles, and after the Troubles in Ulster, continually proclaiming the truth of the gospel.

His focus and message never changed.

It was his life's calling!

Indeed, often he put his life in danger, but such is the precariousness of the preaching profession.

He often met with paramilitary leaders and gave as good as he got.

He didn't ignore political issues, but he offered a divided society a solution by proclaiming the gospel. Generations have come and gone, but the Pastor has never lost his passion for reaching men and women with the gospel. He has continued to be a voice crying in the wilderness - and sometimes into the wind - but calling nonetheless on behalf of the nation. From the emergence of terrorism in Ulster to terrorism worldwide to the arrival of earthquakes, famines and pandemics, the Pastor has always had a message for the hour, Jesus Christ and His love!

That is what preaching is all about, a voice that travels far enough to find a lost soul in the crowd and win them to Jesus and a voice that will travel even into the most unlikely of places.

ENTRE
SATURDA
10.00am-4.00p

How then shall they call on him in whom they have not believed?
And how shall they believe in him of whom they have not heard?
And how shall they hear without a preacher?
Romans 10:14

6.

A Date at Stormont

I remember receiving a phone call from Stormont from Gerry Adams asking to see him. I immediately entered the building and passed by some DUP and unionist politicians who saw me walking into Gerry Adams's office. To say there were a few raised eyebrows from the unionist politicians was an understatement. No sooner had I sat down when Gerry got straight to the point, asking me if we were going to Andersonstown to convert Catholics to Protestantism. I replied not at all and told him that I intended to see Catholics born again of the Spirit of God. I explained that once people accept Jesus as their Saviour, labels like Protestant and Catholic fall off, and we become one in Christ. I then invited Gerry Adams to attend the Tabernacle on a Sunday night, but he didn't appear. However, I recall he was very courteous to me, put the kettle on, and made me a cup of tea. We chatted for some time, and once he realised my motives were genuine, I noticed he started to relax. I could tell his defences were coming down. I reiterated how we intended to go to Andersonstown for one reason only – to preach the gospel, and I invited him to attend the same meeting. **James McConnell**

It proved a most unlikely event, a meeting between an evangelical preacher from the protestant part of North Belfast and the republican Sinn Fein leader Gerry Adams from West Belfast. Yet, that's what transpired in the year 2011. It was more remarkable because it was a time when tensions were still high in Northern Ireland, and an uneasy and unfinished peace existed. The peace process had barely transformed many areas, and riots continued in loyalist areas of East Belfast.

To ensure he reached all sections of the community in Ulster with the gospel, however, the Pastor and the witness at Whitewell decided to attempt something unprecedented with the bold and courageous step of taking their outreach to over a thousand people at a leisure centre in a part of republican West Belfast.

If the Pastor and the Whitewell people were under the impression they would all walk along a red carpet to West Belfast, they were severely mistaken.

The advertising and promotion of such an event caused quite a stir and brought no shortage of controversy. Radio debates followed, and strong opposition from a local priest and his church was formed. Not long before the mission, the sectarian division was so strong a visit such as this by a Protestant denomination into the heart of a well-known nationalist stronghold would have been unthinkable, so little wonder it caught the attention of the people, media, and politicians alike.

Then, out of the blue, a surprising invitation to the Pastor emerged to Stormont buildings where former Sinn Fein leader Gerry Adams offered to make him a pot of tea.

You couldn't have made it up!

Nevertheless, the tension in the city at that time explained why the Stormont meeting between Northern Ireland's best-known preacher and one of the country's most prominent politicians not only took place but began suspiciously.

Despite the background of someone like Gerry Adams and the troubled history between protestant and catholic communities, the Pastor recalls he didn't feel threatened or intimidated by such a meeting. On the contrary, he not only counted it as a privilege but was up for it and saw it as an excellent opportunity to influence the former leader of Sinn Fein about Jesus.

After stopping the car one day, I remember seeking God for wisdom and asking for the ability to talk to this man. When we finally met, I remember saying to him, "Gerry, there's no partition in hell." Protestants and Catholics will be there together, and another thing Gerry, there's no partition in heaven because those who accept Christ as their Saviour will enter the same place. I witnessed to him the mercy of God and the power of the gospel to change lives. It was one of those extraordinary encounters Christ has afforded me, and I wasn't going to pass it up. Gerry was very courteous and listened, and I respect him for that. **James McConnell**

To grasp this meeting's extent and the subsequent encounter, one only has to recall how despised Gerry Adams was in loyalist and Protestant communities. And how equally detested the Pastor was viewed with no shortage of suspicion by republicans and Catholics because of his frequently outspoken views about the Catholic Church, Sinn Fein, and republican paramilitaries.

The venue's unusual thing was that it was a leisure centre in the heart of Andersonstown, a staunchly republican part of Belfast.

Not surprisingly, the outreach became a lead story on the BBC Northern Ireland news and was picked up by many other media organisations. The BBC sent a camera crew to cover the event accompanied by one of its leading reporters. There was singing, drama, and preaching, and dozens of souls were won to the Kingdom of God that evening.

However, the unexpected sight of two bitterly and polarised and divided communities worshipping the Lord cannot be either disputed or ignored. It is still one of the most extraordinary moments in the ministerial career of James McConnell and his church and possibly that of any evangelical church in all Ireland. When the Pastor first muted the idea of going to West Belfast, many of his leadership and flock were sceptical, but he was convinced this wasn't only a good idea - it was a God-idea, and he was proved right.

This kind of courage from the Pastor has uniquely played a significant role in bringing divided communities together, particularly in Northern Ireland, because it wasn't the first time he had taken the opportunity to venture into unfamiliar territory or meet with high-profile political leaders and even paramilitaries. In this respect, he's more than played his part in improving relations in his nation.

Pastor James McConnell believes that from the time he became orphaned until the present, Christ put the Kingdom of God within him, and he considers Christ can put the Kingdom of God in anyone willing to receive it.

That said, his ministry and preaching always came across as puritanical, a direct and to-the-point preaching style. However, the essential thing in understanding the puritan preaching style is that they were preachers before anything else; men set apart to preach an undiluted gospel to the "Whosoever."

Okay, call them odd, unique, different, weird, call them what you will, but God had a purpose and plan for their lives by expounding His Word. Most people don't always comprehend or identify with such vessels, but God has separated them unto himself for a greater purpose.

For example, someone once described Pastor McConnell as being like three things:

Number one - a preacher! Number two - a preacher! Number three - a preacher!

Indeed, like the apostle Paul, he believes that his position is "woe is me if I preach not this gospel."

Here we see the sole inspiration and justification of any preacher. Whether it was striding across a platform at a church or gospel outreach or sitting having tea with a prominent politician like Gerry Adams, the Pastor continually desired to preach the Kingdom's good news. He frequently talked about and witnessed for Jesus, and it was his sole function.

Nonetheless, he believes such passion for Jesus is getting lost in many other less important things today. The songs replace the sermon, the preacher is being made redundant, and the entertainer is getting all the engagements.

The Pastor believes the church is in danger of becoming a circus, and powerful messages are also becoming less frequent.

Nevertheless, when apathy rules, that is the very time to preach again and push against the tide of apostasy. So Paul instructed the younger protégé, Timothy, to: "Preach the Word, be instant in season and out of season; reprove, rebuke, exhort with all longsuffering and doctrine. For the time will come when they will not endure sound doctrine; but after their lusts shall they heap to themselves teachers having itching ears; and they shall turn away their ears from the truth. **2 Timothy 2: 2-4**

While Pastor McConnell believes we live in such times, he has repeatedly refused to give in to popular demands during his ministry. As a result, he has met with criticism and opposition but has remained firm in his stance on the gospel message. And here's the thing! Despite giving no corner, the puzzle is thousands still flocked to hear the truth, proving that God will bless them when ministers honour the Word of God.

Remember, the great DL Moody once said: "The best way to start a revival is to build a fire in the pulpit."

Today people use drama and music to get their message across, but perhaps the church needs to light a few fires again in their pulpits!

The great preachers do not rely on gadgets or gimmicks. Instead, they have sought God for their hope. At some point, there must be a clear proclamation of the gospel, namely that all have sinned and fallen short of the glory of God, but that Jesus Christ has provided a sacrifice for sin. If we surrender to Him in obedience, we can have those sins forgiven and inherit eternal life.

In short: no repentance brings no redemption! And no hope equals despair!

If our society is going to change, it must, says the Pastor, get back to the place where preachers are prepared to stand on a platform and say, "thus and thus saith the Lord!"

Is this an old-fashioned view from Pastor McConnell? Is he out of place today, along with anyone else who desires to preach like him?

On the contrary, perhaps today's society is out of step with the Bible, a subject we will examine in more detail later. Christians aren't expected to change the community's worldly view at times; instead, society must hear a message that changes it.

Many believers express surprise at the demise of genuine Bible preaching these days, yet it's no new occurrence. The current generation is not unique to liberalism and indifference. Every generation has experienced an inevitable "falling away." We have been here before! Even during the era of CH Spurgeon's, there was a decline so vast he termed it "the downgrade conspiracy," a reference to the introduction of Liberalism and Darwinism.

During that period of apostasy, Spurgeon remarked: "We shall not adjust our Bibles to the age, but before we have done, we shall adjust the age to our bibles."

Is history repeating itself?

As Paul predicted for the last generation, is there a great falling away?

Is there a shortage of skilled preachers in our pulpits?

Even more importantly, when there is a significant shortage of preaching quality, a fair question is: Will God provide this generation with ministers who know how to preach the Word? Can the glory days of excellent gospel preaching return?

We must trust that the answer is yes! While a world without sound biblical truth is a frightening prospect, God has never lacked a voice or the sound of the Spirit.

Arguably one of the most profound statements ever made by Pastor McConnell came from his very own pulpit on a Lord's Day morning. He left his sermon notes to declare in full flight: Bible schools cannot teach tears; they really cannot because tears are spirit-led. No matter how weighed down a preacher is with degrees and doctorates, he will not go far unless he knows soul bitterness over the sin of this day."

Or, as Paul wrote in his letter to the Romans. "How then shall they call on him in whom they have not believed? And how shall they believe in him of whom they have not heard? And how shall they hear without a preacher? **Romans 10:14**

What makes a great, even an influential preacher, then?

Is it something that can be learned or taught at Bible College?

James McConnell's method in successfully communicating the gospel's message has always been to walk the roads and call unto God.

Even during the period known as the Troubles in Northern Ireland, when it wasn't at all safe to be on the streets at night, a police Landrover would follow him to ensure his safety as he walked and talked to God. Although unaware of it, those same policemen appear to have been sent as guardian angels by a greater authority to protect the servant of God who has always lived to preach, not preached to live.

How do I get the Holy Ghost?" Pastor McConnell once asked his congregation from his pulpit before answering the question for them: "A PhD won't get you it, or a Doctor of Divinity or a BA won't get you it, or a BSc won't suffice. How do I get it then? Walk the roads, call unto God, ask Him to come, and he will visit you! In many churches, today's missing link is the Holy Spirit's power to change lives radically, mainly because ministers have not first sought God. There must instead be a desire to seek God and hear from him. If a person seeks the Lord and gets an anointing from God, they can be helpful anywhere. No matter what culture and language, people will come to listen if a person has a blessing. It is not a personality that brings change and conversion. It is not wit and charm and even education; it is not even faithful hard work; it is solely down to the power of the Holy Spirit. And the only way to discover more of the Holy Spirit is to spend time with God. **James McConnell**

As Jesus said to His disciples, "But ye shall receive power after that the Holy Ghost has come upon you, and you shall be witnesses unto me both in Jerusalem, all Judaea and in Samaria and unto the uttermost parts of the earth" **Acts 1:8**

And again, Zechariah wrote, "Not by might nor by power, but by My Spirit," saith the Lord of hosts." **Zechariah 4:6**

Nevertheless, the gospel is not only to be preached in the power of the Spirit; it is also to be reached!"

And here is where the Pastor shares yet another resemblance to his boyhood hero CH Spurgeon, who was also a great believer that the gospel was for body and soul – a social gospel – a belief system that invoked considerable criticism for the great Baptist preacher.

Like Pastor James McConnell, CH Spurgeon had no formal training, yet he embraced thousands in need, started a Bible College from which 900 of his students graduated, and with no fewer than 12,000 books in his library, he managed to write four books per year. Pastor McConnell's ministry has proven equivalent. With over 60 churches, including current involvement in Kenya and Ethiopia, going to the entire world is scripturally based but imperative, which has left a significant impression on people both at home and abroad.

The unmistakable fruit of preaching is applying the Word that has just been given and the desire to take that Word abroad. So even the greatest preacher and teacher of all the Lord Jesus Christ said: "Go ye into all the world and preach the gospel to every creature." **Mark 16:15**

It has been well observed that the principal point of preaching is to display how much we care, not how much we know.

The prolific preacher Paul the Apostle understood that preaching is only truly effective when accompanied by love. Therefore, preaching based on anything other than God's love is often not nearly as fruitful.

In his first letter to the Corinthians, Paul states: "Though I speak with the tongues of men and angels, and have not love, I become as sounding brass or a tinkling cymbal. And though I have the gift of prophecy, understand all mysteries and all knowledge; and though I have all faith so that I could remove mountains, and have not to love, I am nothing. And now abides faith, hope, and love, but the greatest of these is love." **1 Corinthians 13:1-2 and 13**

Unless scripture and a message of love and hope are at the forefront of the sermon, the church doesn't have good news to share with people, even in the most unlikely places. God's Word is not for an exclusive group, nor should it be tampered with, and it needs no other props. Preaching the undiluted Word of truth is more than enough for everyone to hear, no matter what age we live. It also reveals and announces the arrival of every faithful preacher.

Bank of Ireland
Bank of Ireland
Bank of Ireland
WELCOME TO
RAVENHILL
MOTORS
FIRST TRUST
tabernacle

Passion for People

The true character of the ministry is a servant's heart.
Harold Warner

7.

He missed nothing

Bob Gass, once said, "If you don't, won't or can't love people, the ministry is not for you. The ministry is about people, not buildings. God requires Shepherds and nothing less. So if you don't love people, find a job but don't go into the ministry. I couldn't agree more with it. Loving' not merely 'liking' God's people is crucial in shepherding any church. It is not enough to like people. If a minister cannot love his people, he will not survive, especially in God's eyes. A servant of God must love his people with everything they have, which doesn't just mean loving those they favour. They must love those that are unruly and cause trouble. Naturally, a minister is human and will have favourites and trust people to confide in; although they will not reveal them, they will love all of their people, care deeply for them, and frequently discern when they go missing. Remember, Jesus said: "As the Father has loved me, so have I loved you, continue ye in my love." Therefore, if the Father loves the minister, ministers will love the Father's people they are responsible for. **James McConnell**

One wet Monday morning in 2008, the usual mayhem in the boardroom at the Metropolitan Tabernacle, Belfast, broke out. It was a chaotic time when the Pastors would meet regularly to let off steam before gearing up for another week of fast-paced ministry under Pastor James McConnell's guidance.

At that time, all twelve seats were taken, mine included, and morning prayers had ended. A welcome pot of tea had arrived with the usual selection of delicious goodies on offer. Naturally, no one dared to reach first for the freshly made pancakes with copious amounts of butter on them as these were the Pastor's privilege, but the iced-buns were fair game and caused no shortage of scuffling.

While the men fought over the food that morning, a Pastor, who shall remain nameless, was making mischief throwing paper aeroplanes into the teacup of a colleague. Some of the men were shouting and joking about the weekend football scores, while others were mocking a fellow Pastor's attempts to pronounce Mephibosheth's name during a recent preach when suddenly the table was thumped by the leading man.

"Listen up, guys," said Pastor McConnell, "I've just realised I missed 'Jim and Valerie' yesterday - (not their real names.). Did anyone spot them?"

All of us were speechless. We belonged to a megachurch, not a tiny gospel hall.

At the time, the Tabernacle regularly attracted crowds of thousands to one service. Yet, amongst such a gathering of faces, the senior Pastor was conscious of only one missing family.

With that, he grabbed his coat, asked one of the men to accompany him, and out the door, he rushed to visit his missing parishioners. Over the top?

Not for Pastor James McConnell. He took the work of God seriously and God's people seriously.

Regardless of the many distractions, he would have encountered the day before or any routine examination about his sermon, which most preachers experience, Pastor McConnell had missed 'Jim and Valerie'.

It was all he could think about. A rare gift, indeed!

There was no discussion about the previous evening's sermon. There was nothing uttered regarding the large attendance or other incidental matters; the Pastor didn't seek any pat on the back for 30-something souls coming to know Christ, a regular occurrence in those days.

Instead, the Pastor's sole focus was on who "wasn't" rather than who "was" at church the day before—observing people missing rather than in attendance was one of his unique attributes. He was always more concerned for the one gone astray than the ninety-nine present. He kept track of his flock and thought more of their welfare than his own.

Despite moving to the grander surroundings of the Metropolitan Tabernacle in 1994, the Pastor appeared to have retained the humble attitude he'd started with at a small hall on the Whitewell Road back in the 1950s. Whitewell may have become a big church, but the Pastor still held "small meetings" with the welfare of every person a priority.

In John chapter 10, the Lord Jesus Christ is the Good Shepherd who lays down his life for the sheep. We read of this shepherd in Psalm 23, the Epistle to the Hebrews, the First Epistle of Peter, and the book of Revelation. The words Shepherd and sheep shouldn't be underestimated in scripture. Even today, shepherds and sheep retain a prominent role in the rural life of the Mediterranean world, but it was especially so in Biblical times. Sheep were everywhere in the Near Eastern world. Sheep were essential for sustenance as the primary source of meat, though only rich people could regularly eat sheep. Solomon was so rich that he had 100 sheep and 100 goats to eat on his banqueting table every day! In those days, Shepherds not only knew the sheep, the sheep knew the shepherds.

Sheep and shepherding were familiar themes in the lives of the Old Testament characters, too; men like Isaac, Jacob, Joseph, and his brothers, David and his brothers (the sons of Jesse) were all shepherds, among a long list of others.

God's Word has always likened literal shepherds and sheep to His servants and His people. In this sense, James McConnell became a spiritual shepherd, and the people of his parish at Whitewell became his life.

"Some of God's so-called servants love crowds, but they don't love people," wrote the Pastor a few years ago in his book of one-liners entitled McConnellisms, which suitably describes the priority in his ministry. He attracted crowds yet found a way to love and minister to those crowds, and ultimately they eventually became his people.

It is significant that after Peter was restored by Jesus and given his life's commission, he wasn't told to build a vibrant church. Neither was it suggested by the Lord to become a great preacher or evangelist – even though that is a beautiful calling and what he ended up becoming. No, the first thing Jesus said to Peter was to give him a command in John chapter twenty-one- "Feed my sheep."

One Greek meaning is "pasture (tend) the lambs." Therefore, the totality of the task set before Peter and all shepherds is apparent by this command from the Lord Jesus. Consequently, the pastoral ministry should include Pastors caring for and feeding their people the Word of God.

Many young men from Whitewell entered the ministry after being initially inspired by Pastor McConnell's own ministerial drive and determination.

One of those is Pastor Jonathan Clarke, who attended Whitewell as a young man, and now oversees the ministry at the Welcome Evangelical Church in the Woodvale area of Belfast- a church founded by the family of the world-renowned missionary Amy Carmichael.

No matter how difficult times have proved, Pastor Jonathan has diligently attended to the needs of his people for many years, including completing the adjacent and impressive Amy Carmichael Centre. This Pastor has preached, week after week, month after month, and year after year, to the people in his patch, proclaiming God's goodness and offering God's love and support to those in his community. Yet, significantly, he is not only respected and admired for his considerable preaching ability – but also because he cares deeply for the flock of God and the people of his surrounding district – a quality he saw in James McConnell, a quality off course, all genuine

Christ was first and foremost interested in the flock of God, even though that would bring its share of problems. Of course, while people in many walks of life see an element of ministry in their work, being in charge of a church congregation, small or large, requires a unique kind of commitment and poses unusual challenges. It requires a great love for God's flock (people), and there is an understanding that one will most likely still experience criticism no matter what. It has been said that Pastors cannot win, for people will always find fault no matter what they do. Nevertheless: Pastor McConnell has resorted to some extreme measures over the years to protect his congregation, even outrageous methods. He still recalls the days when he would drive to the homes of people he'd been praying about as late as 2 am, throw stones at their windows and ask them if they were doing okay.

It was a regular habit in those days. He would tell them, "I know you think I'm crazy to wake you up at this hour, but you are on my heart, so please let me pray with you."

Perhaps if a Pastor did that today, the church elders would summons him, or someone else might commit him, yet it was all part of James McConnell having the heart of a shepherd. Simply put, he had a passion for ministry and his people.

Pastor Michael Bunting, who travelled exclusively with the Pastor during his term, remembers fondly one of his earliest memories of the man referred to by his people as "the Bishop" or "Servant." He experienced first-hand the Pastor's concern for his flock, which profoundly impacted his life and the life of another colleague at work.

Not long after joining the church at Whitewell, during the early 1980s, Pastor Michael was then working as a security person at Belfast International Airport.

On a Tuesday morning, he and a colleague were checking in their travel bags when Pastor McConnell arrived at the airport. Spotting Pastor Michael, he asked, "Is everything alright, Michael? I missed you at the prayer meeting last night?"

Michael then explained that he'd been on duty at the airport the night before and couldn't attend.

After the Pastor had made his way through airport security, Pastor Michael's colleague, not a believer, enquired who he was.

"That's the Bishop; he's our Pastor at Whitewell, How many people go to the prayer meeting? Around eight hundred, And how long have you been attending the church? A few months,"

His colleague fell silent and continued with his work before commenting, "You've been attending the church for just a few months, and the Pastor noticed you were missing from a crowd of 800 people?"

That incident not only left a mark on Pastor Michael, a story he recalls to this day but also spoke volumes to his colleague about God's love and care.

Bottom line: the call of God was a vocation to James McConnell, never a job!

People were his business. He was a shepherd, not a "hireling." He was called to the ministry, not appointed to it. He lived to preach, not preached to live.

As CH Spurgeon wrote, "he couldn't help preaching, "so he embraced it and became God's man for the hour.

Is this why he lasted over half a century in one place?

He had genuine compassion for his people and took an interest in them.

His ministry wasn't about sermons, theology, statistics, or even earning a living. Instead, it was rooted in his care for the sheep and the desire to not only remain faithful to them but to God and His work.

The distinction between a God-ordained Shepherd and a church employee is evident when we read the Bible, especially Christ's teachings about leaders and shepherds. In particular, Jesus was at pains to point out the difference between hired servants and God-appointed leaders.

For example, in John's gospel, Jesus explains how the hired hand is not the shepherd who owns the sheep. So, when he sees the wolf coming, he abandons the sheep and runs away. Then the wolf attacks the flock and scatters it. The man runs away because he is a hired hand and cares nothing for the sheep. Therefore, the primary difference between a hireling and a shepherd is their motivation for tending the sheep.

The hireling is interested in his gain, while the shepherd is willing to endure the pain for the sake of the sheep's welfare.

On the contrary, when managing the sheep no longer benefits the hireling, who is nothing more than a paid help, suddenly he is nowhere to be found and leaves the sheep scattered and unprotected.

Such individuals are not called by God but hired by men.

An analogy involves the sheepfolds of the East. These are roofless enclosures made of loose stone or surrounded by thorn bushes. They have only one door. The true shepherd came in the proper and appointed way, through the right door, thus indicating his office as a shepherd. When ministers follow this example and enter in by surrendering to their will, in service, humility, possessing love, and compassion for others, then a church is blessed indeed.

At the beginning of Pastor McConnell's ministry, he came in by the right door. Starting at the bottom, he worked his way up. Beginning, he received a paltry salary which continued for the next thirteen years. Even at the height of his ministerial career, he reluctantly accepted an average working wage – indicating a desire to preach and his dedication to his calling. Prosperity and profit were not on his list of priorities at any time. He accepted God's call to the ministry and the protection of God's people

Even though millions of pounds would eventually be brought into the Whitewell ministry, none of it has ever been used for his prosperity; moreover, it has exclusively been allocated to the Whitewell ministries, both home and abroad.

We examine the rise of the so-called prosperity doctrine and even covetous TV evangelists in the next chapter, which is a most critical subject today; meanwhile, the

Pastor has his doubts about some preachers who it appears unless they are receiving a handsome wage with benefits, will not take the job God has purposed for them. Notwithstanding, he also highlights how it is scriptural for the church to pay their ministers a decent wage without putting them or their families in danger of financial difficulties. Notwithstanding, when the balance sheet is king and personal comfort is the goal of any Pastor or church, people are easily replaced, and the church has lost its way.

The scripture says, "You shall not muzzle an ox when it treads out the grain," and, "The labourer deserves his wages. Therefore, it is proper to meet a minister or church employee's needs and not short-change them. I always tried to do this. Nevertheless, the flip side of this is that some preachers are extremely wealthy today, even personal millionaires, but how did they make their millions? When I was raising money, it was exclusively for God's work, and that's a significant difference, but the way some so-called ministers live today is nothing short of disgraceful. They say things like "the Lord has blessed me" and "the Lord has increased me," but what about Jesus of Nazareth who said – "foxes have holes and the birds of the air have nests, but the Son of man hath not where to lay his head." What about people struggling to make ends meet while they live in luxury? **James McConnell**

Pastor McConnell always had a conscience about any money God had given him. He raised thousands for the work of God and poured all of it back into the ministry at Whitewell and ministries at home and abroad.

While money is the weakness of many individuals, it has never been his God. While he was always trying to raise funds, it was explicitly to further his projects: a church plant, church extension, or even sending money to help young missionaries in foreign countries. The Pastor was too committed to his calling, too busy even to think of spending money on himself. When once asked if he owned a large jet at Belfast City Airport, he laughed it off with the line, "And when would I get time to fly it?"

The accusation about owning a jet was at odds with a man who lived and breathed to minister to his local church. While his church's wealth increased due to God's favour, he never sought to feather his own nest. On the contrary, if the Pastor felt he was receiving too much money personally, he would regularly refuse it or give it back to the ministry.

Once, he even returned an expensive new car as he felt it would send out the wrong signal about his ministry. The congregation and his leadership begged him to take it, reminding him of his faithfulness over the years and that it was a blessing from the Lord and the community, yet all to no avail. He wasn't comfortable with it, and his conscience about money and God was his deciding factor in turning down the generous offer.

The truth is, no matter how much progress the Pastor made in terms of buildings and church growth, even popularity, and regardless of his increasing reputation, he never really outgrew his roots of walking to church and back during the days when he didn't own a car. Then he visited his flock on his feet for many years, wearing out his shoes, and was always saving money to use for the Kingdom of God – something that didn't go unnoticed. One night, for example, a lady noticed holes in his shoes when he was on his knees praying, and she went out immediately and bought him a new pair. He relied on things like that. It was all part of his conscience towards the treasury of God, not to mention his commitment to God's people – people like 'Jim and Valerie'- who were much more precious to him than silver and gold and a generous plate of pancakes and tempting buns.

Be thou diligent to know the state of thy flocks and look well to thy herds.
Proverbs 27:23

8.

Selfish Shepherds and Prosperity Preachers

There's no doubt that some people have become rich on the back of the poor and have discouraged the flock rather than encouraged God's people. The ministry is about people, not bricks and mortar or money. Ministers are called to Shepherd the sheep, caring for the people of God, not to operate like Commanders in Chief running a corporate organisation. They are not army sergeants but God's servants. **James McConnell**

Evidence of a man or woman called by God is humility.

It is the essential attribute of any Christian leader, but especially ministers.

No matter how much one knows and understands the scriptures, God's Word is better carried and communicated by those with a humble heart. Therefore, humility always values people and desires the best for them. Augustine wrote: "Humility, humility, humility, is what every Christian requires."

Jonathan Edwards also stated: "Nothing sets a person so much out of the devil's reach as humility."

In the same way, Christ laid down his life for the sheep; a sincere shepherd puts the people's best interests above their own.

When evaluating any ministry or Church, neither numbers, programmes, or events prove successful outreach. What heralds a ministry as successful, even divine, is when the same assembly people are in unity and spiritual health and love the Lord and one another. Humility in a Pastor or minister reveals God's will and blessing and brings a peaceful place to worship.

We see an example of this humility in his second letter to the Philippians written by the Apostle Paul. Speaking of the lowliness and yet greatness of the Lord Jesus Christ, he wrote: "If there be therefore any consolation in Christ, if any comfort of love, if any fellowship of the Spirit, if any bowels and mercies, Fulfil ye my joy, that ye be likeminded, having the same love, being of one accord, of one mind. Let nothing be done through strife or vainglory, but in lowliness of mind, let each esteem other better than themselves. Look not every man on his own things, but every man also on the things of others. Let this mind be in you, which was also in Christ Jesus: Who, being in the form of God, thought it not robbery to be equal with God: But made himself of no reputation, and took upon him the form of a servant, and was made in the likeness of men: And being found in fashion as a man, he humbled himself and became obedient unto death, even the death of the cross. Wherefore God also hath highly exalted him and given him a name which is above every name." **Philippians 2:1-9**

Humility is contrary to most teaching and survival today. Our world and culture have conditioned us to respond to slick entertainment and media output and follow and promote confident, outgoing people, regardless of character.

Furthermore, the 21st century has embraced a "celebrity-like Church," where the Pastor has become a TV star, accentuated by the arrival of Covid-19 when many churches had to rely solely on their online output.

Apart from the many positives in such a development, which we will cover later, it is worth noting how excessive self-awareness encourages ministers and Christians to prioritise their online status and reputation rather than concentrate on the accurate measure of one's faith: spiritual fruit and the needs of the flock. What a minister wears and how his studio or office looks before broadcasting is not as crucial as genuinely connecting with and meeting the congregation's needs.

The late Margaret Thatcher once said about politicians, "It used to be about trying to do something, but now it's about trying to be someone."

I have used every media technique at my disposal, including online facilities, and they are perfectly acceptable but only if the motive for using them is correct. If ministers intend to promote themselves, social media and online ministry are counterproductive options. On the other hand, if the intention is to spread God's Word, people will be reached, touched, and blessed by the gospel. However, it all begins with humility in the heart of the servant. What is the real motive? **James McConnell**

In the Bible, selfish and self-important shepherds are referred to as "waterless springs" that attract people to themselves rather than God. They build a ministry around themselves instead of for and on behalf of their people and even believe the more seats they fill, the more significant proof it is of a successful ministry. However, the mark of any great church is not in its seating capacity but its sending capacity.

Is spiritual repression a new thing? Not at all!

During the reformation, similar abuse occurred when people became dependent on the Church and the Pastor, saints, priests, or sacraments, rather than being led into beautiful freedom with a relationship through the Lord Jesus Christ. It caused Martin Luther to cry out on behalf of the people, and we may indeed require such a voice again. Protestantism has often pointed the finger at Catholicism for this sort of behaviour, yet the truth is many protestant denominations have also been guilty of spiritual abuse.

All this runs contrary to the fact that a church and Pastor's primary function is to steer their flocks to a meaningful relationship and in-depth knowledge of Jesus Christ and provide their communities with care and consideration.

When there is an understanding of what Jesus accomplished on the cross at Calvary, which was to set people free, the result will be greater humility, which produces greater surrender, one of the most significant challenges for all believers, especially the clergy.

DL Moody once said, "God has yet to find a man surrendered unto himself."

While the Pastor agrees with this sentence, he believes every minister and Pastor must live a reasonably surrendered and humble life.

Despite becoming aware of his imperfections, he remained uninterested in personal prosperity throughout his ministry, sticking rigidly to his religious devotions. It's in stark contrast to what he sees as a "disturbing development" today, where some preachers and Pastors appear more interested in preaching and ministering as long as they are well remunerated.

A minister's objective isn't to gain popularity wealth and line their pockets or establish power but seek their flock's health and prosperity at all times. It is a surrendered life, not a selfish one. In the Old Testament, Ezekiel wrote of a true shepherd: "Blessed is he, who in the name of charity and goodwill shepherds the weak through the valley of darkness, for he is truly his brother's keeper and the finder of lost children." However, Ezekiel warns of counterfeit leaders – "wolves in sheep's clothing" - as Jesus also did – exposing such people who fleece the flock for personal gain. **James McConnell**

In this respect, much criticism has been levelled in recent years at those who build individual nest eggs, having little or no regard for the people they oversee. Stories have abounded in recent years of how some TV evangelists have become comfortable and ridiculously wealthy through preaching the gospel even to the extent of owning grand mansions, having butlers, flying personal jets, and securing numerous luxurious properties worldwide and a comfortable lifestyle.

Is this level of affluence necessary?

Is this acceptable?

Is it the blessing of God, as is often claimed by these same individuals?

Is it a God thing at all?

These are relevant and appropriate questions.

I'm too mixed up about it all. If the Lord meets my needs and the needs of my family, then I am happy. I want God to meet my needs, not my greed, and many Pastors today are greedy rather than needy. **James McConnell**

So what is the so-called "prosperity preacher" or "prosperity doctrine" we hear so much about these days? The prosperity gospel, referred to as the '*health and wealth gospel,*' or the *'gospel of success and faith,'* has become attractive to Christians worldwide because it promises God's blessing both financially and physically, no matter what.

Those who accept it are convinced faith, positive speech, and donations to religious causes will significantly increase their material wealth and hasten such blessings.

Prosperity preachers often view the Bible as a contract between God and humans.

In other words, if humans have faith in God, He, in turn, will deliver security and prosperity. However, this doctrine is entirely erroneous and rarely mentions anything about suffering in a Christian's life or the gift of Salvation through Jesus Christ.

Instead, it concentrates more on personal empowerment, suggesting that it's always God's will for His people to be happy and wealthy. Not surprisingly, then, prosperity theology comes in for severe criticism by leaders from various Christian denominations, including within the Pentecostal and Charismatic movements, where it originated in the United States.

While most evangelicals believe God wants to bless his people; nevertheless, critics of prosperity preaching maintain it is irresponsible to present God as some "sugar daddy" while promoting idolatry, insisting on how it is contrary to Scripture.

Sadly, secular observers have also criticised the prosperity doctrine as exploitative of the poor.

Fascinatingly, many preachers who previously endorsed the message of excessive wealth and prosperity through God are now beginning to backtrack from it. They've become embarrassed because, of course, the Gospel "is not for sale," and some teaching concerning faith and prosperity has become "out of balance."

So, the question remains: is there a need for such extravagance?

Such people confuse the secular with the consecrated! The leadership of any organisation brings both power and responsibility. In church terms, a servant serves others, but a selfish shepherd helps himself. He fails to clothe or feed the sheep. When this occurs, the sheep get scattered and left to all kinds of dangers; the weak become weaker, people remain sick, the injured stay wounded, and the strays never get found. Ezekiel wrote, "Without the shepherd, the sheep become food for all the wild beasts." **James McConnell**

People have become tired of watching their leaders grow rich on the back of their congregations. From the emergence of Coronavirus, many people are more isolated than ever and are crying out for a humble shepherd in their lives to help meet their spiritual needs.

Instead of church leaders introducing their own agendas, I would encourage them to consider God's more mundane and routine work by tending to their and God's precious flock? After all, those building their kingdoms will not be in God's kingdom. These are not my words but the words of the Lord Jesus. I would genuinely encourage modern ministers to think firstly of their flock and help meet their needs. Ignoring your people's plight while guarding one's prosperity is a far cry from what God expects from shepherds of the sheep. In my opinion, it highlights the stark contrast between selfish shepherds and God's servants. **James McConnell**

Uncomfortable as this section may be, the Pastor believes it is both biblical and responsible for drawing attention to the dangers of greed and prosperity in the life of a shepherd of God. He quotes Matthew chapter 25 and the parable about the sheep and the goats to underscore his point.

In it, Jesus had some powerful words, not just for leaders but also for all believers in this parable, challenging every person of faith. For example, after explaining what is expected from a shepherd of the sheep, some replied to Jesus, "Lord, when did we see you hungry or thirsty or a stranger or needing clothes or sick or in prison and did not help you." to which Jesus replied: "Depart from me, I never knew you. Truly I tell you, whatever you did not do for the least of these, you did not do for me. So then they will go away into eternal punishment, but the righteous to eternal life." **Matthew 25: 45-46**

True shepherds have a heart for their people and will defend their people and call to the hilt. They will seek the lost and sacrifice the pleasures of material things. They understand their calling, and they are born Pastors and protectors of people, not prosperity-obsessed.

Concerning Pastors, I recall a day that still leaves me feeling slightly embarrassed. Interviewing the Pastor for his first biography, The Seer's House, I made a terrible blunder, I was not experienced and happened to remark that he wasn't so much a Pastor, more a preacher. That was how I saw things at the time.

Talk about a comment backfiring!

I thought the remark would compliment him, and he'd be pleased with my assessment of his ministry, but how wrong I was. Instead, it provoked an instant reaction from him, forcing the reply, "I disagree; I am very much a Pastor and a shepherd to God's people also."

His reaction spoke loudly of his devotion to his calling as a Pastor. As my face rapidly reddened, he proceeded to tell me how he would visit the hospitals between 7 am and 9 am and how he had a regular visitation route, just like the other Pastors. He then elaborated on a string of other duties he often carried out, leaving me feeling mortified. It wasn't my finest hour in interviewing terms but a lesson well worth learning. Ministry is more than preaching, and no minister will survive preaching alone. People are blessed by good preaching, but they are desperate for something else these days - a humble and surrendered Pastor and a loving shepherd.

Pastoring people is more than preaching and bringing sermons to an audience every week. God is not only looking for preachers; He's searching for Shepherds in the same way that he found a young David in the field tending the sheep. You will never be accepted as a preacher if you are not first a shepherd. I repeat, God is looking for shepherds, but not selfish shepherds or celebrities and indeed not thieves! Remember, the Pharisees were both. They stole the sheep in Messiah's absence, and they slew the Messiah when he came. They did not come in the ways ordained of God. In the words of the most excellent Shepherd of all: "The thief cometh not, but that he may steal, and kill, and destroy: I came that they may have life and may have it more abundantly, A Pastor's priority is NOT to "build a bank account" or even a "reputation." Instead, their calling is to "build the flock" and seek lost souls and let the Lord take care of everything else. The anointing of God meets every need and never your greed. The objective of preaching is to win souls to Christ, not make a fortune for oneself. I used to tell my people: You will know them by their fruits, not their suits! When preachers focus on winning souls, they have no time for material things. A Shepherd seeks the lost and is concerned with the welfare of his people. It is the solitary focus and absolute proof of his calling. **James McConnell**

Greater love hath no man than this that a man
lay down his life for his friends.
John 15:13

9.

God's Shepherd

If the Good Shepherd gave His life for the sheep, then the Shepherd of God will act likewise. That is always the yardstick. Even when people upset the shepherd, disappoint him, and let him down, he's still a shepherd and must act accordingly. The biggest test in a shepherd's life is when bad things happen; what will be the response? The shepherd must answer for the sheep no matter what has taken place. Of course, shepherds are not perfect, and they are mere flesh and blood, but those genuinely called to shepherd the sheep will have surrendered much to please the Lord. They will have even denied themselves their happiness and comfort and will not seek revenge or retribution. A man or woman doesn't have to be perfect to enter the ministry, but they need to care deeply about those they govern. **James McConnell**

The book of Matthew states how, when Jesus saw the multitudes, he was "moved with compassion because they were fainting and scattered abroad as sheep having no shepherd." **Matthew 9:36**

The extraordinary nature of Christ's ministry is His great compassion.

Christ, as the Good Shepherd, had a love for the sheep and the flock of God.

As we address the critical issue of passion for people in ministry, all aspiring ministers face the most appropriate question for our 21st-century generation: what makes a true Shepherd of God?

As we have covered, nothing is more discouraging than a shepherd full of greed and corruption who displays no mercy or compassion towards their flock.

On the other hand, sincere shepherds continually see the best in people and believe the best about their group.

They are humble enough to be challenged and regularly extend mercy and grace, affording chance after chance, and consistently believing and hoping for positive things.

I'm convinced God's shepherd possesses that rare gift of love spoken about by Paul, the apostle in Corinthians' first book – Love is patient and kind; love does not envy or boast; it is not arrogant or rude. It does not insist on its way; it is not irritable or resentful; it does not rejoice at wrongdoing but rejoices with the truth.

Love bears all things, believes all things, hopes all things, and endures all things **1 Corinthians 13:4-7**

God's representatives display His true nature and character, love, joy, peace, patience, kindness, and forgiveness - evident fruits of the Spirit.

Notwithstanding, when a leader discourages the flock of God, the people lose hope, and the beautiful gift of God's restoration is lost. Moreover, it often results in heartache for God's people, incongruously at the hands of those supposed to bless them.

It is possible to possess the necessary qualifications for the job, except for the most important one –deep love and concern for the flock.

Academic achievement is helpful, but the gospel minister requires the heart to go with the job description.

Even during their most significant traits and rejection, the telling feature of all loyal, dedicated servants of God remains faithful ministers focused on their flocks.

Moses was such a man. He prayed continually on behalf of his community and defended them when they had come up short. Even when they criticised him and threatened to stone him, he continued to plead to God on their behalf. Moses was a type of Christ and became a picture of the Good and Faithful Shepherd, the Lord Jesus, who gave his life for the sheep and forgave the sins of many. In this respect, Moses was a man like Jesus. The book of John states: "Greater love hath no man than this that a man lay down his life for his friends." **John 15:13**

Although he lived in a different era to Moses, Nehemiah was also a great shepherd having a heart for his brethren. He stood firm against great provocation, helped rebuild the broken walls of Jerusalem, and even sacrificed his comforts in Babylon in exchange for hardship and danger in Israel. He was indeed a true shepherd of God.

Think about it!

Here is a man who turned his back on prosperity for poverty! He shunned fame and fortune for faith and famine. When others stayed where they were, he returned to Israel as others were leaving yet not without reward. His selfless actions helped save his brethren from tyranny and his nation from apostasy. Nehemiah returned to Israel to face the problems in Jerusalem and rebuild its walls. In short; Nehemiah was a true shepherd, and similar to King David, he became a man revered by his people.

Nehemiah was a mighty man of God, but David was equally an immense example of a sincere shepherd. Regardless of his mistakes, he had the Spirit and love of God all over him, causing God to choose him and anoint him for service. Psalm 89 records: "I have found David, my servant; with my holy oil have I anointed him. Notice how God "found" David!" It proves that God is looking for the sheep and looking for Shepherds and leaders. It is one thing for young aspiring ministers to "catch the eye" of their Pastor. Still, another to be found and handpicked by God! God observed David "following the little ewes great with young and brought him to feed Jacob his people and Israel his inheritance." He saw in David gentleness and a humble spirit that He could use for His glory. **James McConnell**

In other words, in God's eyes, if David could lead the ewes' great with young, he could do the same for the people of God. David's humility is what caught the attention of God, and his care for the sheep revealed his heart for God. David's priority wasn't himself, building projects or business proposals, but people. Jacquelyn K. Heasley wrote: "Use your ministry to build people, not people, to build your ministry."

David has received enormous criticism for his affair with Bathsheba and is infamous for this misdemeanour. He was far from a perfect man. Yet, David is also remembered as a great shepherd prompting God to describe him as "a man after my own mine heart." **1 Samuel 13:14** David loved God, declaring those well-known words in Psalm 23, "The Lord is my Shepherd."

David's trust and confidence were not in himself but in the Lord. Just as Jesus was David's shepherd, the imperfect David became a shepherd to others. Due to the incredible love, forgiveness, and mercy, he experienced from his heavenly Shepherd, David proceeded to lavish understanding to all around him. He could say like the hymn writer, "I have a

Shepherd, one I love so well, how he has blessed me; the tongue can never tell." What an encouragement this is to every minister seeking to please their people and the Lord today! It is worth repeating that, like David, mortal Shepherds and leaders are by no means, perfect people. They make mistakes and fail and require guidance from the great shepherd, but in many cases, they are still people with enormous compassion for others and, through grace, tend to the sheep in extraordinary ways. It is possible to be imperfect and a great shepherd. David is proof! **James McConnell**

Such imperfection, coupled with strength, was a constant facet of Pastor McConnell's ministry. Here is a Christ-like attribute in every sincere shepherd.

Love for the people makes one a great shepherd, not business acumen, theological knowledge, or preaching ability. A shepherd is a leader who cares about and loves his flock. If he loses that or, worse still, doesn't possess it, he might as well quit. A shepherd of the sheep will be judged and remembered for how he cared for the sheep – period! Poor shepherds are always selfish shepherds at heart. When a man is interested in himself, he has become a poor shepherd. Such leaders rarely go after sheep that are leaving. On the other hand, a faithful shepherd never gives up on his sheep, and his passion for the people will ensure that. I have lost countless nights of sleep over people who left the church and those who never returned; I still pray for them today. It's all part of being God's Shepherd. **James McConnell**

When it comes to protecting his flock, over the years, the Pastor has done things that certainly would not be taught or advised at any modern-day Bible college, which he isn't afraid to discuss. For example, some years ago, in one of his early churches at the bottom of the Whitewell Road, he heard about an incident inside a rented building when someone verbally abused some of the church's elders and ladies. It was a shocking incident that left them all in tears.

The Pastor says he told his people and staff to leave the building to deal with the matter himself. When they had all gone, the Pastor recalled giving the person involved a proper good scolding rather than counsel the man responsible.

On another occasion, when the Pastor went to the home of a lady who attended his church, he was told that her husband was giving her a hard time about the grocery bill and regularly raising his hands. The Pastor again recalls taking the husband into the hall, and instead of offering him the usual time of prayer, showed him an alternative and unorthodox form of ministry!!!

Of course, hardly religious practice, but he maintains it was merely a case of a shepherd defending the sheep.

He fondly remembers other extraordinary ways he has had to be a shepherd of the flock. For example, one night, a lady called to say that her husband was in the local pub and needed someone to safely bring him home as she didn't want him to drink and drive. The Pastor went immediately to the public house and was jokingly offered drinks by the locals who recognised him and asked why he was there. "*I'm taking this man home now, and no one will stop me,*" he replied before grabbing the man and putting him into his car and driving him home.

I wouldn't advise anyone to do those things now; I am unsure if Pastors consider such drastic action. But I was younger then, inexperienced and full of youthful enthusiasm for God, and it was love and passion that provoked those things, love for my people and love for the work of God. I genuinely cared about what happened to them. God's shepherd will defend the sheep even when it is inconvenient and often takes courage. It is not the job of shepherds to root out and expose people for their failures. They must help them find restoration. Unfortunately, the ministry seems to be churning out police officers and prosecutors instead of Pastors. I believe Pastors need to learn how to encourage rather than expose. The apostle Peter wrote, "Above all, keep loving one another earnestly since love covers a multitude of sins." **James McConnell**

Over the years, the Pastor has covered and helped many people in distress or who have found themselves experiencing compromising situations. After decades of ministry, he is acutely aware of how imperfect he and his people are. He still recalls how a young couple ran away together to Portrush in Co Antrim while their parents were on holiday. The Pastor knew if the parents discovered this, they would both be in trouble, so he drove to Portrush and found them, talked gently to them, and proceeded to bring them home in his car. It is an incident the parents know nothing about to this very day. Every time the couple, who are now married, see the Pastor, they chuckle and smile affectionately.

People think a Pastor only gets up on a Sunday and addresses his congregation, but there's much more to shepherding the sheep than this. Having a passion for people is what ministry is all about, and where there are people, problems exist.

In many ways, a Pastor is a problem solver and a parental figure. People must feel safe with their Pastor, and the flock of God must have a shepherd they can turn to in difficult times. While a Pastor shouldn't be afraid to wield discipline, if and when required, people, in general, need to be encouraged and reminded of their better side. Therefore, they often need a compassionate, present Pastor, not an absent or uncaring one. **James McConnell**

In this respect, the Pastor insists he always tried to make himself available to his flock, a practice he fears may be "going out of fashion."

People frequently require an appointment today with a Pastor who claims his diary is "full of tasks," but this is not shepherding the people of God. Pastors are not CEOs; they are shepherds and men and women of God, on-call for their people 24/7. I never owned a diary and never needed one. The church must not become a business, which is the opposite of Jesus' words when he said: "Wist ye not that I must be about my father's business". Jesus wasn't referring to administration in this context, accountancy, or programmes, even though a church's administration and organisation are necessary. Instead, he says that shepherding is 'the father's business,' and those who lead, protect the work of God, keep the flock together, and perform the Father's business are genuinely called of God. **James McConnell**

Looking after a few sheep in the wilderness is one thing, and it took considerable faithfulness and dedication during the early days of Pastor McConnell's ministry when he supervised just a handful of people; however, controlling a megachurch, which the Pastor did for the second half of his Christian calling, must have been quite an ordeal also. After all, how does one person look after thousands of people? How does one switch from looking after a few sheep in the wilderness (10 people in 1957) to caring for thousands by the late nineties?

How does one be a shepherd and a businessman at the same time?

By separating the two. God observed David "following the little ewes great with young and brought him to feed Jacob his people and Israel his inheritance." While I fed the people with the Word of God, I was fortunate to have my wife Margaret as support in general. She was a remarkable person to have by my side, especially during my early years, and I couldn't have done without her. In addition, my daughter Linda and her assistant Geraldine Higgins, and other great people around me took care of the administration and finances. At the same time, I attended to the duties of a Pastor/shepherd. Without these people, I couldn't have been as successful in the ministry. A shepherd must continually focus on God's work and his people to succeed, but they require others to help carry out the assignment. **James McConnell**

Teamwork is a subject we examine later in the book, but love and passion for his people earned the Pastor much respect. Worry, concern, care, call it what you will; the Pastor always tried to exude genuine love for his people, despite the daily stresses and strains associated with the ministry.

It didn't mean he was a "pushover," he hasn't claimed to be either soft or perfect, but deep down, he wanted the best for his flock and fought their corner on many occasions. It was all part of being a shepherd of the sheep and showing passion for people – the aspiring minister's most marvellous and admirable attribute.

Passion for Ministry

Preach the word; be instant in season, out of season; reprove, rebuke, exhort with all longsuffering and doctrine.
2 Timothy 4:2

10.

Prophetic Preaching in a Politically Correct World

I have been the victim of political correctness on several occasions and unfairly targeted in my ministry. It has crept in everywhere, and frankly, it needs addressing. Ministers must return to the old days when a person laid all on the altar and preached the message of God's Word. When I was growing up and still had interests in other things, the people of the Church were praying for me and asking God - "Lord help him to lay all on the altar for you." The ministry is something unusual and unique, a God-given and Christ-centered vocation. I have even been prepared to go to prison to stand for the truth of God's Word and stand up to the political correctness in our generation. It is that important to me. **James McConnell**

James McConnell is no stranger to being silenced and even censored in his ministry by the politically correct. Over the years, he's regularly faced opposition when preaching the Word of God, especially when met with a possible jail sentence for remarks he made about Muslims. While he has since graciously admitted that those comments could have been better articulated - even apologising for them publicly – it is also fair to point out that Pastor McConnell was vindicated in court.

Whether we like it or not, political correctness is here to stay, and many ministers face the choice to either appease those who would seek to silence them or take a stand and preach the Word of God. In this chapter, while the Christian reader is encouraged to continue to stand for the truth, there is a cautionary reminder of a healthy balance to be found in preaching God's Word, which should always go forth as a message of hope, love, and grace not just a statement of truth.

During what was dubbed by the Press "The Islam Storm" in 2014, the Pastor was accused of race-hate crimes because of what he had said about Muslims and Islam's religion. Still, he has always maintained he never had anything personal against people who believe in the Islamic faith. Instead, he says he was merely exercising his right to preach the Word of God and hitting out at the more radical forms of extremism.

He accepts that some of what he said, however, could have been interpreted as offensive, following the remarks by the judge in the trial which followed. Still, significantly some of what was in his sermon also came to pass, particularly concerning religious extremism, which seemed to explode globally shortly after his address.

I was tired of watching injustice and inequality towards the Christian faith. So I was merely standing up for my right to preach the Word of God. Unfortunately, prophetic preaching is a consequential responsibility in a politically correct world. **James McConnell**

It's all part of the Pastors' focus, a determination not to be distracted, and because he's always had what many agree is "an authentic prophetic ministry."

The Pastor is Pentecostal and passionately believes in Bible prophecy and the prophetic office. But, of course, such a ministry often courts controversy. Many reject prophecy because it warns of outrageous and sometimes unpleasant things to come. Until prophecy has been tried and tested, it can indeed seem extreme. A prophet's words were not always palatable in Bible days. Still, they often proved instrumental in keeping the flock of God away from impending danger, not to mention bringing clarity where there was previously confusion.

The great prophet, Samuel, was known as "The Seer." After losing livestock, Saul and his Father Kish went to the Seer's House to find direction and instruction, which led to Saul becoming King. Saul also learned a valuable lesson on that same journey; he was told to stand still for a while so that Samuel could show him the Word of God. Throughout his ministry, the Word of God directed Samuel as it did all faithful servants of God. As David penned in Psalm 119, "Thy word is a lamp unto our feet and a light unto our path."

Yet, the most outstanding facet of all the prophets has been pointing to the Messiah's first coming in the Old Testament and the Second Coming in the New Testament. Of course, not every preacher is a prophet, demonstrative, or even outspoken. A softer delivery than the Pastor exuded during his calling to the ministry is acceptable and indeed probably more common these days, but never at the expense of watering down God's Word.

There is a greater need than ever in this politically correct world for a prophetic voice in the Church. The Church requires a prophetic ministry, but sadly too often, instead of "prophetic" ministry, it has produced "pathetic" ministry. People ask what a prophetic ministry is. It shouldn't be confused with shouting and bluster but communicating the words of God to humanity and then seeing those words come to pass. A God-sent preacher will not water down God's Word to please the hearers. But, of course, by remaining faithful to the Bible and the Gospel's message, a preacher invites inevitable controversy and must be prepared to accept this. I am reminded of the story of a German Pastor who went to prison for preaching about Christ. He was visited by a friend and asked, "What are you doing in this jail?" to which he replied, "And why are you not in jail?" Preaching about Jesus comes at a price, and one's message is not always readily received, no matter how inoffensive it seems. **James McConnell**

The Pastor is not alone in falling foul of the politically correct police - a more recent illustration being Franklin Graham, son of the late Billy Graham.

In early 2020, he saw a series of pre-planned gospel meetings in the UK cancelled because of his strong Christian views. Opposition and interference to God's Word through direct preaching need challenging because the state should not stray into censoring church sermons or unwittingly creating a right not to be offended.

On the other hand, Christians often overlook that it is also incumbent on the Church and gospel preachers to wisely steward its freedom of speech to present Christ graciously and appealingly. Not doing so will undoubtedly cause unnecessary offence and create an obstacle to salvation for the hearers.

Is this a difficult balance to find?

Of course, it is. I have said things I regret over the years, but remember preachers are not perfect, sometimes they get it wrong, but God's servants are also right on many occasions and confirm that God sends them. But I accept that words have consequences, and the Gospel's message should always be tempered with truth, hope, love, and grace. **James McConnell**

John the Baptist's story illustrates the importance of finding grace and truth in a preacher's life. When John announced the arrival of the ministry of Jesus Christ, the greatest preacher ever, he said something very revealing - "And the Word became flesh and dwelt among us, (and we beheld His glory the glory as of the only begotten of the Father) full of grace and truth. **John 1:14**

Speaking of Jesus, John proclaimed the Saviour of the world as a man with a perfect balance, being full of grace and truth! Jesus told it like it was but never offended people or condemned them for no good reason. Unfortunately, some preachers today feel they haven't spoken the truth unless they leave people offended. It is a highly distorted form of evangelism and a significant misrepresentation of the Gospel.

During His earthly ministry, Jesus suffered much persecution for preaching the truth but balanced all his sayings with words of great grace. Yet His message was frequently rejected. That said, even though today, the good news about Jesus will prove offensive at times, preachers must still be careful not to add to that offence.

If this occurs, it is usually because the preacher's prejudice had taken precedence over the Gospel's right message.

So, how does the Church navigate a politically correct world, standing for truth without offending unnecessarily? How does a professing Christian, let alone a preacher, remain faithful to God's Word without insulting or losing the person they hope to convert?

One way is to remain restrained in our vocabulary as we use it. However, we may also need to count the cost of practicing free speech, given that society and the court system are trying to smother, silence, and even eliminate Christian messages.

Who would have imagined that we would witness people standing on street corners with a Bible proclaiming the Gospel being arrested by the police? Yet, it has become a frequent occurrence today.

Every preacher's right starting place is to realise that trying to please a politically correct world is a futile policy for any preacher. Loyal followers of Christ will preach the whole truth of the Gospel, but always with the grace of God, and even when the time is not appropriate.

Preaching God's Word is not always convenient, but, despite the opposition, it is still mightily essential in this wayward and perishing generation. Paul, the apostle, knew all about the opposition and political correctness, even during the days of his ministry.

It is no new phenomenon.

Paul wrote to Timothy, who was younger and perhaps a lot less bold, the words "Preach the word; be instant in season, out of season; reprove, rebuke, exhort with all longsuffering and doctrine." **2 Timothy 4:2**

Paul encourages Timothy, the Church, and its ministers to declare God's word and proclaim that all those in Christ Jesus are brothers and sisters in Him. No matter the background, in Christ, God's love is freely available, and the unsaved depend on churches and Pastors preaching the right message of the Gospel no matter what the current climate is.

Every preacher will have a different delivery style, but the content must always be the truth of God's Word. Whether some choose to proclaim the Gospel with great enthusiasm or whisper is not essential. The critical thing is to deliver it without resorting to another gospel. Today, we hear about another Jesus, another gospel, and another God. If this continues, the Church will become unrecognisable and void of any real clout. Sadly, in many cases, this has already occurred. **James McConnell**

Notwithstanding the importance of speaking the truth, words unquestionably have power, and words have consequences.

More than ever, because of the explosion of social media and the internet, words have the opportunity and ability to influence many fields today, such as politics, via Christian and secular forms of broadcasting, and particularly in spiritual environments.

German composer Richard Strauss once said: "The human voice is the most beautiful instrument of all, but it is the most difficult to play."

Good leadership requires self-control and carefully chosen sentences, and it's a sign of respect and responsibility for the position one holds. Leaders - especially those in the ministry - are not just responsible for what they say, and they are responsible for what people hear.

Of course, today, it appears, due to obsession with equality, people can say whatever they like, even if it isn't factual or fair, and even if it is downright offensive

Sadly, it appears worldwide there is an appetite for this sort of reckless politics and radical preaching as more and more people demand freedom of speech. Many politicians and preachers have peddled outlandish statements to sensationalise their message or draw attention to themselves. Unfortunately, all this has accomplished is to confuse and, in many cases, condemn certain groups of people and create further division.

The right to free speech should never be confused with a perceived right to promote hate or limit the freedom of others, especially minority groups. Jesus taught us to obey the land laws and hate the sin but love the sinner. It is not that people are demanding the right to free speech – if they live in a democratic country, they already have that right. Instead, it is rather that some are demanding the right to demonise or promote hatred of others. Such actions lead to the gas chambers of Nazi Germany or the genocides we have witnessed in our lifetimes in Serbia, Rwanda, Iraq, Afghanistan, and Syria. Christians should always ask themselves –what would Christ do? Where would He be standing?

The words we use matter! Solomon wrote: "Death and life are in the power of the tongue, and they that love it shall eat the fruit thereof" **Proverbs 18:21** In the New Testament, the Apostle Paul, one of the greatest gospel preachers of all, is quoted as saying, "Let your speech be always with grace, seasoned with salt, that ye may know how ye ought to answer every man **Colossians 4:6**

Everyone is screaming to say something in our 21st Century age of social media and the internet. Yet, the reality is not everyone has something applicable or appropriate to say. Free speech, therefore, is not careless talk, and it comes with responsibility.

Again, on the other hand, today, there is a genuinely understood criticism of the Christian faith: God's representatives are being muzzled. We live in a time when many Christians believe the Bible will be outlawed, Churches' activities curtailed, and ministers of the Gospel sanctioned if such a time isn't already upon us. It appears you can be anything you like except a Christian.

These days, a question is: has this politically correct generation gone too far, influencing how churches are being run? Is a politically correct agenda the cause of ill-judged statements, especially by frustrated and repressed church leaders?

The answer seems to be an overwhelmingly yes! Preachers are often provoked to say things they later regret because of bullying by politically correct people.

After all, through no fault of their own, many churches are subject to increased scrutiny and are pressured to follow the rules and regulations that previous generations didn't have to follow. At a stage in society when we are trying to avoid saying things that offend, we have reached a point where people get attacked for speaking the truth. So, the result is a more militant response by Pastors and preachers than would have otherwise been necessary. During his ministerial career, the Pastor was compared with a "Trump-like style" following his statements about Muslims. He maintains no malice was ever intended towards any religious faith; instead, he insists he solely defended the Christian faith.

Of course, if being politically correct means that we treat people of different backgrounds with respect and do not stereotype them, then it is, in fact, no bad thing! Yet is this the underlying objective of our contemporary, politically correct movement? On the contrary, many ministers feel that politically correct people seek to "water down" their message and only want pre-approved words. Even the title of a Pastor today or a minister is being changed, which most people may not recognise. In this politically correct era, clerics are often referred to as "ministers of religion." It is a far cry from Pastor McConnell's early days in ministry when clergymen and women were known merely as, servants or Pastors.

So, what does he think of these new titles and a softening of all things godly?

It is how you see yourself and what God has called you to be. Remember the words of Paul: "Paul, an apostle of Jesus Christ by the will of God, according to the promise of life which is in Christ Jesus". He didn't announce himself as some great preacher or use any grand title. Instead, he described himself as an apostle of Jesus Christ by the will of God. In the book of Romans, he even describes himself as Paul, a bondservant of Jesus Christ, called to be an apostle, separated unto the Gospel of God. We rarely hear language like that anymore. Here is a man who considered himself a slave to the Gospel and the call of God. He didn't mention anything about his rights, holidays, and self-interests. He was "separated" unto the Gospel of God for one purpose – to preach Christ and liberate the distressed. The apostle Paul was a man called by God to minister, Christ, not a religion, and, of course, what a minister he became. He brought to his hearers a person, not a politically correct doctrine. He brought liberty instead of bondage, and his messages helped set people free. Finding such freedom is what people crave most. **James McConnell**

The Pastor recites the story of when once travelling to Holland, the plane he was on developed engine trouble, causing a diversion to another airport. The Pastor had to wait with the other passengers for around three hours but struck up a friendship with a man he didn't know. The man told him he was the director of a well-known company and offered the Pastor a drink. However, the Pastor only wanted orange juice. When the man returned with an orange juice and a whisky for himself, they chatted about his business, and after some time with the drinks finished, he asked again if the Pastor wanted another one. To his surprise, the Pastor asked for Coca-Cola.

At that point, the man became curious about why the Pastor didn't drink alcohol and asked, "What is it you do for a living, sir? I am curious. I have talked a lot about myself, but I haven't heard from you."

The Pastor was about to give him the official position – I'm a minister of religion or Pastor - when the Holy Spirit spoke to him and said, 'Tell him that you love Jesus.'

I remember looking at him and saying: "I love the Lord Jesus Christ and serve him. That's all I said. He looked shocked and replied, "My goodness, I've never heard anyone speak like that in my life. You speak about Jesus as though He is alive." I responded: "He's more real to me than I am to you." I told him nothing other than I loved the Lord, and he began to weep in front of me. It was a lesson in my ministry. That is an authentic ministry, just sharing Jesus with the world and allowing him to touch the listeners' hearts. It may not seem spectacular and politically correct, but it will lead people to the Lord. **James McConnell**

Prophetic preaching in a politically correct world is not for the fainthearted. It requires balance and skill, but it is as necessary as ever and unlikely to go out of fashion any time soon. But what about genuine prophecy? If people are going to prophesy, then the Pastor is resolute in knowing they've heard from God.

Sadly, many so-called servants of God have declared "thus saith the Lord," not even knowing the Lord. It is a dangerous thing to do. If they are wrong, their words and predictions can prove very damaging to the lives of those who they address. I have seen and heard some ridiculous prophecies which never came to pass. The opposite happened, bringing confusion and even distress to the persons who had been prophesied over. I was taught as a boy to have respect for the things of God. Saying a "thus saith the Lord" carries enormous responsibility, and those words shouldn't be uttered at every service but only when God truly moves upon a minister or a person. **James McConnell**

Nowadays, we hear that to get people back to the Church, they should experience new things, and many are currently calling for the end of the firebrand preacher and termination of words like hell, the devil, and sin. People want items of current interest instead and shorter sermons and softer content. They demand singing, drama, debates, videos, zoom and conference meetings and testimonies, even online entertainment.

Pastor McConnell has proved, however, as other great preachers have also demonstrated, that when the Gospel is preached in its entirety, that's what people need. It's what they desire more than anything.

As the media and politics seek to marginalise the Christian message and make it a politically correct communication - denying the truth of John chapter 14 and verse

6 that Jesus is the only way to God - then the Church again desperately requires a preacher with both courage and strength to counteract such a distorted narrative.

Moreover, when a country, culture, and people remove the Gospel from the Church, the beauty of Christ, and the glory of God, and concentrates on the seeker-sensitive and consumer-friendly Church, the Church is on a downward spiral. Only the pure Gospel attracts men and women to the beauty of Christ; it draws them to the sacrifice of Christ and the cross of Christ.

It is fair to say that Pastor McConnell became such a prophetic messenger for God at many vital times in our nation's history throughout his ministry, which brought both blessing and affliction and even persecution. In good times and bad, God regularly revealed His Word to His people through the obedience of an ordinary man.

The Pastor received many prophecies too numerous to mention, which sometimes didn't immediately manifest, but eventually came to pass. Throughout the generations, all forms of Bible prophecy have, of course, passed the test of time.

And he gave some, apostles; and some, prophets; and some, evangelists; and some, Pastors and teachers; For the perfecting of the saints, for the work of the ministry, for the edifying of the body of Christ.

Ephesians 4:11-12

11.

The Real Thing

Today, many people are considered Christian ministers. Some believe they are well qualified for the job, promoting themselves as motivational speakers and attending large gatherings in churches that focus more on "exciting events" than bread and butter issues that affect their flock. Unfortunately, man's need for performance has replaced the power of God and the passion of Jesus. If I am honest, it is not hard for any minister to become distracted due to administrative tasks in preference to leading people. However, while a leader's primary function is to preach and teach, organise services, take care of finances, etc., ministering to people is vitally important, authentic ministry. Running a church ministry requires a tremendous amount of work and responsibility. Nevertheless, operating a church is not just about completing daily duties. Even more central is that a Pastor genuinely cares for his people and ultimately becomes a shepherd. When this occurs, the Church will begin to flourish. **James McConnell**

People are continually searching for new methods of how to "do Church." But how did God intend the Church to function? Failing to focus on what is and isn't authentic, the Church sometimes encounters unwanted consequences. The challenge is like previous generations: finding what the Pastor calls "The real thing."

While a personal relationship with Jesus Christ is essential, there is always a need for the Church and the ministry. Highlighting such a point seems fitting in a generation where Coronavirus forced many people to stay away from the Church and rely solely on their relationship with the Lord Jesus, assuming they have one. Notwithstanding, the Bible clarifies that a corporate relationship – the Church - enhances and enriches a personal relationship with Jesus.

The need to meet together as one body and be ministered to by a Pastor is God's intention for His blood washed people, according to the apostle Paul who stated, "Not forsaking the assembling of ourselves together, as the manner of some is; but exhorting one another: and so much the more, as ye see the Day approaching" **Hebrews 10:25**

In other words, only two or three people is sufficient to herald Christ's presence among them.

Of course, the Church is no new thing, and it was alive and vibrant in the first century and should remain so as the coming of the Lord draws near. The Lord Jesus said those powerful words to his disciples, "I will build my Church, and the gates of hell will not prevail against it" **Matthew 16**

The Church is consistently mentioned throughout the New Testament. Its existence is not in dispute, not even today, not even when the Church's doors were forced to close temporarily in unprecedented circumstances! However, given the switch to a lesser dependence on the Church and the Church's ministry these days, it is vital to be careful not to go down the road of individualism as a preferred method, leaving the Church as seemingly optional.

Moreover, a thriving church and ministry that will again attract people are still possible, but that same Church must be authentic with one condition.

The evidence of a God-centred Church is where a relationship with Jesus develops, and relationships with others also flourish. The relationship between a Pastor and his people will determine any church ministry's depth and quality. Hence, Paul wrote in his letter to the Corinthians: "I have planted, Apollos watered; but God gave the increase" **1 Corinthians 3:6**

There is a significant responsibility for the leader to love and embrace his people. Implement the trendiest and most creative programmes all day long, but if the lead Pastor gets detached from his people, not much will happen or grow in that Church. A minister who lacks love and empathy, and becomes emotionally isolated from his people, will soon have a considerable bearing on how staff, volunteers, and other members interact and behave. Therefore, the key to progress and a spiritually healthy church is nothing other than authentic leadership.

Authentic leadership is more than a modern term. It is more than pretending to have authority. It is at the forefront of church leadership, for more than ever, people seek authenticity in church ministries, especially during times of unprecedented challenges. Authentic Christian ministries are not defined by their strength but by impacting and equipping people. It has been said, "Leadership is not wielding authority; it is empowering people." That is always the sign of a healthy, vibrant, and flexible ministry. Authentic ministries are adaptable, not rigid, or stubborn. Leading brands worldwide have always adapted and changed to see growth and continued success, and things are no different in the Church. Real ministry connects with real people and keeps up with the times. It doesn't play Church but provides a church for its members.

In the same way, the Church is facing massive change; one of the leading brands in the world experienced similar challenges many years ago. Coca-Cola's 'It's the Real Thing' campaign was a way of consolidating the vast swathe of changes being made to the brand as it entered the 1970s. Coke's then brand manager, Ira C Herbert, heralded it as a new direction that "responds to research which shows that young people seek the real, the original and the natural as an escape from phoniness."

The dictionary defines *authenticity* as honest, trustworthy, pure, not phoney, and conforming to the original. Unfortunately, today young people still have the uncanny ability to smell phoniness from a mile away. If we are not for real, people will quickly catch on.

People appear obsessed with titles these days, but perhaps a leader without a title is better than a title without the ability to lead.

In 1st Corinthians chapter 3, Paul pinpoints a minister's function to plant and God's response to increasing and blessing. The Apostle Paul gives the Church a clear definition of what authentic ministry achieves – spiritual fruit.

Teaching them on the traits of a true evangelist and what ministry should look like, he said: "And he gave some, apostles; and some, prophets; and some, evangelists; and some, Pastors and teachers; For the perfecting of the saints, for the work of the ministry, for the edifying of the body of Christ." **Ephesians 4:11-12**

Therefore, the ministry's objective is to advance and perfect God's people, accomplish God's requirements through Church, and encourage the flock of God.

It is a place where God reaches His people through the love of God and His servants and uses them for His glory.

Ministry is the great evangelist's spirit, the Lord Jesus coming upon a person and speaking as Christ would. That's a true evangelist, and that's an authentic ministry. So many of the great preachers down the centuries were God's appointed evangelists, chosen to reach a dying world of lost sinners. The apostle Paul perfectly describes a five-fold ministry in the text found in Ephesians 4, I remember hearing years ago how that five-fold ministry is like the hand of God. The thumb is the apostle, the index finger is the prophet, the long finger is the evangelist, the next finger is the Pastor, and the smallest finger is the teacher. But notice how the evangelist is the finger that reaches out. Take away the thumb, and you haven't the exact grip; in other words, a church needs the whole five fingers because that's the hand of God, and that's what makes the ministry effective. Lots of people preach the gospel, but the evangelist wins souls. **James McConnell**

Some have asked: is the fivefold ministry five different people or one with all five gifts? Is it possible to operate all five gifts? Many have often wondered about this premise.

I have also wondered about this, but I've also come to believe that God's chosen servants can operate the whole five to some degree. It's like what Paul told Timothy, "Do the work of an evangelist and make full proof of your ministry." When God anoints a minister, it is amazing what can transpire. Miracles can happen among ordinary men and women." **James McConnell**

Of course, the ministry has changed from the early days of Pastor McConnell and his band of merry men and women in a small hall on the Whitewell Road. There were no significant strategies other than to preach for a verdict every Sunday.

Today many clergies are under increasing pressure to change their churches' methods with more modern ones. However, some are either too radical or not radical enough.

"That's not how we've done it in the past," is something regularly muttered at churches today. An opposing view is: also frequently lamented, such as "why can't we do things differently than before?" These opposites can easily create conflict and division. There's an evident struggle between those who prefer to keep things as they were and those who seek more contemporary and modern ministry methods. And it is not just a confined dilemma but a global issue facing most evangelical establishments.

The latter group now appears to be winning the argument because change is inevitable, and change is happening worldwide. If this change doesn't happen, church ministries get left behind, and no one, not even the traditionalists, wants this to occur.

Notwithstanding: following radical revolution to transform churches globally, the penny also seems to have dropped that change for the sake of change is not always a good strategy either. It has been said: "never change a winning formula" or "if something isn't broken, don't fix it."

So, how do Christians deal with change in our churches?

How can the Church ensure authentic, yet relevant ministry continues?

Do believers welcome change or dread it, dragging their heels at the very thought of it?

Change can benefit all involved if leaders embrace it and plan for it instead of running from it. Adjustment prevents a ministry's direction from stagnating, allowing growth and freedom, and it modernises and makes things more recognisable.

What is even more vital in all of this is learning how to change with the times and meet the current generation's needs without comprising the gospel's message; herein lies the ultimate challenge for all churches.

The times may be changing, but the message must never change!

According to the Pastor, such equilibrium is what all churches should strive for - an idealistic goal still possible to achieve.

Even before the so-called church revolution, I believe we managed to achieve this balance over many years in Whitewell. Of course, during my ministry, I had to adapt on numerous occasions, but I stress that I utterly refused to water down or change the gospel's central message. I believed then, and still do today, that real ministry reveals Christ through the preaching of God's Word, and while methods may indeed change and are to be embraced, the message never changes. **James McConnell**

Rather than remaining central, the Word of God is often "squeezed into a programme" full of many other less essential items. The American theologian from the Presbyterian Church in America RC Sproul once said: "I think the greatest weakness in the Church today is that almost no one believes that God invests His power in the Bible. Everyone is looking for power in a programme, a technique in anything and everything except where God has placed it; His Word."

Has the situation improved any? Some would quickly write off this statement as "outdated."

They are calling for change when, in fact, what they are inviting is "backward steps."

Christ-centred preaching and communicating the life of Jesus is still the most powerful way to do ministry. Ministry has undoubtedly transformed considerably, and it is not the same as in previous years. Then we were brought up under a Christ-centered organisation. The need to be entertained didn't exist. Today, however, the Church appears to be all over the place on all sorts of subjects. It seems interesting, but it is not what people require. When I was preparing my messages, I was conscious of the man struggling with his family and hearing how Christ could meet his need and help him. I considered the young person struggling with temptation and how Christ was once young and understood and could help them. I imagined life as a single parent and struggling housewife. Remember, the Bible says: "For we have not a high priest which cannot be touched with the feeling of our infirmities; but was in all points tempted like as we are, yet without sin." That's the sort of ministry I always sought. I didn't know how else to communicate God's Word. **James McConnell**

So why are some churches and even preachers not preaching as much about Jesus today? Why do preachers prefer to burden their people with complex theological arguments rather than preach about the love of Jesus?

The Pastor believes it is because of an absence of what he calls "the real thing."

As Joseph Parker said of the Corinthian Church, which had so many factions, "Sometimes God must live in poor lodgings." In other words, some believers and preachers are poor ambassadors for God, but this is nothing new. When the apostle came amongst the Church of his generation, he didn't want to hear anything other than Christ. He wasn't interested in their quarrels, theological brilliance, or their hare-brained schemes; he was focused and determined to preach about Jesus. Here is what I call the real thing – preaching Christ! When Pastors in our pulpits begin to expound the story of Jesus and His love again, there is no telling what would occur in those churches. **James McConnell**

Paul wrote: "So then, faith comes by hearing and hearing by the Word of God" **Romans 10:17**

The original Greek relating to this verse is interesting, "So then, faith comes by hearing and hearing by the Word of Christ."

If we observe the original Greek translation, Paul suggests how genuine faith comes when we hear the Word of Christ!

If I were called to address a conference of young preachers, I would encourage them to invest in every book they could on Christ's life and make it part of their inside lining, and when they preach Christ, people will respond and come to hear them. Bring out all the truths about the Saviour and watch your congregation treble in size. Or, as John Wesley once said, "Get on fire for God, and the people will come to see you burn." **James McConnell**

The challenge for every church leader and follower of Jesus Christ, by the grace of God, is undeniably to remain humble, walk in the light and share the hope of glory with the Church they serve. It is to love and care for the flock of God and preach Jesus at every opportunity; nothing more and nothing less.

Here is the real thing, and people won't accept anything less.

But covet the best gifts earnestly: and yet shew I unto you a more excellent way.
1 Corinthians 12:30

12.

Future of the Ministry

I believe we are in a far more inferior place today, yet the potential remains to excel. It is not just an older man talking, but what grieves me is the calibre of ministry today, especially in our part of the world in the United Kingdom. I am more fearful of the United Kingdom than the United States because I believe some great people in the United States are bringing the Word, whereas the UK's ministry seems too shallow. The dedication is light years behind what is required, and the knowledge and experience of God within students needs to improve drastically. Despite this decline, I do believe God can and will raise an Esther or Joseph for such a time as this. In this respect, our current Senior Pastor at Whitewell has birthed a new Bible college, The Shepherds Academy, to train and equip Bible students. Still, it needs to be more widespread than Whitewell if we stop the rot. An international revival is required because there's a noticeable decline in standards, which needs to be addressed. **James McConnell**

All generations' experiences change, yet sometimes you sense you're in a period of unprecedented transformation, the kind that happens only every few centuries.

Increasingly, it is becoming clear we're in such a moment now – a before and after situation - and not only about the massive societal changes due to the pandemic known as Covid-19. The entire fabric of society has altered, especially concerning religious opinion. For example, those in Western culture over age 30 were born into a culture that could conceivably still be called Christian, but not anymore. As a result, many Christians are fearful about the Church's future and what we have always described as the ministry.

So, does the ministry have a future, and what is that future?

The good news is that things may not be as bleak as they are often portrayed. A closer examination of Church and ministry shows that the future can be just as bright as many previous generations enjoyed. Yes, even in this Laodicea period known for "lukewarm Christianity" and "last days," there is potential to shine. However, much will depend on being flexible and faithful to the gospel's message. We will address this crucial crossroads shortly; however, what does the Pastor make of the ministry today compared to when he first started back in 1957? After all, he not only travailed but prevailed through the last half-century with all its many twists and turns.

What is the reason for such a decline? Is it due to changing times or something else? Is it merely the opinion of a man whose own standards have always been a tad high?

None of the above, but due to the low standards in our bible colleges and the emergence of ministers who have been taught theology but have no experience of God's reality in their own lives. Knowing about the book is never a substitute for knowing the book's author. We need people who have been there, done it, and got the t-shirt – Pastors who can teach the next generation how to minister and win people to Christ. Ministers don't study enough. As soon as I hear a preacher, I can tell if they have read the word. Many years ago, I was brought up in a church when rightly or wrongly, young people competed to be the best preacher. Some people may criticise this approach, but there were both zeal and hunger in those days. When you got up to preach, the rest looked at you and hoped you would make a mistake, which drove you to be careful and study well. That's all gone, and getting young people to enter the ministry is becoming more complex. The desire to teach and preach doesn't appear to be the same. A surrendered life is no longer appealing, if it ever was, of course. People are only interested in what is in it for them. What can I get from God, rather than what can I do for God? If this attitude and approach remain, seeing God move as He has done previously seems unlikely, but He has promised to move, so something must change somewhere, and we must be optimistic about the future of the Church. **James McConnell**

The Pastor is spot on. The Church was never designed to meet our selfish desires. Instead, as the Pastor experienced during his ministry, ministers and Christians are called to die to themselves and find the joy of Jesus. Only when this occurs can the true Church of Christ remerge in victory, but much repentance and contrition are required before then.

Qualifications for the Ministry

Apply for any job, and the first thing you are asked for is a list of your academic qualifications. God's work is very different. According to the Bible, the qualifications required are not theoretical but spiritual. Divine experience is better than self-effort. Timothy and Titus speak of the spiritual qualifications of a minister, including faithfulness and absolute surrender. The Pastor has never made any secret that he didn't have sophisticated capabilities or academic competence; instead, he maintains he attended God's school of hard knocks and learned valuable life lessons. Adversity, not academia, led to extraordinary achievement. To quote his boyhood hero CH Spurgeon "God's true ministers don't return from seminary, but a cemetery."

It has certainly been the experience of the Pastor.

Yet, how difficult is it to maintain ministry standards?

It's difficult because, at times, a minister needs to know when to say no, and at other times he needs to say yes. Then he must take a stand and say I am against this no matter the consequences, as I experienced on numerous occasions. He must be faithful and not just to his people but to God. That said, ministers are interested in several things, and this is a cause of distraction. Still, once I placed everything on the altar, those interests faded, so staying focused if a minister hands everything over to the Lord is possible. **James McConnell**

Sacrifice and surrender brought the Pastor considerable respect during his tenure, mainly as he led by example in his long-standing ministry and remained faithful to his calling. But entire surrender is something he did not manage ultimately, nor anyone else he's encountered. So, why then do Timothy and Titus speak about surrendering? Are these standards set by Timothy and Titus merely a goal for ministers to reach rather than a realistic objective?

Spurgeon and Knox were men who sacrificed to God's demands, as did the martyrs who went to their deaths, but still, many of them admitted that they hadn't fully submitted. The only person who wholly surrendered in every area was the Lord Jesus Christ in his humanity and during the days of his flesh. However, that is not to say aiming for greater surrender is a futile experience. God deals with people differently, and each person has a conscience. I've always had a conscience about money and other things in the ministry, although sadly, individual ministers can appear void of conscience and remain in the Church. The men I grew up with loved the Lord with all their hearts and sought to show their dedication, devotion, and consecration to others. That's what I have tried to emulate over the past 60 years. I felt compelled to serve Christ. I couldn't do anything else. I had a passion for ministry and still have it today. **James McConnell**

There will undoubtedly be changes in ministry as society evolves. However, limitless potential still exists when people are in tune with God and what He requires rather than what they desire. But, of course, that's not to say this change is easy to either accept or understand. So prolific is current change it may one day be viewed as a revolutionary period like when the invention of the printing press and the reformation occurred. But, whatever transpires, it will unquestionably go down as a seismic shift from what we've known.

So, again, what is the future of the ministry? And how should we respond?

Firstly, the future is not as daunting as Christians may think. And change should be embraced, not feared. The present shift is viewed with suspicion and negatively, but this doesn't have to be the case. The Church is not our invention, and it is the creation of God Himself. The Church will continue and defeat any cultural change, including our poor choices. We are not only an imperfect society but an imperfect church, yet regardless of the generations, God has always found a way to communicate the love of God and the message of Salvation to a fragmented world.

Most people are not turning their backs on "Church" but instead on "religion," a distinction essential to point out. Of course, the question is why?

It is because religion doesn't cut it anymore, not that it ever did. People are no longer looking for organised religion; instead, they cry out for genuine relationships. Perhaps the current generation is more aware that religion can't lead to God or save a person. And it is also powerless to help when tragedy and disaster strike, such as natural disasters, personal loss, and world atrocities. However, God is bigger, broader, and greater than any religion. He provides relational security and perfect freedom, but people will only feel free when discovering that God never intended humanity to have religion. Instead, he sent a person - Jesus Christ - to free us from religious teaching.

It is no bad thing people reject religion and the Church when they do not hear about Jesus. Could this absence of Jesus be why many religious organisations and churches are haemorrhaging people? Is the name and person of Jesus the key to revival in our churches? Rather than diluting God's Word, preaching it in its entirety may be more fruitful.

Where are the great preachers about Jesus with fire in their bellies? Where is that special anointing required to reach souls for Christ? Unfortunately, the desire to teach and preach Christ doesn't appear to be the same, and there are fewer role models to follow. Is this why the Church is struggling? Many young aspiring preachers wanted to be like my boyhood hero George Jeffreys, even mimicking his Welsh brogue when I was a boy. Smith

Wigglesworth said he would rather have wildfire than no fire, but Jeffreys had a polish with the power. He would stand in front of the mirror and practice his mannerisms; such was his attention to detail. Soon I did the same. I would get to Ormeau Park in Belfast, stand on a woodblock, and preach to the trees pretending they were an audience. If anyone had been passing, they must have thought I had lost my mind, but the desire for souls was more significant than the mockery, which resulted. If people did that nowadays, they would be locked up. Yet this passion for ministry and preaching is necessary again to experience revival in our land. Nothing else will suffice. **James McConnell**

Interestingly, over the years, many young men who came through the ranks at Whitewell started out mimicking and desperately trying to emulate the preaching and pastoral style of a confident James McConnell. Some faded out, while others would eventually find their true self, but it must have been an excellent complement for the Pastor to witness young students using him as their role model. After all, they say imitation is the highest form of flattery; remember, he too had many great mentors to imitate during his youth! Then later, under the Pastor's guidance, many more young students went to pioneer churches on their merit.

For numerous years, Pastor Michael Bunting, one of the Pastors' devoted and longest-serving colleagues, kept a record with all the churches birthed from Whitewell, no fewer than sixty-five – and these are only the ones known. Perhaps one of the most remarkable stories of pioneering a church is the work started by Paul Malcolmson from Banbridge in Co Down. Several years ago, he obeyed a call to minister to Native Americans in Nebraska and is still there today. As a result, the Pastor has seen for himself the remarkable things God is doing in Nebraska.

I preached in Nebraska in 2016, and three hundred and twenty-five souls came to Christ. It was an incredible experience. I remember Paul telling me what God had told him and thinking, "are you sure?" But Paul has more than proved his calling. Suddenly attending a 1200 minister's convention, an Indian lady stood up and asked, please help us? Paul assumed she had been inundated with offers and forgot about the incident, but no one came forward. Finally, after six months, he felt the Spirit prompting him to phone her, and she admitted that not a single person had replied. Having developed a burden for the Native Americans, Paul sold up and went to Nebraska, where he still ministers today. **James McConnell**

Other men have entered into ministry from Whitewell, like Malcolm Duncan, the senior Pastor at Dundonald Elim. A former lead Pastor at Gold Hill Baptist Church in London, He is highly respected among church circles and never forgotten his Whitewell roots.

Malcolm has done a fantastic job and has become an intelligent and progressive Pastor. The late Robert Gass was also saved under my ministry and wrote the renowned book Word for Today, not to mention other men like Ken Davidson at Christ Encounters Church Gilford, NI, and Jeff Wright at Green Pastures Ballymena. There have been many graduates from Whitewell into the ministry. Our own senior Pastor David Purse also came through the ranks at Whitewell, having served in several churches in Ireland and the UK before replacing me following my retirement. I still receive letters regularly from people who came into the Church, heard God's word, got saved, and are today Pastors. In the end, only the Lord knows how many others are out there, having been spiritually motivated and trained at Whitewell. **James McConnell**

Online Church

The fastest-growing aspect of the modern-day ministry of the Church is unquestionably the success of the online ministry – a relatively new and exciting part of church outreach. A developing ministry, it has become, oh, so essential! (*See additional thoughts about the explosion of the online Church in Part Nine Passion for Souls*)

Even in the latter stages of the Pastor's ministry, his preaching went to places and people he never dreamed possible due to online facilities. The benefit, of course, of the online Church, is that it can stream services live to many people's front living room. Online is a perfect way to reach people who cannot make it to the Church in person due to distance or illness, family commitments, or other restrictions. Still, as highlighted in the previous chapter, it is critical to underscore how it will never supplement Church. It is currently serving a significant purpose of speaking directly to a person and their situation and has proved a lifeline during Covid-19, but only as a first objective. There is still nothing like being in the house of God worshipping and praying with the actual blood-washed people of God.

Contrary to some opinion, the Church is not a spent force when assembling for worship and praise. It might not be the same as we remember it, either numerically or in terms of its presentation, but Church it is, and Church it will remain. A properly functioning, God-breathed Church produces unity, strength in numbers, and the power of agreement! Unity is a critical player in the survival of churches today, as the body of Christ refocuses on the great commission.

Take the Lord's Table as an example. It helps the Church understand what's important to Jesus and not us. It brings people together in an equal setting. It reminds us to concentrate on the unsaved individual because of Christ's sacrifice rather than zooming in on ourselves. It also makes one aware of Christ's exceptional forgiveness, love, and grace at the Cross. When people are greeted with kindness and compassion, their spiritual needs are met. When they feel loved and cared for, safe, and sound, the Church will come to life again instead of being merely tolerated.

When the focus shifts from individualism and even mastering spiritual gifts to what the Apostle Paul called "a more excellent way," the Church of Christ will finally look transformed.

That "more excellent way," which is loving God and one another, was the first-century Church's approach; moreover, it's why the Apostle dedicated a section of his letter to the subject of love and loveliness **1 Corinthians 13**. At the close of 1 Corinthians chapter twelve, Paul reiterated the importance of spiritual gifts, but not in place of the greatest gift of all, which is love.

He said, "But covet the best gifts earnestly: and yet shew I unto you a more excellent way" **1 Corinthians 12:30**

By the start of that great love chapter in 1 Corinthians 13, he begins with a profound and "pause worthy" statement – "Though I speak with the tongues of men and angels, and have not charity, I am become as sounding brass or a tinkling cymbal. And though I have the gift of prophecy, and understand all mysteries, and all knowledge; and though I have all faith, so that I could remove mountains, and have not charity, I am nothing." **1 Corinthians 13:1-2**

These words answer many questions for the Church today.

Anyone can preach on love; performing it is the real task.

The ministry's future is not necessarily online or in gathering; it is the same as it has always been, even in the first-century Church. The art of ministry is loving people, and we can achieve this noble goal in any setting, large or small. The future of the Church is not in brilliant ideas and programmes but is made secure by brotherly love, compassion, and concern. If people are to remain part of any fellowship for any length of time, it depends significantly on how loved and accepted they feel when they walk through the doors of the House of God or meeting hall.

An influential and successful church is a place where men and women, even children, can access the love of God and feel safe and secure and valued.

Such an environment helps develop their self-esteem in knowing that all their sins are forgiven, and they feel accepted in the beloved. So, the critical question for our current generation of preachers appears to be: do we build more Mega Churches or Ministry Churches?

The Pastor managed to build both during his ministry, an unusual accomplishment. Despite those humble beginnings, Whitewell became a megachurch, but it was a love-filled Church also. The Pastor says that while meeting the needs of his flock and preaching God's Word was paramount, he was always conscious of the Church's numbers and those responding to the message he'd preached.

Although smaller than some colossal ministries in the United States, Whitewell became a megachurch and a fountain of love during the Pastor's time. Nevertheless, he concedes the days of megachurches may be behind us as many ministries appear to be downsizing to reach the individual. Ministry has undoubtedly become more about a smaller one-to-one outreach, highlighted by the explosion of online services, facilities, and workshops.

All the same, the future is still bright for the collective Church. The ministry is neither dead nor the Church, just a different environment, but alive and kicking and full of potential. It may look different online or offline, but the successful ministry's end game is God-centred, and God's people worshipping together side by side, loving God and each other. Whether it is between a handful of saints or a packed sanctuary, one thing that must remain is hearing about and being introduced to the love of God through Jesus Christ.

There is no more excellent authentic ministry than that.

Passion for Teamwork

Coming together is a beginning, keeping together is progress;
working together is a success.
Henry Ford

13.

There's no 'I' in Team!

I could never have accomplished what I did without the Team God gave me. Yes, God enabled me to spearhead it, but I also firmly believe that God gave me good men and women at that time. All teams have their differences, and we had ours, but the "miracle was," as one young woman once told me, "God gave you the ability to keep your team together." That is true. Looking back, they were all very different individuals with different personalities, but I rarely had to tell them what to do. They were already passionate about the things of God, which naturally brought tension at times, but God helped me keep the peace. My Team also knew that I would ask them only once to do something and not a second time. Authority and strength are vital in leadership if you want to produce results. If a leader lacks this sort of authority, he will be undermined and eventually forced out. A leader needs to know when to be tough and back off. **James McConnell**

Football and athletics are my preferred sports, but rugby provided me with one of the most incredible sporting moments of all time.

In November 2003, in the Telstra Stadium, the Australian Rugby team faced England in the Rugby World Cup final. Australia, the hosts, took an early lead in a physically brutal match, but England gradually pulled ahead towards the end of the first half. There then followed a nail-biting second half. Australia equalised, England drew forward, and Australia equalised again in the last minutes, forcing the final into extra time. The tension was unbearable. Johnny Wilkinson and Elton Flatley went toe to toe, kicking penalties in extra time to put the score level at 17-17.

Then, in the final 21 seconds of the match, in the 100th minute, in the dying seconds, England pulled together in an outstanding example of a team working as a single mind – right to the very end! The hero of the game was Johnny Wilkinson.

The sight of Wilkinson scoring the winning drop goal in the last seconds of that fantastic final was better than Ali versus Frazier, Federer versus Djokovic, and, dare I say it, Ovett versus Coe.

But far more influential in securing the Rugby World Cup for England was Clive Woodward. Rugby enthusiasts will know that Woodward coached England from 1997 to 2004, and his teamwork philosophy is widely credited with turning them into the winning team in the world in 2003. However, it was not an overnight process but took six years and a failed World Cup attempt on the way.

Woodward believed that great performances come from outstanding leadership. He thinks the most important question a leader must ask is not 'how do I make my team play better?' but rather 'what and where my team must be to win?'

Woodward believed that unless you're willing to ask yourself exactly what the Team needs to be doing and what skills it needs, you risk being highly efficient at the wrong thing. In other words, unless a unit is unified, no success can follow.

That's true in business, sport, and, indeed, in church ministry.

For Woodward and a church leader, the most challenging thing is that it takes time and effort to ask yourself that question. Time to think, time to get the best ideas from everyone, time to get everyone to buy into a vision, and time to seek the Lord for His direction and not anyone else's

Of course, only a few leaders are ever willing to invest this time and planning. What isn't commonly known is that before England's World Cup success, no fewer than forty improvements were underscored, which would take two years to implement. Success takes time, focus and patience.

It takes enormous humility to undertake such a brutal call for change and accept that things are not where they ought to be. It also takes acceptance and recognition that no one person alone can deliver success. If matters are not correct, leaders must courageously take an unbiased view of where things are and involve everyone to bring positive change.

In sporting terms, its rivals feared England due to its long-standing reputation for great sportsmen and women, especially on the rugby field.

Still, Woodward understood that no team or organisation could rest on their laurels or past glories. Reputation alone is not a red carpet to success; indeed, it can be a recipe for disaster. England hadn't won anything for a while, including the World Cup, but significantly, Woodward sensed the reason for this decline - they were no longer a team!

When it comes to experiencing success, no business, sporting, or religious organisation can ignore the potential of good teamwork and the importance of unity.

Without it, repeated failure is guaranteed.

One of Woodward's long-term methods to propel England back to World rugby's summit was Teamship. Once he'd got the Team and the leader 'being as one,' Woodward got the Team to write their own set of standards that everyone had to buy into and accept.

It was another great sportsperson Ben Ainslie, the most successful sailor in Olympic history, who claimed, "You need more than one leader; there's no 'I' in a team, and they can't be all leaders." It was this same philosophy Woodward employed. He knew that success would follow if he could develop a genuine team of players who believed in the cause, fought for each other, and defended each other.

Sometimes excellent leadership and inspiration spring from unexpected places and at random times. It is the same no matter what field we choose.

Pastor James McConnell and the ministry at Whitewell are no exception.

He may not have taken the same scientific approach that helped Clive Woodward guide England to World Cup glory; even the profession is vastly different, but the results were very similar due to a deep understanding of the importance of teamship. Get people to work as a team, and success will follow.

From a starting place of 10 people in a little hall in 1957, through tremendous teamship, unity, and togetherness, the Pastor built one of the largest churches in Europe and broadened its reputation worldwide thanks to the explosion of the internet and the online ministry.

How did he accomplish such a feat? He wasn't a technical buff like Clive Woodward, constantly checking stats and facts. Neither did he have the assistance of the Rugby Football Union and their massive administration and PR benefits, not to mention the financial budget. He was just a local Pastor raising money for God's work and serving in a deprived working-class area of Belfast.

True, in ministry terms, he was an anointed man, something we will cover later in the chapter *Passion for the Anointing,* which always helps ministers and ministries find success. Yet, the Pastor's gift of finding unity amongst people from very different backgrounds also brought unexpected blessings to his Church, a level of success that seemed to evade many others.

The Pastor often plays down this accomplishment, suggesting that God loved him or favoured him somehow. While this explanation is credible, it also undermines his rare gift to not only create the right Team but, more importantly, keep that same Team together and improve it year in, year out. I was privileged to watch how he continuously held together with a varied team of people from many backgrounds over countless years.

Of course, there were times when these people disagreed. After all, when committed people meet inside an organisation, conflicting opinions will always surface. When people feel so passionately, they strongly disagree, even separate over issues.

Still, during his 60 years, the Pastor generally managed to keep his flock together in a remarkable way due to a passion for teamship and, more importantly – an understanding of the need for unity!

Enter the Church any Sunday or during the week, and almost to a person, everyone knew their job. Whether it was helping park cars, greeting people at the door, singing at the front, or simply handing out hymn books, people appeared trained to serve the Lord without prompting. It was a secret ingrained over many years from the earliest days when Pastor McConnell was in charge.

Teamship is defined as a group being effective and efficient and pulling in the same direction, and this is what the Pastor always tried to instil during his ministry. He was, in some ways, akin to a business manager or sports coach like Clive Woodward.

"Human beings subconsciously understand that alone I am nothing, but I can achieve great things in a team," said the legendary former Premier League football manager Arsene Wenger. He was a master at motivating many of his Arsenal teams and rarely seemed to look for any credit or prominence, a quality that helped him build numerous successful great sides over 20 plus years. Wenger's boys were a real example of great teams. Similar teamwork is equally essential in the Christian Church if the result is progress.

Former Manchester United manager Sir Alex Ferguson once said, "You must know when to go over the top to get a reaction, and when to be calm to get a reaction."

The famous hairdryer treatment dished out to David Beckham in 2003 would appear to be in the former category. Sir Alex clashed with several of his players during his tenure at the Old Trafford club's helm. However, the most memorable incident occurred following an FA Cup defeat to Arsenal, with David Beckham, the victim.

Ferguson inflicted a wound on the star by kicking a boot in his direction. It became a sensational news story when Beckham subsequently appeared with a paper stitch in the shape of an X over his eye. He has since accepted the funny side of it, joking in 2017 that the flying boot incident gave him an insight into how accurate his former boss was as a player with his feet.

Of course, the term 'hairdryer treatment' is used in football to describe an angry verbal reprimand, usually delivered by a manager to an individual player or group of players within a dressing room.

It does not have to be confined to a dressing room.

Individual managers and coaches are renowned for using the 'hairdryer treatment' to get their point across to their players. It is prevalent among older generations who have grown up in a sporting environment where 'tough love' was a regular landscape feature. However, even those who favour a holistic and less aggressive approach today have been known to let their tempers get the better of them at times. Everyone is human!

The ministry's difference is that it often involves people passionate about what they do yet somehow expected to hold their peace and exercise self-control. However, sometimes conflict is inevitable because they are not perfect, no matter how unified a team might be, and finding restraint isn't always easy. The Pastor agrees, but in the ministry, he points out how he was also under tremendous spiritual pressure and admits that "keeping one's temper" in check and getting the right balance wasn't always possible.

Keeping your cool is essential, but sometimes letting fly is just as effective. I never remember kicking my shoe at anyone, but righteous anger is allowed in the ministry, and I displayed plenty of it. The trick is knowing when to stay calm and when to explode. To maintain unity and good teamship, we must avoid a spirit of individualism from creeping into the Church. Personalities, pride, ego, etc., must not be allowed to trump teamwork and togetherness. **James McConnell**

Many might well find this opinion about teamwork in the ministry of the Pastor contradictory, even dare I say, hypocritical, because, during his term, he was known to be a strong personality and leader; some have even described him as "a dictator," but although he was continuously interested in God's direction and led from the front, he also learned how to rally the troops' so-to-speak and bring others with him – the mark of any great leader.

While I believe in a person leading from the front - that is God's way, and I did it myself- no leader can succeed on their own. A lack of teamwork in many ministries is spoiling God's blessing, and the Church must return to the place of inclusivity and involvement. If leaders think they can press on regardless of the majority's support, they are in for a rude awakening. Yes, there are times when a church leader must stick to God's instruction and refuse to be influenced by others, but in general, we need one another, especially in God's work. **James McConnell**

There's nothing wrong with being a solid leader today; the Church, more than ever, desperately requires such people, but leadership involves a vision to recognise God's place in a church. A leader notices talent and allows that talent to bloom. As the book of Proverbs says, "a man's gift makes room for him."

There is no paranoia or insecurity involved in a genuine leader. Great leaders are comfortable with the brightest brains and the best talent on their Team. Clive Woodward scrutinised his Team's talent carefully before utilising them effectively in their best positions. Leadership is not about creating individual stars or being the best. Leadership is described as 'making everyone else better.'

When a leader imposes himself on his people and refuses to delegate, it can cause problems and leave others feeling left out and, worse, make them unfruitful and leave them isolated and discouraged.

How damaging is a ministry like this?

There is no cure for such a ministry until God breaks in and brings change. Nothing positive will happen in that sort of environment until God moves and sorts it all out but move, He can, and move He does. People may think they are unmovable, even invincible, but remember Jesus said, "I will build my Church, and the gates of hell will not prevail against it". The thing to remember is that it is not our Church, but Christ's. When a man or a ministry or people think it is all about them, that is the most dangerous place.
James McConnell

Teamwork hasn't only helped spiritual establishments; political parties have also known and experienced a team's power, none more so than New Labour, a political party which, through teamship, achieved its remarkable political accomplishments back in the nineties. A dominant political force in the UK for more than a decade under Tony Blair and Gordon Brown's leadership, invincibility entered the party, and eventually, the wheels came off. However, at the height of Labour's success, their chief spin doctor Alastair Campbell said the following: "we achieve more together than we do alone."

Togetherness is and always has been God's way for His people and Church. The Bible says: "Two are better than one because they have a good reward for their toil. For if they fall, one will lift his fellow. But woe to him who is alone when he falls and has not another to lift him! Again, if two lie together, they keep warm, but how can one keep warm alone? And though a man might prevail against one who is alone, two will withstand him-a a threefold cord is not quickly broken." **Ecclesiastes 4:9-12**

Without this teamship or strong unity, progress will be hard to find.

Unity is vital in the work of God. In general, I had a fantastic bunch of people, mostly when we travelled around the country, bringing the gospel to different communities. The list is endless, but there's no doubt in my mind that our passion for unity helped reach a divided nation at that time. I remember we got up early each morning and went out with leaflets and literature to speak to a troubled land, we went to Derry and Dublin and wherever God called us, and everyone worked together as a team. It was teamwork, which made the difference, and cooperation is what God is after. In my experience, if everyone buys into the vision, anything is possible. The old saying goes only the person who isn't rowing has time to rock the boat. **James McConnell**

While great unity in leadership is essential, the agreement of Pastors and the Church's congregations inevitably creates a healthy spiritual environment. Sadly, some leaders demand compliance without first ministering the most critical ingredient: love and respect. Love does not follow unity; unity springs from love.

During the Pastor's ministry, he recalls strong bonds and brotherly love in the Church. That said, it wasn't a perfect church, and often he had to deal with the unruly elements and disorderly individuals. Still, even visitors who frequented Whitewell remarked about the warmth and love in the Lord's House. It was a happy place to be, and more importantly, it was a unified environment and safe location. A constant remark the

Pastor would make from time to time was how God had given him the best people in the world. It sounded like he was trying to motivate his troops, even flattering them, but he maintains it is accurate, and he meant every word of it.

True comradeship came from great love in the Lord, and I never underestimated how important that was. When Judas kissed Jesus, some Greek students believe Christ must have pierced his heart by referring to him as a comrade. Why did Jesus use this word to a man who had utterly betrayed him? Perhaps He showed how it is a great thing to have genuine comradeship in a church, and that's something no church or its leadership should ever take for granted. I constantly reminded the Pastors that the people who paid their wages gave and sacrificed to continue in the ministry. The people prayed for the work's success. So, naturally, I encouraged the pastoral team to look after God's flock, love them and care for them, even the unruly, because the people God gave me were the cream of the crop and deserved looking after. I can honestly say that within a 30-year supernatural period, I believe I served the best God ever gave. The "Whitewellers" were and still are a unique bunch whom God made both faithful and fun-loving. In those days, the people gave anything and everything without thought for themselves or even their families. Many were genuinely "sold out for the Lord." When a legitimate need emerged, and provision was required, no one could meet it like the people at Whitewell. Americans gave much through massive evangelical outreaches at that time, but I believe our congregation was a match for anyone. It was a vintage period to serve the Lord. They were generous and together as a team– and, of course, they had genuine love in their hearts, and what more can a Pastor want? **James McConnell**

Teamwork brings results, no matter the profession or field, and anything is possible when people stick together, and nothing is impossible for them.

God has placed enormous potential within humanity and within His people. When that same humanity is unified, and God's glory is the objective, never underestimate the passion for teamship or the power of unity to achieve the seemingly impossible.

And when the day of Pentecost was fully come,
they were all with one accord in one place.
Acts 2:1

14.

The Power of Two and Vision

At Pentecost, the followers of Jesus stood in one accord in one place, not one accord all over the place. Unity is described as a sweet-smelling fragrance. It is like sweet perfume and fresh aftershave. It smells good, making you smell good. A church in harmony will have this odour. So, when Mary in Mark, chapter 14 anointed the head of Jesus with the precious ointment, the fragrance not only filled the house but probably travelled into Martha's kitchen. In other words, if a church has a genuine love for the Lord, and one another, producing unity, it will permeate every place within that assembly. **James McConnell**

One of the most remarkable biblical examples of teamwork is found in the book of Acts and the story of Pentecost. It was a unique occasion when people came together, and the blessing of the Lord fell due to a mighty visitation from the Holy Spirit.

Whitewell, under the leadership of Pastor McConnell, continually sought New Testament Christianity, copying without apology the instructions of the apostle's doctrine. It is one of the reasons togetherness was fought for even when it didn't come naturally. The scripture from the book of Acts reminds us just how fiercely the followers of Jesus sought agreement.

"And they devoted themselves to the apostles' teaching and fellowship, to the breaking of bread and prayers. And awe[1] came upon every soul, and many wonders and signs were being done through the apostles. And all who believed were together and had all things in common. And they were selling their possessions and belongings and distributing the proceeds to all, as any had need. And day by day, attending the temple together and breaking bread in their homes, they received their food with glad and generous hearts, praising God and having favour with all the people. And the Lord added to their number day by day, those who were being saved." **Acts 2:1** says, "And when the day of Pentecost was fully come, they were all with one accord in one place."

It's easy to read such a verse and become familiar with it, but consider what this verse is saying? First, when the people of God are in one place and of one accord, it leads to breakthroughs and miracles of all descriptions.

"How should one chase a thousand, and two put ten thousand to flight, except their Rock had sold them, and the LORD had shut them up?" **Deuteronomy 32:30**

The extraordinary feat that followed the unity in the early Church was seeing ten thousand put to flight! Suddenly a sound from heaven arrived like a mighty rushing wind, and it filled all the house where they were sitting, and demons fled.

"And there appeared unto them cloven tongues like as of fire, and it sat upon each of them. And they were all filled with the Holy Ghost, and began to speak with other tongues, as the Spirit gave them utterance." **Acts 2:3-4**

Here we read of ordinary people from all backgrounds who had managed to put their differences, pride, and theological disputes behind them and teamed up in one Spirit, in one place and one accord, and the result was that God moved on their behalf.

By contrast, such togetherness is becoming much less common today in politics, sport, and evangelical circles. Instead, disunity is becoming more and more widespread, sadly even in Church and Church leadership. Whether it's down to theology or church policy, many differences of opinion have produced separation and even ill-feeling among God's people. Still, for a brief period during the book of Acts, unity shone brightly, proving how God's way offers hope to all fragmented institutions.

While the Pastor accepts that keeping unity wasn't straightforward during his tenure, he's also convinced he tasted a little of what it means to have a unified body of people, not unlike what took place in Bible days. As a result, Whitewell became a place of comradeship, teamship, and friendship for thousands – and at a time when they and the country needed it most.

Strangely enough, this miraculous coming together of people from all backgrounds and religions arrived during a period of enormous bigotry and bitterness in Northern Ireland when a nation was bitterly divided by the Troubles and when there was supreme hatred between Loyalists and Republicans. Most churches fought long and hard to heal divisions – at a high personal cost in some cases and played what became an overlooked and unsung role in helping to prevent a descent into full-scale civil war. Whitewell became a place like Samuel and Saul's days, filled with a band of men and women whose hearts the Lord had touched.

Someone once said, "The miracle of Pentecost was not just the sound from heaven or the other gifts which the Holy Spirit demonstrated, but also how God brought them all together in one accord and one place. I believe that was the miracle of Whitewell for a long time, too, especially during those dark days of the seventies and eighties and even the nineties and into the new millennium. People from every background were converging and worshipping the same God in love and harmony, during a period when people were afraid to leave their homes due to the Troubles in Ulster. Thousands, and I mean thousands, came and were baptised in the Holy Spirit and spoke in tongues. The background or religious upbringing didn't seem to matter. If anything, the situation made people on both sides desperate for God, and they flocked to Whitewell to receive a message of hope through the gospel. People who didn't regularly attend church or believe in God flocked to the Tabernacle, and people who did believe in God came too.

In contrast, others left their denominations and joined Whitewell, and we all served the Lord together. In other words, true unity is a God thing. None could have healed such divisions except the Lord. No man can bring such a multitude together in peace and agreement. When people from differing backgrounds are united, it is a God thing because who could have done this, indeed not our Church and me. This kind of harmony is more than human. It was almost as if we'd experienced the words of Psalm 133 before our very eyes. **James McConnell**

The Psalmist states: "Behold, how good and pleasant it is when brethren dwell in unity! It is like the precious oil on the head, running down on the beard, on the beard of Aaron, running down on the collar of his robes! It is like the dew of Hermon, which falls on the mountains of Zion! For "there," the Lord has commanded the blessing, life forevermore. **Psalm 133**

This scripture appears to suggest that when a church or people find true unity, it pleases God to the point where He will move and supernaturally bless that Church and the people. Such was the experience at Pentecost, and the result was supernatural. No one will continue to unite with a leader or church that proves unbiblical and in constant doctrinal error. There will come the point when separation is inevitable! But when a church is preaching the gospel of the Lord Jesus Christ, producing salvation and sanctification, the unity mentioned in Psalm 133 is possible to experience.

One of the psalms is attributed to King David, a favourite Bible character of Pastor McConnell. It has the title A Song of Ascents, of David. The time of writing is unclear, but it's thought David penned it when he was finally received as king over all the tribes of Israel, significantly restoring unity among God's people and ending a terrible season of national division and discord. Another possible occasion is when David was crowned at Hebron, where the nation's leaders were again of one accord, all-be-it for a shorter time.

This Psalm contains the secret of success found through God's blessing. Even the opening word "Behold" challenges the reader to notice what's being said in this noteworthy Psalm. The Bible word behold means "look carefully."

The great Baptist preacher, CH Spurgeon, wrote of this Psalm, "It is a wonder seldom seen; therefore, behold it. It may be seen, for it is the characteristic of real saints —therefore fail not to inspect it! Nevertheless, it is well worthy of admiration; pause and gaze upon it! It will charm you into imitation, therefore note it well!"

The commentator Trapp once said, "Precious and profitable, sweet and delectable, dainty and goodly, as **Revelation 18:14**, the communion of saints is the next happiness upon earth to communion with God."

Brotherly love comes from the head (Christ) but falls to the feet (His people). It ran down, and it went down. Where love and brotherly unity reigns – God reigns. One of the outstanding features of Whitewell was the love between the brethren. In those days, people looked out for one another and cared for each other. It was a notable feature of the Church back then. That is always a sign of a unified group. No one asked about any previous religious beliefs. People had found the Lord and were so thankful they had been delivered from religion; it brought them together as one.

Experiencing this sort of togetherness is not always possible for various reasons, but true believers will always seek excellent and peaceable relationships with others. **James McConnell**

Getting everybody on board a unified vision is a nice thought but not always easy to execute. So, how did the Pastor manage it during a time of great division in the land?

Where did the miraculous unity in Whitewell originate, for example?

It wasn't easy but having a genuine sense of the Spirit of God in the place and in the people helped. Unity comes from God's presence. I think one of my former Pastors fittingly remarked how the agreement at Whitewell in those days was fierce, and it was. I even recall the former superintendent of Elim, Pastor Eric McCombe, mentioning how the unity in Whitewell was remarkable, even to the point that when I visited him, he noticed there were always people with me and surrounding me. I had armour bearers but not for show or because I needed protection, it was due to the unity that existed at that time. We were bonded together, and that was the secret of Whitewell. Some of my Pastors wouldn't allow me to face challenging tasks alone. Yes, we had incidents of disunity. Unruly people came through the ranks; even in leadership, every Church will experience tension at times, but in general, unity prevailed and helped propel the Church to a greater level. **James McConnell**

Over the years, men and women from every denomination and every part of Ireland have flocked to the Tabernacle to praise the Lord in unity. Here was the fulfillment of a much earlier prophecy at Whitewell, which stated that people would travel to the Tabernacle from all over the world by boat, plane, and train, a sign that spectacularly came to pass.

Indeed, as he mellowed and aged, the Pastor became more convinced than ever about the importance of unity amongst Christian leaders and the body of Christ. Such an agreement may be rare, but he insists it is not impossible to find.

You must talk to your Pastors and leaders and remind them how important it is to keep the peace. I spoke to them regularly, every morning, and to my people. I talked to them and told them why they were here. I shared a vision with them and my people, and they liked that. If a congregation has no end destination, no goal, and motivation, other ideas will emerge, causing division and considerable confusion. Every Church needs a leader who God has given a vision. Solomon said that "Without a vision, the people perish." There's an old saying, 'those who pray together stay together,' and it worked for us." We prayed together, and unity and vision followed. Look at many churches falling out and falling over; the common denominator is lack of sight at the organisation's top, an apparent shortage of purpose and direction. **James McConnell**

One translation of Solomon's text is "Without a prophetic vision, the people cast off restraint."

Lack of vision is perhaps the major hindrance to progress in churches today. It is not for the lack of money or connections that people perish, or a church fails - people perish for the lack of prophetic vision from the Lord. Many people think they are failing in various areas of their lives because of a lack of the right connections, opportunities, or resources, yet the truth is, the Lord says that what they lack most is God's vision.

Visions are dreams, but dreams and visions come only from the place of prayer, and genuine prayer is in short supply. When Peter, Cornelius, and Paul all had visions, they were in the position of worship and prayer. The Church must stop facilitating leaders who claim to pray and fellowship with God but show no evidence of God's prophetic vision of the Holy Spirit in their lives. We should not be impressed by those who claim to pray yet provide no proof of answers; instead, we should embrace those who refuse to brag about personal sacrifice; yet are happy to give God all the glory for any signs of wonders following.

The greater the outward show, the greater the inward poverty!

When a leader or person prays privately to God, the idea of how to proceed is sure to follow. Habakkuk is but one outstanding example. He positioned himself to receive God's vision, and God responded.

Habakkuk records: "I will stand my watch And set myself on the tower, And watch to see what He will say to me, And what I will answer when I am corrected. Then the LORD answered me and said: "Write the vision And make it plain on tablets, That he may run who reads it. For the vision is yet for an appointed time; But at the end, it will speak, and it will not lie. Though it tarries, wait for it; Because it will surely come, It will not tarry. **Habakkuk 2:1-3**

Following the dreadful year 2020, the unthinkable occurred when the doors of most churches closed. Notwithstanding, the Lord desires to restore prophetic visions from God once the Church has again positioned itself for God to speak a word of direction. Of course, this applies in the individual lives of believers also. No one can prioritise television shows and social media and expect God to show them a vision of the future, their Church, or personal situation. Therefore, it is vital for church leaders and their congregations to "get alone with God" and spend time with the Lord, enabling Him to reveal a fresh vision.

Significantly, divine vision doesn't only arrive due to purposeful prayer times and the Holy Spirit's seeking; it frequently visits places where there is also genuine evidence of unity. While unity is the goal, it is fair to say that perfect harmony on this side of heaven is an unrealistic, even utopia-like, objective. Still, it must be strived for like the book of Acts. Solomon also wrote, "Iron sharpens iron, and one man sharpens another" **Proverbs 27:17**

There is power in two, and when this happens, vision follows! The challenge for the Church today is the same as it was in the first century - to try and attain unity with God and each other. No mean feat by any stretch, but it is indeed no accident that at Pentecost, fierce agreement and the Holy Spirit's presence resulted in tremendous vision and thousands being added to the Church daily.

If we are together, nothing is impossible, but if divided, we all will fail.
Winston Churchill

15.

A House Divided

Most churches have suffered from disunity at some point, but sadly unwelcome church splits are becoming more common. Even Whitewell endured an awful period of conflict towards the end of my ministry when we suffered in this way. The fallout was catastrophic. Stuff happens in church, and sometimes it can be both heartbreaking and even life-changing. But remember, the Master was himself abandoned by those closest to him. Divisions that cause people who have worked together for years and loved each other to separate don't happen overnight but leaving churches doesn't always bring the results people expect. Disunity still proceeds from disengagement from God's pure vision of building the Church as one. **James McConnell**

On June 16, 1858, the Republican State Convention met in Springfield, Illinois, and chose Lincoln to run against Democrat Stephen Douglas. Abraham Lincoln's speech that evening was explicitly about the problems of slavery in the United States, especially the effect of the U.S. Supreme Court's recent decision. Drawing attention to the dangers of disunity, Abraham Lincoln paraphrased the following passage from the Bible when he spoke of a house divided: And Jesus knew their [the Pharisees'] thoughts and said unto them, "Every kingdom divided against itself is brought to desolation, and every city or house divided against itself shall not stand." **Matthew 12:25**

Abraham Lincoln hoped to use the opportunity to help rouse the people to recognise the magnitude of the ongoing debates over the legality of slavery and the importance of a single vision. In essence, he stated that success is likely where there is unity on a matter, but where there is division, nothing will last or be accomplished.

Abraham Lincoln used this text because Christ's statement that a house divided cannot stand is not just for the Church. Lincoln was trying to rally the troops to be united in a single cause. Similarly, the Master says that any home, organisation, marriage, political establishment, or whatever will not survive if unity is not present in that house. In other words, agreement and harmony is part of any successful partnership. Without this, marriages break down, businesses fail, and the doors of a church will close. As experienced in Northern Ireland with the consistent government breakup, the institutions fail without cooperation. Disunity has been the cause of many hindrances both in political and spiritual circles, at home and abroad. Indeed, it appears it is still the number one cause of lack of progress, so Lincoln's point about the importance of unity is well taken. **James McConnell**

While the Whitewell congregation remained unified for almost sixty-plus years of Pastor McConnell's tenure, a split in 2009 saw the loss of numerous members and the breakup of previously loving and lifelong relationships. In addition, it was disappointing for a church that had always prided itself on unity.

Naturally, the aftershock of such a split was profound. Following the fallout, significant public relations work was required to heal the wounds that cut deeply, of which I was at the forefront. Looking back, it was an incredibly uphill battle because strong divisions caused a tremendous amount of ill-feeling. Finding unity and harmony at that time was never going to be comfortable, and pitching the church as a place of tranquility and restoring relationships proved challenging. As it states in the book of Proverbs: "A brother offended is harder to be won than a strong city: and their contentions are like the bars of a castle." **Proverbs 18:19**

Church splits, which are sadly quite common, are never calm and sadly produce ill-feeling and severe consequences. Given the Pastor's lifelong passion for souls, the loss of people and stability in his Church proved unbearable to accept or endure. For years afterwards, he lamented the loss of people who were part of the work at Whitewell for well over a quarter of a century before the divide occurred, people he had loved and nurtured. Of course, every church has its problems, and even great leaders have feet of clay like all mortals.

Nevertheless, he made no secret that the separation broke his heart and that of his devoted wife, Margaret. However, instead of becoming bitter, the Pastor decided to become better and reach out to those he had lost in the most challenging times. Immediately following the exits he made a passionate appeal to his disaffected churchgoers to return, even writing a heartfelt letter to all his members to tell them of his heartbreak over the split dividing one of the province's best-known churches.

The wording in the message revealed his deep hurt and his apparent love for his people. He also agreed to have the letter published in full in Northern Ireland's largest national newspaper, the Belfast Telegraph, in a genuine attempt to win back the people he had loved and cared for during many years of his ministry.

In an extraordinary attempt to win many of his people back, the Pastor appealed to his people to rethink their decision if some had responded to a knee-jerk reaction. For them, he sent a heart-warming message of encouragement. But his greatest motivation was to see unity again in the House of God!

Most churches have suffered from disunity at some point, but sadly unwelcome church splits are becoming more common. Even Whitewell endured an awful period of conflict towards the end of my ministry when we suffered in this way. The fallout was catastrophic. Stuff happens in church, and sometimes it can be both heartbreaking and even life-changing. But remember, the Master was himself abandoned by those closest to him. Divisions that cause people who have worked together for years and loved each other to separate don't happen overnight but leaving churches doesn't always bring the results people expect. Disunity still proceeds from disengagement from God's pure vision of building the Church as one. **James McConnell**

Listen to many Pastors and leaders, even congregational members today. They can rhyme off every reason in the book why their Church is not growing while failing to address the elephant in the room - disunity and no vision.

Excuses are offered such as - it's a generational thing; people have many other distractions, parents have children who need help with homework, it's the fault of the growth of online ministries, it's not convenient to travel to our Church, the pandemic, and on and on the excuses go. But, notwithstanding, there is an unseen factor in the lack of church growth that most people overlook – a lack of unity amongst the brethren.

Most revealing is how the Bible refers to the Church's unity even more than it does about heaven or hell. Unity is that important to God! While churches are made up of people, and, of course, there are no perfect people, God's strongest desire is to see them bonded together in the spirit of unity.

Where people gather, problems follow. So, naturally, from time to time, divisions emerge. Finding it hard to experience unity at churches is nothing new, yet togetherness can be achieved.

The Apostle Paul's First Letter to the Corinthians demonstrates that even the early Christians struggled to live as a united Church, but he still preached about the importance of unity. The Apostle wrote four biblical letters from prison: Ephesians,

Philippians, Colossians, and Philemon. The common denominator in each letter is a challenge for the believers to be unified, to recognise that their new standing with God must profoundly impact how they relate to others in the family of God.

Paul challenged the Church at Ephesus to "diligently [keep] the unity of the Spirit" (4:3). He did not challenge them to "create unity" because they were already unified by the "one hope at your calling—one Lord, one faith, one baptism, one God and Father of all" (4:4-6). WE cannot make unity, but we can keep it. Unity is a choice. We move away from the blessing of God and the favour of God when we drift from the principles of unity. Church division is not only dangerous, but it can also be fatal for any faith aspiring assembly

The division is disastrous to any church. If a church is in discord, one may as well close the doors. Take the Corinthian Church. It was torn apart, and the Apostle Paul had to intervene, and his argument was, "I was determined to know nothing among you – save Jesus Christ and him crucified." By preaching the love of Jesus, Paul was helping to restore the unity amongst the brethren. He reminded them of the dangers of a divided house and emphasised the importance of pulling together in the same direction. There is no unity in the Church without true humility. Arrogance and self-interests destroy any chances of agreement. Brokenness attracts God's presence, but arrogance repels and repulses Him! God first works in you before he works through you, and that is through having a prayer life with God. If a man or a woman has a prayer life, they will soon possess a great desire for unity in the Church because it will be the first thing God brings to their attention. **James McConnell**

The Apostle Paul commanded the body of Christ to remain unified with a heart that is filled with the grace of God. But, on the other hand, a church at war has been described as an army turning and shooting its people and how the devil must celebrate!

Instead of uniting to advance God's kingdom, a church that fights within itself wastes countless amounts of energy and time-devouring its members. All this is contrary to God's ideal church. Throughout history, Christians have generally been recognised as a group that loves each other well, not a group that takes great delight in destroying one another.

Even the Greek philosopher Aristotle, who once wrote scornfully of the early Christians, accepted that they deeply loved each other. It was the one thing that appeared to impress him. He said, "If these Christians hear that any one of their numbers is in distress for the sake of Christ's name, they all render aid in his necessity."

Is this true of most churches today?

Unity prevails when we view others as better than ourselves and put their needs first **Philippians 2:3**, and the only way we are empowered to do so is if our minds and hearts are continually reminded of how Christ served us.

The Apostle Paul stated: Now I beseech you, brethren, by the name of our Lord Jesus Christ, that ye all speak the same thing, and that there be no divisions among you; but that ye be perfectly joined together in the same mind and the same judgment. **1 Corinthians 1:10**

It isn't just in the Church where disunity exists in the modern age. Many countries, governments, and their leaders are today at loggerheads frequently. One of the greatest hindrances to political and spiritual progress is the lack of agreement amongst politicians and church leaders. The Bible teaches that Satan will do everything he can to cause division as the Church grows. Well-meaning people, even believers, can be used as Satan tries to hurt the body of Christ. As Pastors, as shepherds of God's people, it's essential, therefore, to protect congregations from Satan's greatest weapon – disunity.

In a Covid ravaged world, even the disturbing development of differences between those who received their vaccines and those who didn't bring a two-tier society and caused considerable division within households and even church assemblies. It is all the masterstroke of Satan, and believers must never fall for such a divisive tactic.

Biblical prophecy and the words of Jesus have come to pass: "The father shall be divided against the son, and the son against the father; the mother against the daughter, and the daughter against the mother; the mother in law against her daughter in law, and the daughter in law against her mother in law" **Luke 12:53**

Without the unity of the spirit, in Christian circles, society suffers at every level. When political and secular turbulence erupts, a "divided Church" no longer influences or has anointing or healing power.

The way of peace and reconciliation is one of the most critical and creative of human actions, but the only way to ensure a house doesn't remain divided is to live together in peace and strive for unity at all costs.

While not every relationship, many people were restored following the split at Whitewell, and ultimately many people did find a way of making up. The Tabernacle returned to a place of peace and goodwill, and reconciliation reigned. Of course, constant obstacles to genuine peace and understanding remain in this life, so it will take humility and determination to experience peace in our time, churches, and nations, but it can happen.

Paul urged the followers of Jesus to "make every effort to keep the unity of the Spirit in the bond of peace." Adding: "If it is possible, as it depends on you, live at peace with everyone."

As we conclude this section on the importance of unity, by seeking to live in peace with one another and promoting the "gospel of peace," it cannot be understated how much the Church can play a huge role in helping restore order even within secular establishments. Leading by example can shine a torch to help others see the benefits of brotherly love more clearly, and it can again impress the unbelievers in this world like it once spoke to Aristotle.

Once church representatives strive to promote greater unity in their privileged positions of authority and within their congregations, then anything is possible. To remain entrenched in bitterness and hostility is quite unthinkable for the Church and its community. Jesus has warned that when there is no harmony and agreement between household members, that house can't stand and be successful.

Former British Prime Minister Winston Churchill, who kept the nation of Britain together during its darkest hour, said: "If we are together, nothing is impossible, but if divided, we all will fail."

A house divided cannot stand!

Only absolute unity within the body of Christ can transform a church and a nation because there's both power and strength when the body is together. There is no limit to a unified church.

Passion for the Word

Study to shew thyself approved unto God, a workman that
needeth not to be ashamed, rightly dividing the Word of truth
2 Timothy 2:15

16.

Rivers of Living Water

Some believers are, but just as many others seem to be more interested in reading Facebook rather than God's book. Okay, some are listening to tapes and reading theological books, and while there's nothing wrong with these things, there's nothing like sitting down and lifting the Word and reading it for you. Even if you don't understand it, read it and ask God to help you. Remember what Paul said to Timothy, all scripture comes from God's inspiration, and it is profitable. But I might add how the 'Greek New Testament states' All scripture is God-breathed. In other words, every time I open the Bible, I am experiencing the breath of God. Imagine that! The thought of God breathing on me every day, enabling me to overcome every situation. As you know, in my early days, I read and read and read and asked God to make my mind like a sponge, especially about the Word of God. Jesus said when the Spirit of truth has come, he will bring all things to your remembrance. Now having done that, today, you could quote me any verse of scripture, and I will tell you where it is. It is not arrogant to say this, merely a fact because after immersing myself in the Word of God throughout my life, my mind and heart are full of the Word of God.
James McConnell

There has always been tremendous scepticism surrounding the truth and legitimacy of the Bible. Cynics regularly use an obstacle they describe as "fictional accounts" and "unbelievable miracles" to justify how the Bible isn't accurate and how the Word of God is not really from God but instead has somehow arrived by the imaginations of men. Notwithstanding, the fact that numerous different authors—writing at other times, locations, and cultures—have intertwined a single, combined, straightforward story of the redemption of all things through Christ is quite remarkable. It is more than coincidence and is undoubtedly not human-made but evidence of a divine origin.

The unregenerate mind can never see past human logic, and so without the born-again experience in life, such people will continually struggle to believe the Bible is true. Indeed, trying to persuade sceptics is no easy task.

The Bible records in the book of Corinthians, "But the natural man receiveth, not the things of the Spirit of God: for they are foolishness unto him: neither can he know them because they are spiritually discerned" **1 Corinthians 2:14**

The Bible, which is the Word of God, is more than facts. It's not just any book, but a spiritual book only revealed by the Spirit working in God's people. So when the apostle Peter was taken by Christ to Caesarea Philippi with the other disciples, he declared how Jesus was "the Christ" and "the Son of the Living God." But Jesus replied, "Blessed art thou, Simon Barjona: for flesh and blood hath not revealed it unto thee, but my Father which is in heaven" **Matthew 16:17**

Only by the grace of God and the goodness of God can one's eyes be opened to understand that not only is Jesus Christ the Son of God but that God's Word is true. No amount of schooling will produce this breakthrough. It comes by revelation, not education! Christians believe the Scriptures are God's Word because they hear the voice of their Lord in them. As Jesus declared, "My sheep hear my voice, and I know them, and they follow me" **John 10:27**

Rather than becoming influenced by sceptics or atheists, it is natural that people like Pastor McConnell, and all men and women, continue reading the scriptures to increase their faith.

As mentioned in the chapter, Passion for Preaching, the practice of reading and studying God's Word has proved one of the secrets of success in the Pastor's life.

He has always maintained a passion for the Word of God. He is convinced and captivated by the words found in the second book of Timothy: "Study to shew thyself approved unto God, a workman that needeth not to be ashamed, rightly dividing the Word of truth **2 Timothy 2:15**

Yet as was prophesied in Thessalonians, a great falling away is taking place today, leaving a question - are people interested in the Word of God in the same way as previous generations? Are they reading the Bible as much as previously? Do they still regard the Bible as reliable and relevant today?

Pastor McConnell's congregation came to know the truth all too well.

On numerous occasions during his ministry, while in the full throws of a sermon, he would begin to quote a Psalm or verse of scripture before going on to finish the entire chapter. Like a walking Bible, the Pastor parading up and down the platform was an extraordinary sight that often thrilled his listeners with great joy. Knowing they had a Pastor who engrossed himself in the Word of God brought many of them enormous comfort.

It was evident that he didn't waste away his days watching television or spending time on other activities; instead, he would rush back from his daily church duties, open God's Word and prepare the freshest of bread for his people. It was a habit he didn't break for over half a century. Once his morning duties were accomplished at the church, his only focus was returning to his home, getting into his casual wear and slippers, and starting his devotions and preparation for yet another sermon.

Memories of Pastor McConnell's extraordinary focus and desire for the Word of God are precious to the Whitewell people and ignite legitimate questions such as: are Pastors seeking God in the same way through the pages of his Word these days or is their ministry and research dependent more on things like self-effort, Google statistics, and other easily accessed modern media? Let's leave this thought until the following chapter and fully explore this subject.

Meanwhile, another appropriate question is: do the people of God still desire the sincere milk of the Word when attending Church?

The answer might surprise you.

In days when many churches are trying to offer everything but the Word to their congregations in a desperate attempt to maintain interest levels, a survey held by a Christian TV network in 2019 asked why people still come to church. None of the expected responses followed, such as enjoying fellowship, worshipping God, meeting people, paying tithes, etc.

Instead, 76 percent of people surveyed stated how they still go to church for one reason alone – to hear the Word of God. It proved a surprising yet most encouraging revelation. It highlighted how people remain hungry for the Word of Life even in our technologically advanced world, no matter what happens elsewhere.

Regardless of what generation has passed, the power of God's Word has never lost its attraction. Some new revolutionary teaching methods are excellent, but the central gospel message never changes, and the gospel is still the power of God unto salvation.

The accuracy of neither God's Word nor its relevance is in any doubt. As the Second Coming approaches, the Word of God has burst alive before our very eyes. Many prophecies are being fulfilled as God sets the stage for the coming of the Lord.

The Bible is still much loved and read by millions of people who study it daily. It is no exaggeration to state how it is the most fabulous book globally, soaring high above all other books.

Of course, the question is, why?

Why, indeed, has this book become the book of books and endured the test of time? The answer is that the Bible is not man's book but God's book. Yes, God significantly used those appointed to pen it, but they were only the secondary authors. The primary author is God Himself, Who came upon others to write what He wanted.

It was frequently the practice of the Pastor for over 60 years to keep his flock familiar with the Bible-based on those words found in 2 Timothy "Study to shew thyself approved unto God, a workman that needeth not to be ashamed, rightly dividing the Word of truth" **2 Timothy 2:15**

I have followed this verse all my Christian life and noticed how "Unto God" are the keywords in this text. I wanted to show God how earnest and sincere I was during my life and ministry, rather than trying to impress men. Many of God's so-called workers today are ashamed due to not understanding their calling and job. The importance of those words "unto God" can't be overlooked. The highest goal was to show God I was serious about his work and the Church during my ministry. I grew up with men and leaders like that. I saw them studying the Word and seeking God, so I tried to follow them. I wanted to be like them. Of course, I saw their weaknesses, and they were just men, but I wanted to follow them because their hearts were seeking after the things of God. My weaknesses became evident when I did follow them, but I hope no one can doubt my passion for reading and preaching God's good Word. It sustained our Church and me for years. Like Elijah, who lived off a cake and a jar of water for 40 days and nights before arriving at Mount Horeb, many times, the Word of God has kept our people and me alive. **James McConnell**

While the Pastor has nothing against daily devotionals or podcasts and tapes, he fears if this becomes the only form of reading or learning, even the norm, the Church will become spiritually sick. He maintains Christians need to be planted and deeply rooted in the Word, and gimmicks are no substitute for God's Word!

If you feed someone sweets every day, they will eventually become ill. The body needs proper nutrition and calories, like a decent meal, not ice cream and jelly all the time.

No one could or has ever survived on such a diet. In the spiritual sense, it is the same. If our spiritual diet is top-heavy with things only designed to assist our daily bible reading or what we call "light entertainment," we will inevitably lose our way. There is nothing like the Word of God to build our spiritual foundation. In the book of Hebrews, "For the word of God is living and active, sharper than any two-edged sword, piercing to the division of soul and of spirit, of joints and marrow, and discerning the thoughts and intentions of the heart." While Timothy states: "For the prophecy came not in old time by the will of man: but holy men of God spake as they were moved by the Holy Ghost". Timothy also wrote: All scripture is given by inspiration of God, and is profitable for doctrine, for reproof, for correction, for instruction in righteousness: That the man of God may be perfect, thoroughly furnished unto all good works. **James McConnell**

The Bible is not just God's inspired Word; it is His gift to humanity. The Word inspired simply means "breathed out by God." Therefore, the difference between the Bible and other books is that it didn't originate from men's lips but God's very mouth. Terms like "God spoke" or "Thus saith the Lord" appear thousands of times throughout the Bible, showing how it is dangerous to assume it is just a book written by men. The Word of God didn't come from men or even the Church; it came from God alone. It has come from the very mind, mouth, and hand of God.

Down the centuries, the Bible books have been subjected to the keenest scrutiny and received the most demanding inspection by contemporary academics. Yet, time and again, the Bible books have proved themselves to be historically reliable and worthy of our trust and the prophets. The Word of God is not only the most reliable but the most enduring book ever written. While many other books get consigned to the literary scrapheap, within just a few years, Jesus said concerning the Word of God in Matthew's gospel, "Heaven and earth shall pass away, but my words shall not pass away." **Matthew 24:35**

So, for all his regular reading of God's Word over the years, who does the Pastor view as his favourite character in the Bible and his favourite book?

I love King David's story and Samuel's book because David was such a complicated and genuine person, having been through many things, even his child's death, adultery, and murder. He was able to identify with his people and meet them at the point of their needs and find the mercy and forgiveness of God. He found forgiveness with God, and because of this, he loved Him much. And yet, with all the negative things in his life, the Bible still maintains how David was a man after God's own heart. Think about that! What a compliment! God wasn't and isn't looking for perfection because only Jesus is perfect. He's looking for people who have a heart for Him. Of course, David is only one of many spiritual giants in scripture, who though not perfect, pleased God, and their stories bring hope to us all. Read the Word and study all of these remarkable characters. You find spiritual giants like Abraham, Moses, Joshua, Joseph, Gideon, Samuel, Ruth, Esther, Daniel, Elijah, Isaiah, Jeremiah, and all the apostles, to name but a few. Study all these great characters, and you will grow leaps and bounds in your faith, for you will see that they endured life's ups and downs as we do and yet found the grace and mercy of Almighty God. **James McConnell**

The Pastor is indeed living proof of a psalm many have heard him quote verbatim on countless occasions throughout his ministry – a psalm which God still offers today to all who will believe His Word is accurate. It says: "Blessed is the man that walketh not in the counsel of the ungodly, nor standeth in the way of sinners, nor sitteth in the seat of the scornful. But his delight is in the law of the LORD, and in his law doth he meditate day and night. And he shall be like a tree planted by the rivers of water, that bringeth forth his fruit in his season; his leaf also shall not wither, and whatsoever he doeth shall prosper. The ungodly are not so: but are like the chaff which the wind driveth away. Therefore, the ungodly shall not stand in the judgment nor sinners in the congregation of the righteous. For the LORD knoweth the way of the righteous: but the way of the ungodly shall perish. **Psalm 1:1-6.**

The Pastor's life and ministry have been like this tree, planted by rivers of water. He has based everything upon the words of John "He that believeth on me, as the scripture hath said, out of his belly shall flow rivers of living water." **John 7:38** He has consistently stood on the promises, reliability, and enduring steadfastness of God's Word, and much fruit has followed. His stream has continually flowed through the forest of God's Word, making its way towards God's eternal sea.

I am the bread of life. Whoever comes to me will never go hungry,
and whoever believes in me will never be thirsty.

John 6:35

17.

Bread Again in Israel

Many nations are starving due to a natural food shortage, yet a famine of God's Word is equally severe, especially when scarce in the church. It brings chaos and confusion and paralyses nations and individuals. Without the bread of life, homes and lives are destroyed, people are left malnourished, and blessing decreases. In Samuel's days, the Bible describes how there was "no open vision" – or "frequent vision" - a reference to a lack of bread and the preaching of the Word in God's house. Solomon wrote, "Without a vision, the people perish." There is nothing to compare to the Word of God, and thankfully that is something I have always had a passion for. Modern Israel and the true church of Jesus Christ cannot hope to survive without the bread of life. The church is trying many newfangled ideas, but the greatest need is to return to reading and hearing the Word of God. It's counterfeit to believe that more original, creative, and intelligent sermons are better than addresses based solely on the bread of life. Many reasons are cited for the apparent deficiency of people at church in this generation. For example, too many distractions, apostasy, and the lukewarm age we live in, yet only when there is bread again in the church will the masses begin to return, and the Spirit will start to move back. Only when people rise like Naomi did and return to Bethlehem (House of Bread) will they see a positive change in their lives. **James McConnell**

Have you ever wished you could go back and start all over again? Ever messed up so badly or wandered off from God's path? You just wanted a clean slate and the opportunity to shine again? Maybe you haven't messed up at all? Maybe circumstances rearranged the fixtures in your life so dramatically it was out of your hands, yet you wish you could go back and start all over again and follow the perfect way of God. But is it even possible to go back and begin again?

Is it possible to put behind you the hurts, disappointments, regrets, and even broken relationships that may have occurred?

If this is a picture of you, then the answer is yes, it is, and the best place to restart is with the Word of God. Psalm 119 says, "Thy word is a lamp unto my feet and a light unto my path" **Psalm 119:105**

Starting all over again was Naomi's desire in the book of Ruth after she found herself starving for food, both spiritually and materially.

A godly woman whose name means "pleasant" or "beautiful," she left the land of Israel for the land of Moab in a hasty moment that seemed right to the eyes, yet instead was met with only tragedy and heartache. To suggest that life in the land of Moab didn't work out for Naomi is something of an understatement.

For example, while there, she witnessed the loss of her husband and two sons, who died prematurely, and was left to fend for herself and two foreign daughters named Orpah and Ruth. In the beginning, of course, the thought of a new life elsewhere seemed exciting as both Naomi and her husband Elimelech tried to avoid the famine in Israel, but what's that old saying about "Far off fields?" The book of Proverbs states, "There is a way that seemeth right to a man, but the end thereof is the ways of death." **Proverbs 14:12**

New Testament believers should not quickly overlook Naomi's Old Testament story, for not only does it produce much hope of restoration, but her life is also a picture of modern believers and their relationship with God and His Word.

Following the calamities she'd experienced in Moab, there was only one road left to take for Naomi — the way back to Bethlehem – which means House of Bread!

The book of Ruth states: "So she got up with her daughters-in-law to return from the land of Moab, for in the land of Moab, she had heard that the Lord had visited His people by giving them food." **Ruth 1:6**

Do you think God is angry with you because you have stepped off the spiritual train and taken a break from spiritual things? On the contrary, God understands our weaknesses, and He is just waiting for us to return to Him and His Word to begin our recovery.

There are multitudes of people who have lost hope today and consequently stopped attending the house of God; people, who have given up, and who appear content to blame God and others for their mistakes to justify no longer turning to the Word of life as a solution to their problems. Once filled with the Spirit of God and alive to the joy of the Lord, today, they are living in Moab and running on empty. Many justifiable reasons explain this demise, but one prominent cause is likely - the absence of fresh bread (the Word of God) in the house of God and their devotional lives.

The words of Psalm 119 are worth repeating "Thy word is a lamp unto my feet, and a light unto my path" **Psalm 119:105**

No one could accuse Pastor McConnell of failing to serve up fresh bread to his congregation week after week. On the contrary, he regularly worked on new weekly sermons to feed his flock with the finest of the wheat, and like the manna sent from heaven to the children of Israel in the Old Testament, the supply never ran out.

The Word of life lasted for generation after generation, and the people of God prospered materially and spiritually.

Let's revisit the question we raised in the previous chapter - do Pastors continue to seek God from the bread of life, or is modern research shallow and based on social media statistics and from other easily accessed forms of media?

Do God's people also view their daily devotional time with God as important as their natural food, or are they content to live off scraps and social media posts?

It is an essential subject because only the Word of God can radically transform lives. A nation, church, and people scarce of the Word of God will live in misery, confusion, and even in defeat. People often ask, "What is God's will for my life?" God's will is not as difficult to unravel as is often portrayed. His intention is where there is bread, both physically and spiritually. While God understands we require food that feeds our stomachs, He is also determined to teach us the importance of what the Bible calls - the bread of life — the Word of God.

Even more than natural food, the thing we all need most is was what Jesus would later describe in the New Testament as "the bread of life." Without this bread, no one can be satisfied. Jesus said;

In the past decade, denominational church attendance in the UK has decreased by fifty per cent; notwithstanding, the same people who have walked away from the church and the Bible can yet be encouraged to return and be filled again by looking to Jesus and finding a church which believes that still, the "gospel is the power of God unto salvation." **Romans 1:16**

Imitations can never compare to the preaching of the Word of God. Nothing can satisfy the soul like the Word of truth. It is more than enough. I would encourage preachers today to stick with the Word of God, which has stood the test of time. By all means, try and appeal to your listeners and people with illustrations and creative methods, but the Word worked before, and it still works today and will work in the future. If preachers and ministers starve the people of the Word, it won't be long before their churches begin to struggle and resemble graveyards, and sadly in some cases, this is happening. We must return to the bread of life. **James McConnell**

But what is the benefit of this bread of life the Pastor mentions?

Bread is one of the necessary foods of many cultures worldwide; it is a staple in many diets, and for centuries it would have been one of the most available foods for people of all wealth and social statuses.

During the life and ministry of Jesus, bread would have been recognised as a nutritional necessity. It also has historical significance for the Jewish people, harkening back to God's life-sustaining manna, which helped keep their people alive in the desert. In other words, it was no accident that Jesus chose "bread" as His figure of speech intentionally.

When Jesus says He is the bread of life, He says He is more than necessary.

Metaphorical and storybook language exists in many places in the Word of God. From the Psalms' poetry to the parables of Jesus, imagery and metaphor are a part of how God speaks to the world in His Word.

The Bible magnificently sheds light on heavenly concepts that are difficult to put into words and is a way for the Holy Spirit to speak to the soul providing concrete images to help individuals grasp abstract, metaphysical ideas.

Remember, Jesus, fed 5,000 men plus women and children. Still, after speaking to the crowd again, it is interesting how he offered them a very different kind of bread that would never perish and would continually satisfy them.

When the people demanded this bread, the Bible records, "Jesus said to them, 'I am the bread of life; whoever comes to me shall not hunger and whoever believes in me shall never thirst" **John 6:35**

The point to make is that the bread of life is not physical, but the bread of spiritual renewal found in the salvation of the blood of Jesus Christ.

Why Does Jesus Say He Is the Bread of Life? First, it is a huge claim.

If we read the gospel of John, it is clear the writer is keen to stress not just what He did while here on earth but also on who He is. The Apostle John, therefore, emphasises the deity of Christ. Chapter six, for example, focuses on one of the Lord's miracles and its fallout. Because the Lord performed healing miracles and taught the Scriptures with authority, many people followed Him.

In one of these instances, the Lord takes five loaves of bread and two fish and feeds thousands of people with twelve baskets leftover. Later the same evening, He even walked on water. The next day, thousands gathered again to be provided.

This time, Jesus offered them salvation – eternal nourishment – rather than just temporary sustenance. The following verses in the book of John show how He was no ordinary man, for He even knew the intents and motives of those following after Him. "Truly, truly, I say to you, you are seeking me, not because you saw signs, but because you ate your fill of the loaves. Do not work for the food that perishes, but for the food that endures to eternal life, which the Son of Man will give to you. For on him God, the Father has set his seal. For this is the will of my Father, that everyone who looks on the Son and believes in him should have eternal life, and I will raise him on the last day" **John 6:26-27**

The Lord highlights how, in this life, humanity must toil and labour for the food that only temporarily nourishes the body, which will eventually die. Still, if we trust in Him, He has the power and authority to multiply that food and can do so much more, even the ability to offer eternal life.

Are you struggling at present due to a lack of spiritual sustenance? Are you preoccupied with Social Media rather than God's book?

Fear not; God longs for you to draw close to Him, and He can pull you back to what matters.

Zechariah wrote; "Return unto me saith the Lord and I will return unto you." **Zechariah 1:3**

A good question is: why are people today so reluctant to either return to the bread of life or continue in it and thus experience this blessing of God in their lives?

It's a different generation with many distractions like daily devotionals, videos, and short podcasts. People don't appear as eager to open the Word and read it, even some Pastors, which is a shame because it is that very thing that will bring change and transformation to their churches. People tell me that they are confused and lack spiritual growth, but the problem is obvious – a genuine lack of reading and hearing fresh bread. Reading through the Bible in a year and systematic study is good, but I believe the quickest way to make people return to reading the Word is good preaching, including the bread of life. If our pulpits flow again with fresh bread, miracles will take place. Unfortunately, today there are too many boring sermons from clergy who, although sincere, appear to have little or no inspiration. People respond to inspiration, not aspiration! People are moved by the Holy Ghost, not by Holy teaching, no matter how sincere it may be. I have always said there is no substitute for the Holy Ghost, and there is nothing like fresh bread in the pulpit and our lives. I have given the analogy many times of going to the bakery and buying bread only to find it is stale and, in some cases, blue mould. Is there anything worse to eat? Yet many Christians today, churches and Pastors alike, are trying to survive on such bread. It is not possible! The true church of Jesus Christ cannot hope to survive without the bread of life. **James McConnell**

During his ministry, the Pastor would often make his congregation hungry by painting a picture of fresh bread just out of the oven with lashings of butter on it.

"Even use jam if you want," he would joke before adding, "but make sure the bread is fresh. There's nothing worse than stale bread!"

In the beginning was the Word, and the Word was with God,
and the Word was God.
John 1:1

18.

Back to Basics

For ministers to produce inspirational preaching that travels beyond their congregations into the culture, it requires nothing short of the Holy Spirit and a thing called the anointing of God. There is no substitute for the Holy Spirit. A preacher must be prepared to let fly and speak what God the Holy Spirit wants, not what the preacher prefers. It is essential if the Holy Spirit has His way. A Pastor should often sense his people's needs, and giving them a word for the hour and a word in season is fundamental. That same sermon may only be preached once and never be repeated because it was for someone's situation at that time. A Pastor preaches for the need of the hour, and if ever there is a time to produce this sort of ministry, it is now, but without the Word of God in a person's heart, how can this happen? More than ever, people require revelation and transformation, and only the Word of God and the Holy Spirit can provide it. **James McConnell**

Despite advancements in our civilization, some prominent voices advocate returning to the Bible and its principles. However, current thinking and methods are not always as successful as previously, so going back to move forward is not as risky as some might fear.

Linda Hobson, his personal assistant for four decades is convinced that society and the Church will, in her words, "have to come full circle before there is another revival like the one my dad and many people at Whitewell experienced. We will have to go back to go forward and only after every new toy has been tried. The Bible speaks about the 'old paths' being 'necessary paths,' and, in this respect, the Bible hasn't changed. It is a society that has changed."

According to James McConnell and his daughter, as discussed in an earlier chapter, there's more than a tendency today to find other things to replace the Word to keep people interested and motivated, but a most dangerous development exists herein.

Instead, they both recommend "starting all over again" or going "back to basics" to borrow a legendary quote from John Major's speech in 1993 regarding the conservative party. People weren't expecting that iconic speech from a man who recommended going back to go forward. Naturally, when any vision is proposed, people hope to hear something about the future, not the past. Yet, Major shocked the listeners by suggesting that going "back to basics" was the way to progress and help rebuild the conservative party and a better society.

Of course, several other conservative politicians continued this approach, including David Cameron, who boldly declared back in 2011 in a speech to mark the 400th anniversary of the King James Bible, how "Britain is a Christian country, and we should not be afraid to say so." Cameron told the Church of England clergy gathered in Oxford that a return to Christian values could counter the country's "moral collapse" and blamed a "passive tolerance" of immoral behaviour for that summer's riots, Islamic extremism, City excess, and Westminster scandals.

In 2020, a new MP used his maiden speech in the House of Commons to defend Christianity and argue that returning to Christianity values will help shape Britain for the better. Danny Kruger, MP for Devizes in Wiltshire, lamented that Britain had moved away from its shared Christian heritage and said many of today's problems could be solved by restoring Christianity to society. Kruger, who formed a prisoner rehabilitation charity with his wife, said that "traditionally," British people had felt that we were all capable of both great wrong and great virtue, stating, "Even those who didn't believe in God, there was a sense that our country is rooted in Christianity, that our liberties derive from the Christian idea of absolute dignity. However, today these ideas are losing their purchase, so we are trying to find a new set of values to guide us, a new language of rights and wrongs, and a new idea of identity, based not on our universal inner value or our membership of a common culture, but our differences." Is he wrong?

Even though some secularists are not comfortable with politicians preaching theology in their spaces, perhaps if we had more of this impressive honesty both in the Church and politics, the country and even the world would be in a better place.

Calls for a reoccurrence of Christian principles like Cameron's and Kruger's, which have included respect for the Word of God, have, of course, come from several other politicians. Including the former President of the United States, Donald Trump.

Far from a piety model, Trump has been accused of being an opportunist who cynically plays to his audience –i.e., the Christian right-wing in America and a promoter of hate and division. Yet whether you believe Trump to be a piety model or not, it is undeniable that the former American President has consistently defended the Christian faith and Israel's country. For example, in January 2020, Trump gave his blessing to religious organizations for easier access to deferral programs, and he reaffirmed students' rights to pray in public schools.' He has also consistently defended Israel. On 6 December 2017, he formally recognized Jerusalem as the capital of Israel, reversing nearly seven decades of American foreign policy and setting a plan to move the United States Embassy from Tel Aviv to the fiercely contested Holy City. Then, following civil unrest in America provoked by George Floyd's death, Trump incensed many people when he appeared outside a church in 2020, holding a Bible and appearing to use it as authority and stability during a time of national chaos. Of course, co-opting Christianity in the service of power is almost as old as Christianity itself, yet few incidents have proved as unforgettable and striking as this one.

Many Americans and people, in general, were outraged that a man who they believed had consistently stoked the flames of racism and white supremacy was hiding behind a Bible and effectively claiming how God was on His side. Nevertheless, regardless of his politics or what side of the fence you stand regarding Donald Trump, those powerful images and media footage of him holding high a Bible sent a subconscious message to the world, namely - let's get back to the Bible.

From coast to coast, country to country, and computer screen to computer screen, that image of a single Bible remains a powerful one. God's book still gives clarity and direction around the globe through His Word. The Pastor believes that returning to the Word of God and aligning ourselves with God's Words is the only answer for the Church and the public square. So many times, he has held the standard of truth high at a most inconvenient time.

Society has moved away from Christian values and principles without question due to ignorance of God's Word and lack of interest in it, and things have deteriorated. Therefore, he believes that encouraging "back to basics" when building devotional lives and the ministry is the way to progress.

In short, going back to go forward is not as outlandish as it may seem, nor should it be confined to politics.

People may think going back is an antiquated approach because we live in a generation with so much technology where leaders pressure their people to keep moving forward. All we hear is how to embrace this new thing and that new thing, but show me where the Word of God has failed before? There is an old saying, "never go back." Still, it is not valid in everything, especially regarding tried and tested methods in the ministry or what I have described over the years as "porridge principles." There is no more excellent foundation to build your personal life upon your Church than God's lovely Word. Moreover, studying God's Word is essential because it puts "inside lining" inside the preacher or person reading it. Then when it is required, it will flow out of your belly according to the words of Jesus "He that believeth on me, as the scripture hath said, out of his belly shall flow rivers of living water". The Bible and reading have never failed before, so it is entirely reliable.
James McConnell

Making room for the Word of God would seem to be a good idea in our political establishments, but most significantly, of course, within our pulpits again. How else will a confused and even fearful world derive hope? How else will people in bondage find deliverance?

People object to the Church interfering in political matters and society, but it is the Church's job to help steer the world in the right direction, not the other way around. Notwithstanding, the problem is that neither our politicians nor preachers seem capable of giving such leadership. Leading and directing a ship through troubled waters takes great skill from the captain and crew, and no one can dispute the fact that a flood of critical issues currently engulfs the world.

The preacher and the Pastor must aspire to find a sense of the Holy Spirit again rather than be confined by religious structures and theological boundaries.

The preaching style emphasized by the Pastor is known as 'a Rhema word,' a Greek term referring to the spoken Word. *Rhema* means an utterance, individually, collectively, or expressly. It is also more commonly referred to as 'now' - a word for the present.

Significantly, a Rhema word was a regular occurrence in the New Testament, not an exception. In Luke chapter one, we are told, "And Mary said, Behold the handmaid of the Lord; be it unto me according to thy Word. And the angel departed from her. **Luke 1:38**, while in the book of Acts, Peter, filled with the Holy Spirit, said, "Then remembered I the Word of the Lord, how that he said, John indeed baptized with water, but ye shall be baptized with the Holy Ghost **Acts 11:16**

During his ministry, the Pastor frequently approached the pulpit with a well-prepared message for his people only to toss his notes aside at the last minute, open the Bible and then produce an utterly different Word to the one he had sweated over during that week. It took courage, of course, to stand in front of a packed assembly with nothing but a blank page in front of him, but he knew the Holy Spirit, and he regularly tried to obey His voice. God's message took precedence more than the will and desire of the preacher. Most spirit-filled preachers would readily admit that one of the most challenging jobs they face is hearing that inner voice of the Holy Spirit speaking a different word to them than the one they have packed away neatly in their bibles. The flesh cries to bring the Word prepared and not waste labour hours, while the Spirit calls to get something else out there.

Only a preacher who has walked with God and in-depth knowledge of God's Word would feel comfortable forgoing their prepared message favouring a different text, notably when any notes do not support that exact text. However, it is folly and counterproductive to proceed against the wishes of the Spirit in such situations.

To repeat the words of CH Spurgeon, "No man should preach on a text unless it has first leapt at him like a lion from a thicket."

It has been said: "The Word of God is like a lion. You don't have to defend a lion, and all you have to do is let the lion loose, and the lion will defend itself."

Spurgeon conveyed this idea at least three times, but he never said it this way. The closest quote is found in Spurgeon's 1886 sermon "Christ and His Co-Workers" when he stated: "Suppose several persons were to take it into their heads that they had to defend a lion, full-grown king of beasts! There he is in the cage, and here come all the army soldiers to fight for him. Well, I should suggest to them, if they would not object and feel that it was humbling to them, that they should kindly stand back, open the door, and let the lion out! I believe that would be the best way of defending him, for he would take care of himself, and the best 'apology' for the gospel is to let the gospel out."

Pastor McConnell believes that "Letting the gospel out," as Spurgeon puts it, will transform not just the Church but also our politics and civilization.

But how did the Pastor become skilled in listening for God's Rhema word instead of his weekly masterpiece? How could he remain faithful to the Word when the temptation was to go with the crowd? His congregation lost count of how many times he could make this crucial switch from a regular sermon to one God had appointed for a specific time.

Many a time, after watching him dispense with his notes, I recall sitting in the Church, praying that God would give the Pastor the words he required, but 40 minutes later, he was still going, and fresh bread was being served. Out of his belly flowed rivers of living water.

When I went out in the car, I always had a sheet of paper, an exercise book, and I would jot down thoughts or texts from the Lord. It is good to teach on the Bible but remember God's Word is a divine, life-changing message to the world, and it is instant and transformational. A congregation's needs compel a Pastor, and for a week or two, they will preach on it for the condition of the hour, but occasionally God will overrule and present the Pastor and the Church with a challenge. When a national disaster arrives or tragedy strikes your church members, they require hope and a fresh word from heaven. A Bible series is excellent in its season, but great preachers don't only preach what they fancy. Instead, they are guided by the Holy Spirit to be the spokesperson of God and bring what is termed 'a word in season.' People frequently require a word for their current situation, and ditching a pre-planned sermon is the way to do it if God has spoken. If we believe those sixty-six books are God's Word, it will show in the preacher and the congregation's life. And as you translate God's Word under the Holy Ghost's anointing, people will receive it and be built up through it. It is the only way to explain it. I wouldn't know how to do anything other than read it, believe it, and apply it. And remember, it is the applying that makes the difference." **James McConnell**

The Pastor loves the words of a quote by the late Billy Graham, who, when once asked if Christianity is valid, and why is there so much evil in the world, profoundly replied: "If there is so much soap, why are there so many dirty people in the world? Christianity, like soap, must be personally applied if it is to make a difference in our lives."

As we prepare to leave the subject of passion for God's Word, the gospel is God's power unto salvation, yet various churches and congregations do not seem to believe in it the way they used to. It is almost as if they view the sacred Word of God as less critical. While some might think the Word is no longer relevant and doesn't reach people in their circumstances today, the Pastor completely disagrees.

He quotes the words of the book of John: "In the beginning was the Word, and the Word was with God, and the Word was God. The same was at the beginning with

God. He made all things, and without him was not anything made that was made. In him was life, and the life was the light of men. And the light shineth in darkness; and the darkness comprehended it not. **John 1:1-5**

To suggest the Word is not relevant merely exposes the Holy Spirit's absence in the lives of those who think like this. On the contrary, the Word is incredibly relevant today, in fact, more relevant than ever, with Bible prophecy being fulfilled every day before our very eyes. I like how the Bible says, "and the spirit moved upon the face of the deep, and God said." Here we have the Word and the Spirit working together, and God says, let there be, and there was. If you believe that the sixty-six books of the Bible are divine and that they are the Words of God, miracles can take place in your life. Look at my life! I was an orphan boy with no parents and no future, but I began to read God's Word, and an explosion of hope visited my heart; more than this, God also sent divine purpose and direction into my life. Dreams were fulfilled, and miracles took place. **James McConnell**

That Word the Pastor speaks so confidently about did more than provide a future and hope for him; it also, of course, inspired the building of a soul-saving centre known as Whitewell - a place that helped transform the lives of countless thousands who have passed through its doors. A mighty anointing blew through the Church and not just for a time, but decade after decade after decade, resulting in many souls being swept into God's Kingdom.

Passion for the Anointing

And it shall come to pass in that day, that his burden shall be taken away from off thy shoulder, and his yoke from off thy neck, and the yoke shall be destroyed because of the anointing.

Isaiah 10:27

19.

The Need for the Anointing

The anointing is not optional but essential in evangelical churches. It gives one power and confidence and delivers people from all sorts of things. It even opens the door to salvation. And yet, the missing ingredient in many churches is quite often a lack of anointing. What could the Church do if we can swap tinsel with truth and gimmicks with grace and performance with the anointing? Remember, the anointing made Whitewell such a success; it wasn't the work of a man or men. There's an overwhelming need for anointing again in the Church with many pressing issues today. **James McConnell**

There is a word and crucial component seemingly absent in church life today – it is the word "anointing." Many other terms define and describe potential success and breakthrough in the Church, but rarely do we hear of any evangelical success associated with the anointing.

Too many churches today strive to provide everything except the essential element – the anointing of God. Sadly it appears education, eloquence, and the power of personality are given priority above the one thing that churches, ministers, and converts crucially require – the influence of God's mantle. It matters little what else transpires; without the anointing in a church or a ministry, everything else gets spoiled. The Church becomes a place of no pasture, even open to what the Bible describes as "strange fire." Minus the anointing, the people are deceived by smokescreens, which cannot replicate the real thing. The anointing ensures people are delivered and set free; souls are saved and relationships healed; however, how often has Church felt like a fruitless feast? For example, have you ever sat in a service and enjoyed the overall experience but still felt something was missing?

Have you ever listened to a word preached by the Pastor, and while it was perfectly acceptable and appropriate, even theologically well constructed, something was still missing? Your soul didn't feel satisfied, and you didn't feel comforted or instructed.

Have you worshipped and praised the Lord and been left wondering if God heard your heart's devotion? Deadness permeated the air, and frustration replaced faith.

In such instances, you've no doubt experienced Church but not Christ, and empty preaching rather than an anointed word. You probably witnessed a ministry void of signs and wonders and souls finding salvation, which, according to the New Testament, is why the Church was created.

Church organisers can dim the lights, surprise their guests with exciting programmes and events, and even prepare a good service with the right motive and intention. Still, without the most crucial ingredient – the anointing of God - the service will stagnate and not amount to much. One of the greatest mistakes is to judge policies and programmes by their intentions rather than their results. The anointing always produces results! Without the anointing, both confusion and disillusionment are the results. The Apostle Paul wrote: "For God is not the author of confusion, but peace, as in all churches of the saints **1 Corinthians 14:33**

The well-known Christian writer AW Tozer also said: "If the Holy Spirit and the anointing were withdrawn from the Church today, 95 per cent of what we do would go on, and no one would know the difference," adding: "If the Holy Spirit had been withdrawn from the New Testament church, 95 per cent of what they did would stop, and everybody would know the difference."

The Pastor believes without the unequivocal evidence of this anointing of God in our midst; the Church is wasting its time. During one of our interviews, I reminded him of his statement while preaching in his pulpit following his ministry's retirement. It spoke to many of his parishioners because even in retirement, it was clear that he remained desperate for the special ingredient – the anointing of God. Talking about the mantle God had given him, he said: "the mantle is the anointing of God, and if I don't have the anointing, I don't want to live."

Was he serious, or was this just another useful one-liner? Was it an attempt to interest, even shock his watching audience, or did he mean he would prefer to stop living on this earth than continue without the anointing of God?

I meant every word of that. I believe the anointing has kept me alive because, as you know, my family was wiped out due to Tuberculosis. But all sorts of other disasters happened in my home and left me an orphan and sleeping under the trees in Ormeau Park in Belfast. Yet even then, it was the anointing that kept me going. The anointing has been with me from the age of eight, and I can honestly say I have never lost it. No matter what difficulty or situation I have been in and have failed many times, the anointing has always encouraged me. If that anointing is no longer there, I genuinely don't want to live. There would be no purpose in living. As for ministry, it is even more crucial to have an anointing from the Lord. Indeed, I have concluded that a minister minus the anointing and blessing of God is wasting time. **James McConnell**

That may seem like a harsh conclusion from the Pastor, but he insists the ministry is not like any other vocation. The results do not depend on the employee's efforts or even ability but are dependent on the Holy Spirit's measure, which is upon a minister and his congregation. No amount of hard work and sweat can produce the anointing of God. Yes, ministers must be dedicated and work hard to experience success, but hard work alone has never won a soul to God. Of course, it may be possible to continue like this for a while without the evidence of the Holy Spirit.

Still, if the anointing is genuinely absent, eventually, the cracks will show, and the ministry will appear as a work of the flesh rather than a heavenly-sent church.

An excellent example of this was in Acts chapter five, when the anointing was in full flow from the apostles but attracting severe scrutiny and even potential persecution. Suddenly a Pharisee named Gamaliel, a doctor of the law, with a good reputation, urged caution regarding taking action against them, stating: "Refrain from these men and let them alone, for it this counsel or this work be of men, it will come to nought, but if it is of God, ye cannot overthrow it, lest haply, ye be found to fight even against God" **Acts 5:38-39**

All the 'playacting in the world' cannot disguise a lack of anointing. The best personality and oratory will not suffice. The smartest sermon or the most delightful singing won't be adequate either. Only the anointing will make a difference in changing people's lives and converting men, women, and children to God. It is not man but God who makes the necessary changes. In God's Word, the apostles and prophets had a special anointing, but only for God's glory, not their own. I've discovered that finding this anointing takes time but holding unto it is the real trick. It's like a famous heavyweight boxer once said, "To get to the top is great, but staying at the top is the difficult part." The anointing enables ministers to continue and enjoy continued success even in strong opposition. It is essential in the Christian ministry, or a man or woman will be destroyed. I can't emphasise enough how vital the anointing is for every minister and indeed every child of God. There is a great need for the anointing because it protects us, provides for us, and empowers us to carry out God's purpose for our lives. It is also the ingredient that one needs to see natural fruit from their ministry. There's nothing like it! **James McConnell**

The ministry at Whitewell can be grateful for many things over the years, dedicated people, beautiful worship, outstanding preaching, but the Church, which has experienced a genuine move of God on several occasions, owes most of its success to nothing other than the anointing of God.

Thousands of men and women and children have been saved and drawn to God under that same anointing, people far too numerous to count or mention.

The life of James McConnell has always known the divine help and assistance of the anointing. But what is this anointing, and who should desire to seek after it?

The anointing was a common ancient cultural practice. Shepherds often poured oil on their sheep's heads to protect them from insects that would burrow in their ears and kill them, contributing to anointing becoming symbolic of blessing, protection, and empowerment. The Jewish people anointed the altar when making sacrifices. In other words, spiritually speaking, the term anointing was related to the idea of strength or blessing. Hence, without the anointing, our assemblies become weak and sickly. Priests were anointed with oil, with Samuel anointing Saul and then David as kings of Israel. This anointing signified a person as a chosen one among other people. The anointing is not just important; it is vital and a sign that God is with a person and their ministry!

During the coronation of a new monarch, they are anointed with holy oil. When George V & VI And Elizabeth were all crowned, their coronation ceremonies were all filmed; however, the anointing with oil was considered too sacred a moment to be seen by anyone, including the congregation in the Abbey, so a screen was erected and only the new monarch and the Archbishop of Canterbury were present.

Of course, the ministry of the Lord Jesus was supremely anointed. The book of Luke revealed how God anointed Jesus with the Holy Spirit, saying, "The Spirit of the Lord is upon me because he has anointed me to proclaim good news to the poor" **Luke 4:18**

The word "anointed" was used to emphasise Jesus as the chosen one of God. However, after Christ left the earth, He left the Holy Spirit and the Church's anointing to continue. **John 14:16** says: "And I will ask the Father, and he will give you another Helper, to be with you forever,"

Acts 10:3 records how "God anointed Jesus of Nazareth with the Holy Spirit and with power."

It is vital to understand that in addition to Old Testament leaders and Jesus being anointed, the apostle Paul also spoke of all Christians' anointing. People sometimes assume that the anointing is only for the Pastor or leader of a church, but that is not scriptural. The Apostle Paul regularly taught how every sincere believer had access to their anointing. John wrote: "But you have been anointed by the Holy One, and you all have knowledge **1 John 2:20**

In his second letter to the Corinthians, Paul states: "And it is God who establishes us with you in Christ, and has anointed us, and who has also put his seal on us and given us his Spirit in our hearts as a guarantee" **2 Corinthians 1:21**

Observe how Paul uses the term anointed in the plural sense. So, where and how is the anointing to be found?

I think some of it comes down to desire. I accept that all believers can have an anointing, but how much do they desire it? That is the question! If you are a Christian, God has graciously given you an anointing; you have been chosen for a specific purpose in furthering God's Kingdom, but how much you desire it is the key. How much do you want this anointing to show and shine? It cannot be turned on and off like a tap or taken for granted. Time and sacrifice with God will help establish the anointing. Remember, when Moses came down from the mountain, having spent many days in God's presence, the Bible clarifies that he wasn't even aware that his face was shining. **James McConnell**

If the anointing is from God, it makes sense to commune regularly with God.

Oswald J. Smith stated, "I am perfectly confident that the man who does not spend time alone with God will never know the anointing of the Holy Spirit," which suggests the anointing or more significant measure of it can be greater found by entering the presence of God more regularly.

Christ means *anointed one*, so does it naturally follow that they have the Anointing if a person has Christ?

I don't think we can say it is as simple as that. The anointing doesn't grow on trees, and it costs to have a great blessing. Many preachers are not prepared to seek it, and they are unwilling to surrender things to obtain it. For many years, I cried unto God for it. When

I was a boy, I remember one man saying, what makes an apostle, prophet, and evangelist? An apostle is a man anointed by the great apostle of our profession, which is Jesus. As for me, the Spirit of the great evangelist comes upon me, and I speak in his place with an anointing. Sadly, there are still ministries and churches that don't even know what the word anointing means. They believe in Jesus and are saved, but where is their anointing? It is as if they think they can exist without it, but that is impossible. Without the anointing, a church will never see souls saved, never experience healing, and never truly experience transformation in how the New Testament church experienced. I believe there's a severe need for a re-examination of the anointing of God currently in our history because if it becomes absent in the Church, the consequences are unthinkable. But if men and women will seek it again, all is not lost, and great things are yet possible. **James McConnell**

We have covered earlier how the Pastor was influenced by spiritual giants who he's convinced all possessed a divine anointing for the Lord, but when did he become conscious of the anointing in his life? What happened during his youth, would result in a unique and unusual anointing to win souls.

Pastor James McConnell is like every other person. He is imperfect and admits to having faults and failures, but that didn't stop him from carrying an incredible anointing to win souls and help build the ministry for over 60 years.

I first became aware of the anointing many years ago when I had a remarkable experience as a boy when leading the Easter Convention in worship. After the service had ended, I sat down beside Pastor Gordon Magee and Pastor James Forsythe and a man named Virgil Hughes. Next thing I knew, Mr Hughes rose to his feet and walked over to me and began to prophesy over me, saying, "You have been chosen from your mother's womb, I will take you around the world, equip you with the gift of the evangelist, and put my anointing upon you, but you must first separate yourself, and my anointing will be upon you. When Mr Hughes had stopped, Pastor Gordon Magee then stood up and said, "What are we going to do about this situation?" So, at 17 years old, they decided to ordain me, and within two weeks, I was full-time in the ministry. I took this prophecy to heart and immediately separated myself from my peers. My best friend noticed something was up and commented that I was like a hermit, and I was, but that was the price of having the anointing. I am not suggesting young people shun their friends, but the more time you spend with God, the greater your anointing is likely to be. Again, how much are you willing to let go to gain the anointing of God? Young people go to Bible school and learn to preach, which is good. They are decorated with degrees and accolades. Still, the blessing will be absent from their churches without a supernatural anointing, and without the hard knocks of ministry, no anointing will flow from their pulpits. I discovered that the anointing comes from life experience, not a college curriculum. **James McConnell**

Worth repeating is the words of his boyhood hero CH Surgeon who said: "Great Preachers do not emerge from a seminary; they return from a cemetery."

If a person desires the anointing, they should be crushed because the oil comes from the crushing. Similarly, during his youth, which, of course, is the most challenging time to say no to self and personal desires, the Pastor separated himself from the flesh's wishes to gain a greater anointing. Later, it paid off as he outstripped many of his peers and enjoyed an unusual and long-lasting anointing throughout his life and ministry. Like many others, I had the privilege of witnessing countless first-hand sermons and extraordinary moments during Pastor McConnell's remarkable ministry. Still, one stands out for me above all the others.

"How do I get the anointing?" the Pastor asked his congregation during the full throws of a Sunday morning message. Then, he answered the question for them: "Walk the roads, call unto God, and He will visit you."

He was on fire for God that day, in the prime of his preaching and oozing the anointing of God that same Sunday morning. While it seemed too simple an answer, it became correct in his life and has proved the difference for many other servants of God down through the centuries. The common denominator amongst all great preachers is a powerful anointing from the Lord instituted in the solitary place.

In the case of Pastor James McConnell - walking the roads worked for him. Yet, he insists that the solitary place is still the most likely place to get in touch with God even today.

As history is repeating itself, there is perhaps more than ever a great need for the anointing of God. Just as people were oppressed and sick and sinful in the New Testament times, it is clear that our current generation suffers from similar afflictions and cries out for comparable deliverance. In addition, the global pandemic Coronavirus has left the world reeling and looking for answers. Ours is a world crying out for the anointing and a ministry bringing hope and direction. Playing Church doesn't suffice any longer!

Other than God's anointing, what will deliver our generation from the evil that is not just approaching but has already arrived? According to scripture, if these are the last days, and all the signs suggest they are (see the final section - The Last Generation), only when the anointing is par for the course rather than being the apparent missing ingredient will the church return to its intended state of authority and purpose.

In the words of Isaiah: "And it shall come to pass in that day, that his burden shall be taken away from off thy shoulder, and his yoke from off thy neck, and the yoke shall be destroyed because of the anointing." **Isaiah 10:27**

The anointing breaks and destroys every yoke, every illness, every financial drought, every broken relationship, and every scourge of poverty, every hindrance, and setback. But when the Church is missing this vital ingredient of the oil of gladness and deliverance, it is a sad day for evangelicals and all people, especially those who require God's intervention at this awful and stressful time in history.

Jesus is coming, and the only thing that will wake the dead and heal the world is the anointing of God. The only component that can restore the Church is God's precious anointing. Therefore, today's greatest need is still the blessing that is the anointing of God produced through the Holy Spirit's power.

When you come into contact with the anointing of God,
it not only affects your moment, it affects your tomorrow.
Creflo Dollar

20.

The Purpose of the Anointing

I always felt an anointing from God even when I was a boy, but there's no doubt the angelic visitation rubber-stamped it. I always felt an anointing to win souls from I started preaching and ministering by God's grace, but when the Angel visited me, he told me every time I would preach the gospel, souls would be saved. It is what transpired. An example occurred during my youth. I was asked to go to Gateshead, Newcastle, in the North of England, and I experienced God's presence like never before. All I can say is it was unique. The resident Pastor had gone to America, and I was stationed there for six months, and inside those few months, the church grew to 500 people. I was just 18 years old at this point, which looking back, is hard to understand. I used to walk to church because I only received 15 shillings per week, and the people said they knew when I was coming because the anointing started to rise. Even my housekeeper used to hurry out of the meeting, leave my supper out, and go on to bed because she was frightened of that anointing. One Sunday night, the church's front row was praying, and I remember walking in and seeing the Angel of the Lord in front of me; this time, he was dressed and in his bare feet. Anytime the Angel had come before, he was dressed like a shipyard worker, but not this time. He then walked up to the platform, and some Methodists at the front fell on their faces. People were saying to me did you see him; did you see him? And that was before the first hymn was announced. Some healings took place even before a chorus was sung, and I recall having a vision of a lady putting her head in a gas oven, and when I pointed her out, she repented and came to Christ. It was a remarkable experience and became almost normal in that little church. While rare, such angelic occasions helped shape my life and ministry. **James McConnell**

Therefore, God does not anoint things, He anoints people. EM Bounds wrote something similar: "God's plan is a man, therefore, God always anoints men, not machinery."

And, to guide many thousands of people through the darkest days of the Troubles in Northern Ireland and more, God found a young man from East Belfast named James McConnell. If ever people required a mighty anointing in their midst at such a critical stage, it was the people of Ulster. Battered and bruised, frightened by the ferocity of the violence that lasted for over 35 years, finding hope and a purpose became so imperative for people from all backgrounds. It was especially those from both the protestant and catholic communities.

Of course, God raised other men for such a crucial time as the Northern Ireland troubles –who, similar to James McConnell, displayed fearless faith and determination to preach Christ and Him crucified. You didn't have to agree with these preachers or even like them, but you knew where they stood. Yes, they were controversial during their lives and often misunderstood, yet required to bring robust leadership during a dreadful period of darkness.

When Jesus preached the Word, He also spoke to people who were no strangers to trouble, fear, and problems. Christ's anointing was essential because multitudes were suffering without answers or solutions.

The Pastor's anointing touched not just generations; he led and confronted courageously for God. He still recalls visiting ruthless paramilitary groups for face-to-face summits pleading on behalf of some poor soul who managed to become a target. He paid their dues and had no fear of who he was confronting.

On two occasions, he visited leading figures in the UDA and UVF in East Belfast and North Belfast, asking for mercy for men who had once been involved in the organisations but had since found Christ and were trying to turn their lives around. His faith was the channel through which the anointing flowed. He would walk in and out of those back street meetings unscathed and even gained the admiration of some of the most hardened criminals in Northern Ireland.

They liked him because he called a spade a spade and had no backdoors. In turn, God protected him because he was His servant. Still, the Pastor was covered by the blood of Jesus and felt he had a mandate and the mantle to confront even potentially dodgy situations.

The Pastor has always believed he was the apple of God's eye, and his anointing is the proof. That anointing wasn't only for his benefit; however, it was all part of God's greater purpose for the Pastor's life to help a nation in trouble.

In the book of Luke, we read of Jesus: The Spirit of the Lord is upon me because he hath anointed me to preach the gospel to the poor; he hath sent me to heal the brokenhearted, to preach deliverance to the captives, and recovering of sight to the blind, to set at liberty them that are bruised, **Luke 4:18**

Nothing has changed in respect to people requiring deliverance and solutions. There are a lot of bruised individuals today, and only the anointing can set them free. Unfortunately, as mentioned in the previous chapter, the anointing appears to be one of those terms we once knew but has lost its popularity, relevance, and continuation due to the current generation's independence. Notwithstanding: without the anointing of the Spirit, no one can perform a single miracle or expect to lead a soul to Christ.

Isaiah said: "the anointing breaks every yoke."

Consider this: the anointing is the answer to marriage difficulty, health issues, financial problems, work dilemmas, a problem with your children, and loved ones who are lost. When the anointing is present, there's always a feel-good factor afterwards. As a result, people leave your presence and a church different from how they arrived. When the anointing is present, hairs stand on the back of one's neck. Change occurs in one's life, and expectation and anticipation rise in one's heart.

The Whitewell people lost count of the numerous times they experienced all of the above. The Pastor was a preaching machine with an anointing so strong it could only have come from one source – Almighty God, Himself. How essential is this anointing? It helps people overcome economic catastrophes, the spreading of diseases, and other global setbacks. The anointing also helps a preacher lead people to Christ in what is known as a "soul-saving ministry."

Here is the primary function of any gospel preacher and the purpose of the anointing – to reach the lost! The ministry is not to be used to provide a personal income, a job, or security – its function is to help secure the eternal destiny of the souls of men and women. A soul-saving ministry became especially noticeable in the Pastor's life but especially following a special visitation from the Angel of the Lord during the 1970s. His ministry took off following this incredible event, which he has always felt uncomfortable speaking of.

The proof of James McConnell's anointing and that promise from the Angel is not solely in his recollection of it but due to what took place after that. Just like the Angel promised, not a single week passed without him winning souls from that time.

Even in his so-called retirement, where his passion for preaching proved as intense as ever, souls were continually reached for God.

But the story of how his housekeeper used to hurry out of the meeting because she was frightened of the anointing is perhaps a great sign of the authenticity of his mantle from God to both attract people and repel them.

As stated in the prologue earlier, the Bible records how, when God wouldn't speak to Saul of Kish, the troubled King visited a witch, and when the great prophet Samuel arrived, the witch recognised the Spirit of God on him, describing him as "the man with the mantle." In 2 Kings Chapter two, we also read how "Elisha took the mantle of Elijah that fell from him 2 Kings 2:14. In other words, Elijah transferred his mantle (anointing) to Elisha. It also says of Gideon that the Spirit of the Lord came upon him. The Pastor loves the Hebrew translation: "And the Spirit of the Lord put Gideon on like an overcoat."

There's a lot of rain and pain about today, so it is futile and ineffective to preach without your overcoat (the anointing?) Nothing will transpire, and no one will be influenced for long. Jonah wrote salvation is of the Lord, while Jesus said, "No man can come to me, except the Father which hath sent me draw him: and I will raise him on the last day." Man's ability is nowhere near enough – it's God's power and presence that makes the difference. Neither can anyone be healed without the anointing. It is the power of God and not the ability of humanity that made the difference. Isaiah 53:5 says, "But he was wounded for our transgressions, he was bruised for our iniquities: the chastisement of our peace was upon him, and with his stripes, we are healed." Only when people preach Jesus and Him crucified will there be a sense of anointing. Luke 5:17 says, "And it came to pass on a certain day, as he was teaching, that there were Pharisees and doctors of the law sitting by, which were come out of every town of Galilee, and Judaea, and Jerusalem: and the power of the Lord was present to heal them." It is the power of God and not the ability of humanity that made the difference. It was present then, and it must be present today. **James McConnell**

Scrutiny of that verse in the book of Luke outlines how the purpose of the anointing is to reach the poor, heal the brokenhearted, set the captives free, and bring liberty to the damaged." Zechariah states: "Not by might, nor by power, but by my spirit, says the LORD of hosts." Here is the purpose of God's sweet anointing.

In this respect, Whitewell has always been more than a soul-saving centre. Many people call it "home," and in some cases, the church is their home, a safe house, and a refuge from the storm. All of these souls have been touched by God's anointing on the Pastors' life; no wonder then he still passionately believes in the power of the anointing and the miracles it produces.

Jesus said, "And these signs shall follow them that believe; In my name shall they cast out devils; they shall speak with new tongues; They shall take up serpents; and if they drink any deadly thing, it shall not hurt them; they shall lay hands on the sick, and they shall recover. **Mark 16:17-18**

If signs and wonders and an anointed ministry are essential, why does the western world not experience healing in the same way as Bible days or other parts of the world? There are no doubt several reasons, but could it be the Church is too preoccupied with why people are not coming to church as they used to, meaning leaderships become obsessed with implementing many different ideas and initiatives to try and address that problem, rather than trusting and allowing the Holy Spirit to fill the pews and meet the need.

When the anointing trumps all, none of those mentioned above are required.

Creflo Dollar said: "When you come into contact with the anointing of God, it not only affects your moment, it affects your tomorrow."

In short, it leaves a legacy and brings change. It was the result in the ministry and life of the Pastor at Whitewell. Of course, Jesus was anointed, and the Church is supposed to carry that same anointing. Still, again, a relevant question is: why do many today appear to view this necessary component as secondary and not display the power of God's anointing either in pulpits or their personal lives?

Again, one significant reason exists. It is not enough to preach about the book (the Bible); a preacher must reveal its author (God). Thus, one reason for any perceived lack of power may indeed be when preachers feel compelled to tackle political subjects and exciting topics rather than preach the gospel and "stick to the gospel plan."

On the contrary, the successful preacher will avoid complex theological issues, legalistic sermons, and even political matters. Christ didn't come to point the finger at politicians and the unsaved or to condemn anyone for that matter. Instead, his function was to address spiritual issues and reveal Himself as the antidote to all sin. In this respect, Jesus always appeared to stand separate from the things of this world. His Kingdom and teaching were reserved for spiritual things, not political matters.

Staying true to the message of the Kingdom, which is to "seek and to save that which is lost," is the mark of all great gospel exponents.

In one of his interviews the late Billy Graham revealed something quite profound. He stated: To understand Jesus, we must first understand what he was against. Think about it. He never did say one word against Rome, and Rome ruled the world, including the country He came from. He never said a word against Rome. He was against the religious system and dealt primarily with spiritual questions. When they tried to trap him and get him to say that he gave Caesar allegiance or was against Caesar, he said, "Bring me a coin.". And he said, "Whose picture is on that?" And they said, "Caesar." He said, "Render unto Caesar the things that are Caesar's and unto God the things that are God's. He made that distinction, and he never said anything against Rome. The system he was against was an evil, corrupt religious system – a hypocritical religious system. Now I make pretty strong statements against what I believe to be the theological and moral corruption in some church regions today. One of the things we must distinguish is the difference between the religious system and the political system. Jesus never did say anything against the political system, even though it was corrupt. He seemed to think this was outside His jurisdiction.

Billy Graham was right, but sadly many ministers and even myself have veered off track at times if they are honest. Preaching Christ and His message in the same way Jesus did is the answer for this and every generation. It is a mystery why people who profess to know the Lord never talk about the Lord. The mention of the name of Jesus is authoritative, and we need more sermons about the Master and the Saviour again. It is hearing about Him and His life that changes our life. The Bible states, "And I if I be lifted from the earth, will draw all men unto me. It's no rocket science. Avoid politics and other side issues and preach about Jesus, and the person of Christ and people will get saved. In other words, "make the main thing the main thing." **James McConnell**

Another explanation for any noticeable lack of anointing today might be due to self-love and self-adulation. The book of Timothy warned how this would be one of the critical signs of the last days.

Timothy records: This also know, that in the last days perilous times shall come. For men shall be lovers of their selves, covetous, boasters, proud, blasphemers, disobedient to parents, unthankful, unholy, Without natural affection, trucebreakers, false accusers, incontinent, fierce, despisers of those that are good, Traitors, heady, highminded, lovers of pleasures more than lovers of God; Having a form of godliness, but denying the power thereof: from such turn away **2 Timothy 3:1-5**

A far cry from the words of John the Baptist, who said, "He must increase, but I must decrease." **John 3:30**, or as an old Pentecostal preacher once said: "Don't touch the glory, and God will keep touching you."

What can damage many ministries is a fascination with intellect, creativity, and what we call the contemporary Church, rather than a desire to preach Christ and exalt the Master. But, unfortunately, that's too simple for many people today! Yet when Jesus has all the glory, God's anointing will flow.

It can't be so simple? It is that simple! Preach Christ and Him crucified, or as John Wesley once said: "Build a fire in the pulpit, and people will come out to see you burn!"

The anointing is proof of an authentic ministry – full stop! Counterfeits kill the anointing in the Church. They appear religious or, as Paul said, "having a form of godliness they deny its power." I reiterate, without the anointing, the Church is wasting its time, and no one or nothing can ever replace its value. There is no substitute for the anointing of the Holy Spirit. The purpose of the anointing is to touch people with the Spirit of God and transform them. The Apostle Paul understood the need for this anointing, saying– "And my speech and my preaching were not with enticing words of man's wisdom, but in demonstration of the Spirit and of power." Then he added: "That your faith should not stand in the wisdom of men, but in the power of God."
James McConnell

The best educations and brains in Britain, America, and Europe struggle to solve many of the significant issues facing our world today, including Covid-19.

Brexit, the Middle East, the under-pressure world economy, and global pandemics and disasters, floods and extreme weather conditions, which are prophesied about relating to the last days (see Matthew chapter 24), all cry out for a special anointing and no more so than in the Church today.

God's Spirit touches some good men and women in the Church today, but it appears mainly in America and not closer to home. Without wishing to discourage anyone, in my opinion, only a minority of ministers are truly showing evidence of the anointing of God.

People like George Jeffreys, William Branham, Oral Roberts, and, as we've mentioned, Billy Graham are hard to find right now. I do like TD Jakes in Dallas, it's clear he has a great anointing and a fantastic imagination, and the anointing anoints that imagination, and he's brilliant. I heard him say "If you can't figure out your purpose, figure out your passion. For your passion will lead you right into your purpose."Still, I believe an anointing such as this is hard to find today. If the Church's purpose is to lead men and women to Jesus and deliver the captive and set them free, then the anointing remains the chief need in the Church today and in my life. Remember, that's the whole purpose of the anointing, and it never fails. **James McConnell**

SSEY
A

There is no use in running before you are sent; there is no use in attempting to do God's work without God's power. A man working without this unction, a man working without this anointing, a man working without the Holy Ghost upon him is losing time after all.

Dwight L. Moody

21.

The Result of the Anointing

People are trying everything today when they need a Bible, a relationship with God, and anointing will follow. Christians also need the anointing for everyday living, but until our generation is prepared to put Christ first and seek the Lord, we will have to do secondary things that never meet the need. The anointing result is always souls saved, healings, power and authority over the enemy, and so much more. How futile is it to preach without the anointing? Nothing will transpire. Neither can anyone be healed without the anointing. Only when men preach Jesus and Him crucified will there be a sense of anointing. Notice it was the power of God and not the ability of humanity that made the difference when the power of the Lord was present to heal. A fresh anointing gives you strength and confidence. And yet, the missing ingredient is often a lack of anointing or worse. Replacing it is usually a thing the Bible describes as "strange fire." **James McConnell**

People have witnessed many demonstrations of the power of the anointing in James McConnell's life, incredible events that are too numerous to mention. However, one season of soul-winning stands out during his ministry.

Significantly, it came when the Pastor was at an all-time low and feeling broken and disheartened in his religious life. Left reeling from the split in his church, he was distinctly off-colour, off his food, not on form, and not feeling at all well. The emotional strain of losing so many members of his longstanding congregation became quite a burden, and he found it hard to recover. Remember, the Pastor had previously managed to "move on" from scores of setbacks over the years - proof of his great focus and resilience. Even the loss of his church building in his earlier life hadn't managed to deter his focus on souls and the work of God. Nevertheless, following the split at Whitewell, the untimely separation from people he had loved and nurtured for so many years had left him feeling shell-shocked, and he was struggling to put things behind him.

One day, during a difficult moment, he called one of his pastoral staff aside and invited him into his office in what became a life-changing moment. The Pastor needed someone to reveal the extent of his dilemma, and Pastor David McClure was that man.

"David I know you want to get on with things and fight, but I just can't. My heart is broken, and I am at an all-time low," revealed the Pastor.

As he even shed tears, something he wasn't in the habit of doing, the Pastor was encouraged not to give up but to keep doing the one thing he had always done well – winning souls for Jesus. Then, in what appears to have been a divine moment, He was implored to get back out there and rebuild what had been lost.

Pastor McClure, proceeded to encourage the Pastor to consider a province-wide tour of the country, bringing the gospel to every town and city.

"You can do this; it's who you are," insisted Pastor McClure. He then offered to lead the meetings, bring a worship team, and watch the Pastor do what he does best - preach the Word!

At the time, it proved precisely what Pastor McConnell needed to hear.

His facial expression changed from gloomy to excitable.

Immediately the Pastor quickly agreed and sprang up from the table, saying, "When can we start?"

The rest was history.

A series of yearlong gospel meetings and worship nights in homes, halls, and all kinds of venues throughout the country were organised – events that would change and touch many lives for Christ. It was as though the Pastor had found another gear and even stronger anointing, and the result was hundreds of people being swept into the Kingdom of God.

Those who attended these meetings were undoubtedly exposed to some of the most inspired preachings of the Pastors' long vocation.

Despite already having "been there" and "done it," so to speak, it was as if the Pastor had found another level and, at the most unlikely time in his life.

Missions were held in private homes in Belfast, Ballymena, and Portadown.

Dromore Secondary School was visited twice and also Larne Leisure Centre. At the Jethro Centre in Craigavon, no fewer than thirteen women came to Christ. In addition, there were outreaches at Newtownards Town Hall, Hamilton House in Bangor, and several other community centres throughout Northern Ireland.

The Pastor "shot from the hip," as he recalls, and numerous souls were converted to Christ. At these inspired and anointed soaked events, people were healed of illnesses and delivered from drugs and all sorts of addictions. Many others, who arrived with no interest in the things of God, gave their hearts to the Lord. But what was striking at these rallies was how the Pastor would open his Bible and begin to preach without notes on many of the beautiful stories of Jesus and his compassion before leading scores of people to the Saviour. He was a new man with a mission, and it became apparent that the Man with the Mantle was back in business.

No Bible school prepares a person for this moment in life. It is the result of the anointing of God and nothing else, and it springs from life knowing nothing other than preaching God's Word with signs and wonders following.

Jesus said, "And these signs shall follow them that believe; In my name shall they cast out devils; they shall speak with new tongues; They shall take up serpents; and if they drink any deadly thing, it shall not hurt them; they shall lay hands on the sick, and they shall recover. **Mark 16:17-18**

We will deal more closely with signs and wonders in the Pentecost section by considering how the Church is mainly ineffective and redundant without this ministry's supernatural element.

Meanwhile, throughout his ministry, "seeking God" and "finding one's anointing "is something the Pastor has passionately believed in and the power of the anointing and what it produces.

The story of a man who sold everything and moved abroad during the 20th century is particularly poignant. He barely had enough money to buy a ticket to a ship to the U.S. because he was already short of cash. He decided to buy some cheese and crackers to eat during the U.S. journey, so he ate his cheese and crackers every day for breakfast, lunch, and dinner. One day as he was eating, everybody else was in the ship's dining hall, and he could smell the aroma of delicious food. Sick and tired of just cheese and crackers, by day six of the trip, he visited the ship captain saying, "I'll do anything you want. I'll do the dishes. Clean the bathroom. Sweep the floor. Anything! Just let me have one meal in the dining room."

Suddenly, the captain looked puzzled and replied: "But sir, the meals are included with your ticket."

Imagine the shock it must have been for this man to know that he had been living well beneath his privileges aboard that ship for almost a week previously?

Of course, the moral of the story is that God hasn't called us to live cheese and cracker lives. Delicious meals are included with the ticket, and we have been invited to God's dining hall every day. Do we desire a delicious banquet or cheese and crackers? Or, let's look at it another way. Do we want the anointing of the Holy Spirit, or are we happy to settle for the second-class church services and personal progress due to the limitations of our flesh?

Do we expect to see healings and our churches filled with the fire of God and overflowing with God's blessing? Or are cheese and cracker meetings the best we can hope for? Have we experienced the benefits of the power of God? Or are we content to live in poverty beneath our privileges?

CH Spurgeon made arguably one of the most profound statements of all about the anointing of God and the God of the anointing, saying: "Never try to live on the old manna, nor seek to find help in Egypt. All must come from Jesus, or thou art undone for ever. An old anointing will not suffice to impart unction to thy spirit; thine head must have fresh oil poured upon it from the golden horn of the sanctuary, or it will cease from its glory."

Similarly, DL Moody also preached, "I believe this is a mistake a great many of us are making; we are trying to do God's work with the grace God gave us ten years ago. If it is necessary, we say we will go on with the same grace. Now, what we want are a fresh supply, a fresh anointing, and new power, and if we seek it and seek it with all our hearts, we will obtain it."

Anyone who witnessed the weekly miracles at Whitewell over a phenomenally long period knows all too well about Pastor James McConnell's soul-saving ministry.

He would often say, "The greatest miracle of all is the saving of a soul," and indeed, thousands of souls were converted to Christ at Whitewell because of his unique anointing. However, he never claimed to be the greatest preacher – although he could undoubtedly preach. Instead, the Pastor relied solely on the Spirit of the living God to change the hearts of men and women, boys and girls, and save their souls from death and destruction.

He began at Whitewell in the late 1950s until establishing the Metropolitan Tabernacle in 1994, and his anointed preaching attracted large audiences.

In soul-winning terms, James McConnell's name is synonymous with the likes of evangelical greats like Smith Wigglesworth, William Branham, Billy Graham, and Reinhard Bonke, to name only a few. He is indeed regarded by many as one of the greatest soul-winners of his generation, and all of this he attributes to God's precious anointing.

However, that anointing isn't only to bring men and women to Jesus, as the Pastor has always believed his Mantle extended well beyond the saving souls.

In his case, it was at least two-fold! Before now, he's rarely spoken about or even recognised fully this additional gift within his ministry. Looking back, however, he now firmly believes that the Holy Spirit granted a diverse mantle in raising money for God's work.

It happened one evening after he'd returned from a preaching engagement in America. Having all but decided to put his local Church's finances in the hands of his church elders, a lady at one of his church services brought him a message from the Lord. She proceeded to walk right up to the platform, took both hands of the Pastor, and declared: "Thus saith the Lord, you will not put finances in the hands of anyone. You will control the money yourself, and I will give you millions of pounds."

Who was this lady?

According to the Pastor, just an ordinary member of the Church, who prophesied about twice per year; yet her words became representative of the Lord.

He recalls how she even slipped into the healing line of the renowned evangelist William Branham. He immediately discerned her problem: the desire to have a son but unable to do so. When she confirmed this, Branham prayed for her, and the following year, she gave birth to a new son.

Of course, during his ministry, Branham displayed evidence of a Man with the

Mantle and a considerable anointing on numerous occasions and the supernatural events associated with such.

As we have covered, God can always find a man when he needs one, and if money is required, it equally proves to be no obstacle.

That early prophecy came to pass stunningly as the work at Whitewell went from a local assembly to a multimillion-pound ministry that has stretched well beyond the Belfast Lough where it is situated – quite remarkable given it had all started in a tiny hall on the Whitewell Road when the Pastor had no choice but to wear shoes with holes in them.

An illustration of just how far the Pastor and the Whitewell ministry had come is seen in the story of how one day, he handed his daughter Linda a cheque for what he thought was a hundred thousand pounds. He'd just received it from a member of his congregation who wanted to support the outreach, and, naturally, to say he was delighted was an understatement. When Linda read it more carefully, however, she gasped and replied: "Daddy, you need to go to 'Specsavers', this cheque is for one million pounds!!!"

The money was eventually used, along with an additional funds, to build the beautiful McConnell Youth centre, which today sits adjacent to the main sanctuary and has become a stunning activity centre used by not only the Church but also a building that has become a great blessing to many families in the local area. Of course, collecting such vast sums of money wasn't easy, but God made it look easy. The Pastor often raised the required amount before softening the blow to his congregation with the words: "may your giving hand never falter," - a trademark McConnellism, which frequently saw the Whitewell members searching their pockets and handbags; for an extra fiver!

Such events are supernatural to us but reasonable to God, and the retelling of such miracles can help to motivate the current generation that miracles are normal to God.

While God provided every financial need, the only regret Pastor McConnell maintains he has during his prolific ministry is not having a good education. He readily confesses to "making mistakes" but believes God still blessed him despite those errors. However, he significantly attributes God's anointing in his life as the reason he survived for so many years. From the age of eight to well into his eighties, that anointing carried him through many trials and temptations and, of course, ill-health. There are educated people in ministry, yet they display little or no evidence of the anointing, but the Pastor wonders what he might have achieved if he had both an education and an anointing.

Still, what he accomplished with the anointing alone was, and still is, quite an achievement. People from his church always affectionately refer to those times as "the glory years."

I believe what they mean is "The anointed years."

If one has ever experienced the anointing flowing, either at Church or in their personal lives, they will know that nothing can ever replace it. Neither church events with spectacular lighting, world-beating performances, nor even the best professionals singing nor preaching can match the anointing of God.

Without the authentic anointing of God, people will be playing Church for the rest of their days. They will feel not unlike that man in the earlier illustrations, restricted to cheese and crackers instead of a five-course banquet.

How easy is it to recall the benefits and the encounters when the anointing was flowing and people came away walking on air?

What made the difference? One thing alone – the anointing of God!

Someone had ministered God's sweet anointing, which breaks every yoke, and freedom was the result. It would be impossible to list all the miraculous things regarding God's anointing in the Pastor's life. Still, another is worth recalling when the Pastor attended a preaching engagement at the Cottonwood Church in California. Accompanied by Pastor McClure, they had travelled through the night, and the Pastor had wakened earlier that morning, feeling exhausted and looking dreadful. He was already experiencing some major health issues in his life during this period. His close friend, Bayless Conley, the Senior Pastor at Cottonwood, noticed the Pastor looking exhausted directly before the service. He immediately offered to find a replacement for Pastor McConnell if he felt too unwell to preach.

However, once the Pastor hit the platform, he was different. Anointed by the Holy Spirit, he went on to preach three times that same Sunday, including at a Spanish-speaking church in the afternoon, witnessing in the process hundreds of people coming to the Lord.

Again, the anointing of God had helped His servant in the hour of need and when the message of the Holy Spirit was required. The power of God had quietened the weakness of the flesh, and the power of the spirit proved enough.

How important is it to be mantled with an anointing?

Remember, before Christ commissioned the disciples to go and spread the gospel, He told them: " And, behold, I send the promise of my Father upon you: but tarry ye in the city of Jerusalem until ye be endued with power from on high." **Luke 24:49**

The Word tarry means staying or waiting. Jesus advised against going out into the world or ministry without power and the anointing of God. Or, as Moses said: "If thy presence goes not with me, carry us not up hence" **Exodus 33:15**

That was a fantastic day at Cottonwood, and only the Holy Spirit could have lifted me to that level and reached so many souls, especially at the evening service when almost half of the Church seemed to raise their hands in response to the appeal. But, of course, we don't display this anointing like a magic potion; we must want it, desire it, and seek for it and wait for it. Having the Holy Spirit is lovely, but combined with the anointing power, it makes the difference. So a question for today's generation might be: Are we happy to do Church without the aid of the anointing of God? Or, if we understand it is impossible to do without it, how badly do we want the anointing to be revealed? If we accept nothing less, the results will be worth it. **James McConnell**

Notably, Jesus was led by the Spirit into the wilderness to be tempted by the devil and then returned in the power of the Spirit. He had the Holy Spirit before He went out to the desert, but He came back with power because Jesus was commissioned and anointed for a purpose.

The anointing is vital in the Church because it fulfils God's goal – to save humanity's souls, deliver the captives, and set them free.

Have we been to the wilderness lately like Jesus? How much do we value and desire the anointing of God? Are we willing to wait until we are filled with the power of God from on high?

If you are a believer and born-again, God's sweet anointing waits to flow from you. If you are a minister and preacher, it will make a difference not only in your life but in the lives of others you meet and minister. That is always the result of the anointing of God.

Passion for Pentecost

But you will receive power when the Holy Spirit comes on you, and you will be my witnesses in Jerusalem, and in all Judea and Samaria, and to the ends of the earth.

Acts 1:8

22.

No Substitute for the Holy Spirit

I have always had a personal time to worship the Lord, and when I arrive at Church, it is the most normal progression to feel God's presence again. Surrounded by other believers, I am even more conscious of that presence and desire it all the more. The Church should be a cacophony of praise and worship, not a cemetery. There's nothing worse than a church full of dead ducks and dead religion! God's presence has everything we need for our souls and more, and I recall as we worshipped the Lord, all our needs were met at that time. Neither is true worship shouting and bluster. No one sweats to discover the anointing; it flows naturally as an incoming tide. So how do we recognise the anointing? The anointing is sweet, beautiful, and unmistakable, and once you have bathed in it, nothing else will meet your requirements! **James McConnell**

For as long as the Pastor can recall, he's had an insatiable desire for the presence of God. Whether it has been seeking the Lord during his devotions, out walking with the Lord, or praising God at his Church in Belfast, he's made the presence of God his focus and solitary goal. Easy to recall is his passionate sermons, which won many thousands of people to Christ. Still, those associated with the Pastor for decades are conscious of another aspect of his ministry that was quite extraordinary. He could worship God and bring the presence of God into every service – yes, at every turn!

His consistency was remarkable and evidence of a man with an unusual anointing. He didn't require a vast orchestra behind him, just a "corny chorus leader," as he used to describe himself, and "a willing voice" to touch heaven.

As mentioned earlier, he would even start in the wrong key (and rarely apologised for doing so), something of a nightmare for the accompanying musicians seated behind him. It was soon forgotten, though, as the anointing began to flow, and the Holy Spirit's moving touched many hearts. Watching those old videotaped services, one can still sense and feel a palpable sense of God's presence amongst His people. It was a time when God's move was evident, and God's presence so transparent one could almost reach out and handle it. It was a privilege afforded to few people in life, but those who experienced such a presence have never forgotten it.

No one spiritual can fail to spot the anointing of God, or indeed lack of it. The Church must return to a House of praise and prayer.

Here is not only a sign that Biblical Pentecost is alive and well but the way to breakthrough and victory.

A passion for God's presence and Pentecostal roots is substantially required to conquer the forces of darkness in this world.

Having worked alongside him for many years, of course, I've always known the Pastor had a passion for Pentecost and the presence of God, but it became even more evident to me during the time of the national health crisis.

Following the arrival of the dreadful health pandemic Covid-19 and Coronavirus's spread in early 2020, like many others, the Pastor became housebound for months as the nation came to a stand-still.

All previous interviews for the book Man with the Mantle had been recorded in various locations, so with most of us unable to leave the house and not allowed to meet each other, we had no option but to press on with the latter part of the book by telephone interviews.

There's something about merely hearing a voice at the other end of the line and not seeing a face. Like listening to the radio, you pick up on things you would otherwise have missed.

Even in today's digital communications world, listening can convey vital information that watching doesn't always accomplish. Listening intently to the Pastor, I distinctly detected his powerful passion for Pentecost.

It was as if he'd come alive as he began answering a list of questions on the subject. He was 82 at the time, coming 83 years old, but as he spoke about Pentecost's origins, he sounded like a young man talking about his first week in the ministry.

It was truly inspiring to hear.

His knowledge of the Pentecostal movement was equally impressive as he reamed off remarkable stories that took place during his ministry, but what became clear was that just like his faith, there's no halfway house with Pastor James McConnell. He is a Pentecostal through and through. Indeed, for as long as he can remember, Pastor James McConnell has been a Pentecostal. His preaching and Pentecost are inextricably linked.

Even before he joined his first Pentecostal assembly, the Bible Pattern Church in Belfast, at the tender age of twelve years old, he was already a Pentecostal at heart, having been visited by God in his home at 14 Spring Street, Belfast, before becoming the 'boy preacher' at Craven Street also in the city. Even his ministry at Whitewell has enjoyed Elim affiliation for many years.

Elim grew out of the Pentecostal movement, born at the beginning of the twentieth century. Its origins date back to 1915 in a provincial town in Ireland. Over one hundred years later, it grew to over five hundred and fifty churches in the U.K. and is involved in missionary work worldwide.

Elim's theology reflects evangelicalism in general and the beliefs of what has come to be known as classical Pentecostalism.

The people who attended the Bible Pattern were of similar belief and didn't just take the young James under their wing; they also played a significant role in teaching him the things of God and, just as importantly, about Pentecost's meaning.

George Jeffreys was one of many great Pentecostal preachers in those days. Still, I became significantly influenced by men like Smith Wigglesworth and Howard Carter, yet Jeffreys was undoubtedly unique. For reasons I can't explain, from I came to know the Lord, God has given me a tremendous knowledge of the workings of the Holy Spirit and opened my understanding to the entire subject of Pentecost and its importance. Even in the first Church I attended, the Iron Hall in Belfast, which wasn't Pentecostal, Towell Evans, the Welsh Pastor, often spoke in tongues, introducing me to supernatural workings. It may seem hard to believe, but I understood it from those early days when I heard someone speaking in tongues and even interpreting. Unknown to others at that time, I'd already had a visitation from the angel to my bedroom in Spring Street, which made these mysteries easier to comprehend. I had been reading the life story of William Carey, the cobbler sent to India, and had asked God to make me like him. It was one of the first books I read, and one night I recall a person emerging from a small gas mantle in my little room and commissioning me for ministry. I was just a boy, but by the age of thirteen, I was already fulfilling that incredible prophecy preaching about Pentecost and witnessing the signs and wonders found in the New Testament. **James McConnell**

That may seem overstated, yet by age 15 at the Bible Pattern church, his experience of Pentecostal power reached even greater heights when he received a second visitation from the Lord. While many other youths his age were kicking a football, dating their childhood sweetheart, and finding various ways to entertain themselves, the Spirit of God was visiting James McConnell in a manner most people of any age could only dream. So privileged he unquestionably was, and, perhaps not surprisingly, he still recalls those days as if they were yesterday.

After being handed the keys of that little church, I was coming in and out to put the heat on in the mornings, and I often used it as an opportunity to seek the Lord in prayer. I remember clearly one particular morning kneeling before God and singing, 'Take my life and let it be consecrated Lord to thee.' Suddenly a lady emerged and made me the subject of a God-inspired prophecy, saying, "You will preach the gospel to many nations, and God will give you a mighty work which will reach out to other people. God will use you in a mighty way,' and then she left. At the time, it frightened me because I knew I had locked the doors of the Church when I arrived. It was the start of my Pentecostal experiences. **James McConnell**

But what is a Pentecostal in a real sense?

Pentecostalism truly began during the first century when the early Christians displayed the Holy Spirit's gifts – something all true 'Pentes' believe.

Contrary to some spurious opinions, Pentecostalism is no new thing, even though it has had several revivals throughout the centuries. Pentecostals still have their roots firmly in New Testament Christianity.

For example, Acts 2 records: "And they were all filled with the Holy Ghost, and began to speak with other tongues, as the Spirit gave them utterance **Acts 2:4.**

And also, 1 Corinthians 12:28 records, "And God hath set some in the church, first apostles, secondarily prophets, thirdly teachers, after that miracles, then gifts of healings, helps, governments, diversities of tongues."

Here is the Biblical evidence of Pentecost and Pentecostalism - the workings of signs and wonders accompanied by wisdom, knowledge, faith gifts of healing, miraculous powers, discerning of spirits, tongues, and interpretation of tongues. Therefore, Pentecostal's term relates to early Christians' experience of what is known as The Day of Pentecost. It proved a day unlike any other, as the Holy Spirit was graciously poured out upon the first followers of Christ, and tongues of fire rested on their heads. This remarkable event is recorded in the book of Acts: "When the day of Pentecost arrived, they were all together in one place. Suddenly, there came from heaven a sound like a mighty rushing wind, and it filled the entire house where they were sitting." **Acts 2:1-2**

While the Church has included various other belief groups, Pentecost is regarded as starting the Church's mission to spread the gospel to the world.

It took place as far back as 50 days after the resurrection of Jesus Christ and fulfilled prophecies by both Jesus and John the Baptist, where both said the people would be baptised in the Holy Spirit. It's believed that the Azusa Street revival in 1906 marked the birth of modern Pentecostalism or a resurgence of the early church version. However, there is no doubt this period was a revival that the Church could benefit significantly from again.

I believe this part of history was a rebirth of early Pentecostalism, and it was a particular time in America. But the Pentecostal movement also spread well beyond America, even to the U.K. and Preston England. For example, there was a mighty move of the Spirit in Sunderland's Northeast city, a region I had laboured as a youth when I served at Gateshead. I remember a vicar was holding communion one Sunday when the Holy Spirit fell on him and baptised him in the Holy Ghost, and that Church, which had previously been in debt, was delivered and set free. Another evidence of the revival of Pentecostalism, which followed Azusa Street, came when the brother of George Jeffreys, Stephen - himself a mighty evangelist - saw great miracles and won over 3,000 souls to Christ. One powerful testimony tells of a man who had a withered hand and got healed only to return to the bar to buy a drink, where his withered hand returned. That was how real things were in those days. The incident impacted the people of Sunderland greatly, and many turned to the Lord following the event. **James McConnell**

Around the same time, the Pastor recalls George Jeffreys filling the King's Hall in Belfast seven times, preaching to around 10,000 people per night, and witnessing all sorts of miracles. Divine appointments like these are what the world needs again, but they must not be confused with more extreme Pentecostal experience versions.

Known as "Charismatics," this form of Pentecostalism leaves the Pastor deeply troubled. Throughout his entire ministry, he has continuously taught and believed in order and expression.

He thinks the Charismatics are void of scriptural discipline and sadly have often sullied the name of genuine believers and true Pentecostals on numerous occasions.

We've had many a circus come to town, including the infamous Toronto Blessing, and all of them have left again. Some of it was crazy and an insult to faithful followers of Jesus and the purity of Pentecostalism. I never liked any of it, mainly because it lacked order, reverence, and respect for God. People said God had given them "gold teeth" and other crazy things like that. The difference between such' over the top showmanship' and the men who preached about Pentecost following the revival in the early to mid-1900s was the latter group not only spoke in tongues and exercised the gifts of the Holy Spirit properly, but they also were great theologians. They knew the scriptures and taught them correctly, rightly dividing the word of truth. In my formative years, I learned a no-nonsense approach from my early mentors like James Forsyth and Gordon Magee, and others, and so I never accepted the outrageous stuff we have had to endure over the years. Instead of theologians, I have referred to them as 'meologians.' **James McConnell**

During his tenure as a Pentecostal leader, the Pastor tried NOT to quench the Spirit and has always been conscious not to allow any strange fire or extremism to interrupt his meetings. Neither has the Pastor suffered by staying true to what he describes as "true Pentecostalism." Moreover, he recalls the moment he was baptised in the Holy Spirit with great warmth.

It was like having a blood transfusion. That's the best way I can explain it. I only thought I was operating in the Spirit beforehand, but everything changed once the baptism came. Suddenly this was the real thing. Back then, there was a well-known saying: "Don't give up religion until you've tried Pentecost," or as I've commented over the years on many occasions, there's no substitute for the Holy Spirit.' No pantomime, programme, or event can replace the move of the Holy Spirit in a church. People ask: what is the baptism of the Holy Spirit? The answer is not rocket science. It is having a biblical experience similar to that in Acts. In Acts chapter 8, we read how Phillip went down to Samaria, and the people heard and saw the miracles he did. Later in the same story, the disciples laid hands on people and received the Holy Ghost. These were supernatural experiences that often resulted in people speaking in tongues. Then, by Acts chapter 10, we read that "While Peter yet spake these words, the Holy Ghost fell on all them which heard the word. And they of the circumcision which believed were astonished, as many as came with Peter, because that on the Gentiles also was poured out the Holy Ghost's gift, for they heard them speak with tongues and magnify God. Then answered Peter, Can any man forbid water, that these should not be baptised, which have received the Holy Ghost as well as we? And he commanded them to be baptised in the name of the Lord. Then prayed they him to tarry certain days. He went on to ask, "Have ye received the Holy spirit from ye believed?"

The incident was followed by many of them getting baptised in the Holy Spirit and speaking in tongues. Here is Pentecostalism in a nutshell. No pranks, no gimmicks, no performance, and substitute for the Holy Spirit. If you have been disappointed with your faith, religion, or even denomination, you can still find reality. So, again, my advice is: 'Don't give up religion until you've tried Pentecost.' **James McConnell**

He maintains there is no substitute for the Holy Spirit because the Spirit guides the people of God personally and is always present; The Spirit is exclusively involved in the process of salvation. The Spirit is an unlimited resource for believers. The Spirit gives gifts to believers to be used to build up the Church. The Spirit enables and expects believers to improve their lifestyles. The Spirit, who brings together the Church as the body of Christ, is concerned for the unity of the body and seeks believers' cooperation in maintaining that unity. The Spirit is eternal and omniscient and helps believers enjoy the salvation that God has given to them. The Spirit also enables believers in Jesus to allow them to be witnesses throughout the world.

The book of Acts declares: "But you will receive power when the Holy Spirit comes on you, and you will be my witnesses in Jerusalem, and in all Judea and Samaria, and to the ends of the earth" **Acts 1:8**

The purpose of experiencing the Spirit's empowering is to evangelise and introduce anyone to know God naturally and powerfully regardless of the background. It is beautiful when ministers and people generally desire to have more of the Holy Spirit. Still, in doing so, they must remember the sacrifice of such is a noble ambition.

In Luke's book, he revealed something quite profound when addressing His disciples and promising them the Holy Spirit. He told them that first they must "tarry" or "wait" in the city of Jerusalem before being "endued with power.",

Just as prayer promises to produce a Pentecostal experience, so, too, waiting on God and His ability, rather than one's own, evokes the power of Pentecost in the believer.

Jesus said so!

A false balance is an abomination to the LORD: but a just weight is his delight.

Proverbs 11:1

23.

Countering the Pentecostal Critics

To quote an old Scottish preacher, "Some things are better felt than "telt." There's no doubt that our Christian lives won't be the same once we have experienced speaking in tongues. Therefore, not seeking after or using the gift of tongues as a Christian is unscriptural and counterproductive.

For example, many times, when I found myself unable to pray in my everyday vocabulary, I turned to tongues to communicate with God. As a young man, I would walk to work at the Belfast Shipyard from my home, and the whole way to the Yard, I spoke in tongues. It was an enjoyable experience and enlightenment for my soul. People have suggested that tongues are from the devil, yet the reality is the devil can't understand tongues because it is an unknown heavenly language. If you are praying about things you don't wish the devil to know about, then use the gift of tongues, and the results will follow. God will understand everything you say. When you run out of vocabulary, God will give you language.

As the apostle, Paul wrote in Romans, "Likewise the Spirit also helpeth our infirmities: for we know not what we should pray for as we ought: but the Spirit itself maketh intercession for us with groanings which cannot be uttered. **James McConnell**

Pentecostals have been referred to as "Pentes" and singled out for their adherence to the Bible's authority and belief in the baptism in the Holy Spirit. Even today, they are still maligned, criticised, and mocked for these beliefs. Such empowerment includes spiritual gifts like speaking in tongues and divine healing. Pentecostals believe it is impossible to live a Spirit-filled empowered life without this.

Like many evangelicals, Pentecostals also believe that one must accept the Lord Jesus Christ as a personal Lord and Saviour. However, by sticking rigidly to what they see as the "full gospel," it's fair to say Pentecostals have been maligned, misunderstood, and at times even persecuted for their convictions perhaps more than any other denomination.

Of course, it's not just Pentecostals who have suffered rejection, even persecution for their faith. All believers have, at various points, experienced rejection in some form.

Acts record many instances of persecution among early believing communities, but what perhaps makes the Pentecostals unique is that they are often not only attacked from outside Christendom but also within the family of God. It is one thing to be hated by your enemies, but another to be despised and disliked by your friends, even brethren. Jesus knew all about such rejection. The gospel of John records, "He came unto his own, and his own received him not" **John 1:11**

For example, mention the term Pentecostal and many other denominations think of the church that speaks in tongues and is quite radical in its approach to spiritual matters. Insults like "They're from the devil" or "They're not right in the head" are just some of the insults dished out to tongue-speaking, prophetic Pentecostals. That's because one of the most highlighted aspects of the Pentecostalism movement is the church's belief in speaking in tongues and its confidence in divine gifts such as healing and water baptism by immersion.

Tongues

So, let's firstly address the issue of tongues.

Most Pentecostal assemblies in various countries allow speaking in tongues within their services, prophecy, and divine healing. Despite being ridiculed, most Pentecostals remain unashamed, unwilling to play down the power of the Holy Spirit or ignore the reality of the New Testament church.

So, are tongues Devilish or Divine?

The New Testament provides the answer. Speaking in tongues was a regular part of Christian life and experience in the early church. The scriptural evidence is overwhelming, and most Bible students would agree. However, controversy and even confusion arise when discussing the existence of tongues in our generation. A considerable percentage of the Christian population is under the impression that tongues have ceased while others, as stated, despite overwhelming evidence to the contrary, believe they are from the devil.

Unlike the Pastor, I attended a non-Pentecostal church in my youth and can recall having genuine reservations about people who spoke in tongues. My scepticism was down to lack of knowledge and ignorance of spiritual matters, more than anything else.

Then, in my mid-twenties, I was introduced to Pentecostalism when I joined the fellowship at Whitewell. Several months after properly recommitting my life to the Lord, I was baptised in the Holy Spirit by a Newcastle lady in Co Down who didn't attend the Whitewell fellowship. It was one of the most memorable days of my life. I received the Holy Spirit's baptism, spoke in tongues, and have continued to use this wonderful gift ever since.

Following my baptism experience in the Holy Spirit, I met one of the non-Pentecostal church members I had known during my youth who asked what had made me believe in speaking in tongues.

I replied: "It happened to me."

Can there be more considerable evidence of the power of God than when someone experiences it?

Even the great Methodist minister, John Wesley, preached for many years, bound by the law and without assurance of faith in Christ. However, once faith entered his heart, and the grace of God arrived, he remarked: "I felt my heart strangely warmed." Due to a visitation from the Holy Spirit, suddenly Wesley felt he could trust in Christ alone for salvation, and assurance came that God had removed his sins and saved him from the law of sin and death.

From here on, John Wesley served the Lord to reform England.

His Methodists became a national force. He rode thousands of miles - as many as 20,000 a year - preaching as only a man filled with the Holy Spirit can preach, telling the gospel to all who would listen.

That is the power of personal experience, and it is the same concerning speaking in tongues and the Holy Spirit's baptism.

There's no further need for any debate.

The apostle Paul was not only a great example of someone who spoke in tongues, but he also encouraged the church to do likewise. In his first letter to the Corinthians, Paul wrote: "For one who speaks in a tongue speaks not to men but God; for no one understands him, but he utters mysteries in the Spirit. On the other hand, prophecies talk to people for their encouragement and consolation. The one who speaks in a tongue builds up himself, but prophecy builds up the church. Now I want you all to speak in tongues, but even more to use prophesy. The one who prophesies is greater than the one who speaks in tongues unless someone interprets so that the church may be built up **1 Corinthians 14:2-5**

Here is a challenging issue for today's Pentecostal family. Is the Pentecostal church genuinely Pentecostal? A strange question, perhaps, but remember, the most outstanding feature of the early church was speaking in tongues following the Holy Spirit's baptism and the exercising of numerous other gifts, including healing. Again, we are permitted to ask, is this happening today?

People wonder why we do not regularly see these signs and wonders, yet the answer is obvious; the leaders are not filled with the Holy Spirit. It is not the people's fault for any Pentecost's lack in their lives, but the leaders. Falling attendances and lack of interest in church services are not the people's fault, but leaders void of the Holy Spirit. It is the responsibility of a Pentecostal church leader to teach Pentecost's message, but how can these leaders do this if they are not filled with the Holy Spirit? I believe there is a neglect to speak in tongues, mainly because church leaders haven't instilled this relevant teaching into their congregations. Paul talked about mysteries and spoke in an unknown language. The Christian church is losing out by not following the lead of the apostle on this essential issue. When I first spoke in tongues, it was like a tonic to me, and I could get results in prayer like never before. Yet, perhaps the church feels defeated on specific issues because it is not using this vital weapon of tongues. The Bible says, "For the weapons of our warfare are not carnal, but mighty through God to the pulling down of strongholds; Casting down imaginations, and every high thing that exalts itself against the knowledge of God, and bringing into captivity every thought to the obedience of Christ. Therefore, one of the best ways to execute this powerful form of prayer is to add the gift of tongues when interceding with our heavenly Father. **James McConnell**

Women Preachers

Another feature of the Pentecostal church is the willingness to use women preachers and women in various roles. It is probably fair to say that women are now more accepted in the ministry in many Pentecostal churches than ever before - something else that has seen the Pentecostal movement attract further criticism from other denominations.

Of course, it used to be the case that a woman could serve as a Pastor or missionary in a foreign country if there were a great need, and no one would blink an eye. But, on the other hand, today, women are being used as preachers and Pastors regularly in Pentecostal churches, both at home and abroad, and their influence increases.

While modern Pentecostalism approaches women in leadership positions, many churches ordain women or even place them in roles to lead congregations. Attitudes have changed dramatically and even in the more diehard traditional churches.

The emergence of women preachers may even be an additional sign of the last days and something to consider. For example, in light of Joel, chapter two, is a greater acceptance of women in the church fulfilling prophecy?

Writing about the last days, which many evangelicals believe we are currently experiencing, Joel records: "And it shall come to pass afterwards, that I will pour out my Spirit upon all flesh; and your sons and your daughters shall prophesy, your old men shall dream dreams, your young men shall see visions: And also upon the servants and upon the handmaids in those days will I pour out my Spirit" **Joel 2:28-29**

Notice how Joel speaks not only about sons but "daughters" with the ability to prophesy, and "handmaidens" will be touched by the Spirit of the living God. Should women be in ministry? It is a question much debated. I would answer it like this: Like men, it all depends on the woman's calibre. Some men and women should not even consider entering the ministry because they are not adequately equipped, but exceptions to the rule always exist, and God can find them. The same principle applies to women. It is the exception to the rule rather than the norm. Even when I was a boy, there were lady preachers, but they were usually unique vessels, and I vividly recall how some of them could preach the men under the table. I have found that women make impressive servants of God throughout my ministry and often outstrip men in their devotion and giving. They have a sweetness and compassion often lacked by men. There are also many issues women would not feel comfortable discussing with a man, which is why there is a need for women in the ministry. We must remain balanced in these issues. **James McConnell**

Literal Interpretations

However, one more sideswipe at Pentecostals relates to their literal interpretation of the Bible. Many have suffered ridicule for taking the words of Jesus literally. The point to emphasise is that while some of this mockery is valid, and the church can at times produce terrible extremism, other criticisms are not. For example, one verse cherished by Pentecostals appears in the gospel of Mark, which says: "And these signs shall follow them that believe; In my name shall they cast out devils; they shall speak with new tongues; They shall take up serpents, and if they drink any deadly thing, it shall not hurt them; they shall lay hands on the sick, and they shall recover **Mark 16:17-18**

Not all Pentecostal assemblies hold strictly to this standpoint; nevertheless, biblical literalism is generally used in a fast-changing, highly educated, and technology-driven world. Finding the truth is significant in modern society, but not at the expense of total common sense, so the abovementioned verse is a case in point.

There's a delicate balance to be struck. There are real dangers with some literal interpretations of the Bible.

In the words of Solomon, reputedly one of the wisest men who ever lived: "A false balance is an abomination to the LORD: but a just weight is his delight" **Proverbs 11:1**

While I believe much of the Bible is to be taken literally, there's also much common sense to be employed. For example, in the book of Mark, Jesus said They should take up serpents; and if they drink any deadly thing, it shall not hurt them; they shall lay hands on the sick, and they shall recover. But when Jesus speaks about "taking up serpents," it is metaphorical. I remember hearing the story of one critic who tried to defend this literal view of the Bible when visiting a George Jeffreys meeting. The man held up a bottle of poison and told Jeffreys to drink it because the Bible says that believers will not be hurt by drinking anything deadly. Jeffreys replied: "read the text; it says ***'if'"*** *they drink anything deadly, and I won't be drinking anything like that on purpose." He was a wise old boy, and the church could do with people like him today. I've even heard of people cutting off their own hands or gouging out their eyes to try and follow the words of Jesus. But, of course, this response to the Sermon on the Mount is OTT and is religion gone bonkers. There are Pentecostals, and then there are crazy Pentecostals, just as there are believers and fanatical believers. It is essential to make the distinction. I spent a lifetime discerning the difference.* **James McConnell**

During the Sermon of the Mount, the Lord said: "You have heard that it was said, 'You shall not commit adultery.' But I tell you that anyone who looks at a woman lustfully has already committed adultery with her in his heart. If your right eye causes you to stumble, gouge it out and throw it away. You should lose one part of your body than for your whole body to be thrown into hell. And if your right hand causes you to stumble, cut it off and throw it away. You should lose one part of your body than for your whole body to go into hell." **Matthew 5:27-30**

In light of this text, was Jesus teaching people to take up dismemberment as a way to fight sin? How should these sayings be understood? Does Jesus want us to do things like this or rightly divide the Word and understand who He spoke to in that passage?

It is essential to distinguish that Jesus was not speaking to the church, but the Pharisees, who, of course, trusted in their perfect law-keeping. Christ ensured that the Pharisees realised they couldn't keep God's perfect law and required a Saviour. There's considerable confusion in the church today because many believers read their bibles without rightly dividing the Old and New covenants. Many of the words Jesus spoke in the four gospels, Matthew, Mark, Luke, and John, are part of the Old covenant. He told these things before the cross as He had not yet died. The new covenant began only after the cross when the Holy Spirit was given on the Day of Pentecost. Understanding this is vital for Christians and ministers to demonstrate and believe how the cross made a difference in their lives.

Of course, many Christians claim that the cross has made a difference in their lives. Yet, the same people are bound by legalism and the law and display little evidence of the liberty or forgiveness found following that wonderful Day of Pentecost.

Therefore, if the church was to follow everything Jesus stated above, not only would there have been no need for Calvary, but the Christian church could probably also open an amputation ward! Jesus often exaggerated a story to get the truth across; because even if someone has no eyes and no hands, it still doesn't stop them from lusting after others. After all, sin arises from the heart, and Jesus knew this and taught it elsewhere in the Scriptures.

The Lord used this literary device to emphasise the seriousness of sin - it would be better to end up in heaven physically maimed than end up in hell with both eyes and both limbs. It may not always be possible to give an exact answer to the question - "Do you take the Bible literally?" but common sense and wisdom are also required when determining spiritual truth. The words of Solomon are worth consideration again: "A false balance is an abomination to the LORD: but a just weight is his delight" **Proverbs 11:1**

This would apply to most aspects of spiritual gifts and biblical interpretations. Solomon's advice also ensures Pentecostals are not unfairly persecuted or criticised without cause. When a man or woman is operating with the anointing of God and filled with the Holy Spirit, there is no more beautiful sight because God is not the author of confusion but life, love, and peace.

And they went forth and preached everywhere, the Lord working with them
and confirming the word with signs following.

Mark 16:20

24.

The Growth of Pentecostalism Through Prophecy and Prayer

Religious organisations are collapsing all around us, providing a golden opportunity for true believers and churches to shine. Even though I believe in Pentecost and Pentecostalism, I don't think people are necessarily looking for this, albeit many join the Pentecostal church. It is what Pentecost represented and still represents that they are searching for, which is new life in Jesus and eternal life through His sacrifice at Calvary. The other benefits of Pentecost are only a bonus compared to God's promise that all who believe in Christ will not perish but have everlasting life. ***James McConnell***

The fastest-growing church in the world is often reported as the religion of Islam, but the Pentecostal church, of course, represents Christianity, is also on the rise. Indeed, according to recent statistics, the fastest-growing ministry globally is currently thought to be an underground, persecuted Christian movement in a country notorious for exporting radical Islamic terrorism — Iran. People in Iran, a Muslim-majority nation, are fleeing Islam as believers bow their knees to Jesus and become aggressively pro-Israel.

According to a 2011 Pew Research survey, there were more than 2.2 billion Christians worldwide in 2010, more than three times as many as the 600 million recorded in 1910. Moreover, that figure has increased considerably since.

While God is moving powerfully inside Iran, He is moving everywhere as it is also believed that a quarter of all Christians in the world identify as Pentecostal.

An estimated 35,000 people join the Pentecostal church each day, and it is predicted this surge will increase considerably by 2025.

Despite this great sign of growth, however, switch on the news daily, and you will hear consistent reports about the decline of the Christian church and even of a significant switch to other religions like Islam.

Questions like "why do people not go to church anymore?" or "why are people turning away from organised religion?" are often debated, yet the reality is quite different. Notwithstanding; while it is undoubtedly true that people reject organised religion today like never before, what isn't being reported is how they are also accepting and running to join authentic and vibrant places of worship in line with Bible prophecy that predicts in the last days a genuine conversion by multitudes to Jehovah God. There is an actual reason for this often-unreported revival.

Most people no longer seek a religion; instead, they have become aware and alive to a relationship with God, their Creator, a move accentuated by Covid-19 and other atrocities showing how religion cannot, of itself, comfort or bring anyone to God or save a person. The pandemic also exposed just how vulnerable we all are and finally had the world looking upwards rather than looking inwards.

As has been shockingly evident, religion is powerless to help when disaster strikes. This is because the church's assignment, and purpose, including that of the Pentecostal movement, is not or never has been to provide organised religion. Instead, the goal is to afford people the opportunity of allowing God to invade their lives with His love, grace, and mercy and introduce them to the Saviour of the world, Jesus Christ, and the Kingdom of God.

So, is the church fulfilling this mission?

The central message Jesus preached was repent (have a change of heart and thinking), followed by the announcement that God's Kingdom has arrived. So, again, an appropriate question must be - is this happening today within the Christian denominations, including the Pentecostal churches?

While many churches and denominations are sincere and dedicated in their faith, too much of the Christian church has ignored the Kingdom of God's message, preferring to preach on alternative themes such as prosperity, healing, baptism, divisive doctrine, and many other things. While these subjects are to be taught, the central message Jesus preached was the Kingdom of God, and it was how the First-Century church and the Pentecostal movement came to prominence.

This assignment is still the mission of the church and the unique key to Christ's return according to the words of Jesus – "And this gospel of the kingdom will be proclaimed throughout the whole world as a testimony to all nations, and then the end will come." **Matthew 24:14**

Following the Azusa revival, which we mentioned earlier in this section, what began with just a handful of early Pentecostals soon soared to more than 50,000 in just a few short years. The Pentecostal church has long been considered one of the fastest and largest growing forms of Christianity. While pubs are closing in virtually every region and village (something that was happening long before Covid-19), there are now more church buildings than pubs, according to figures produced by the National Churches Trust. Again this is in total contrast to what secular media reports. You would think the church was dead and buried by listening to some programmes.

It is true that many established churches are disappearing, but not the Pentecostal movement, which, conversely, is experiencing remarkable growth and worldwide acceptance and development. Christians today fear secularisation, believing that the current church is under pressure to exist, but this is untrue and unlikely for several reasons. First of all, the National Churches Trust survey shows that even people of no recognised faith admit that they believe in God and accept they have a soul and still need to pray or read the Bible. World atrocities and prophetic signs are driving people to their knees and God. People feel a greater sense of insecurity and have become acutely aware of their mortality. Therefore, due to substantial growth among particular churches, especially the Pentecostal church, secularisation is a long way off, regardless of what doomsday commentators say. Instead, secularisation is faced by none other than the Lord Himself who said in Matthew chapter 16, "And I also say to you that you are Peter, and on this rock, I will build My church, and the gates of Hades shall not prevail against it." **Matthew 16:18**

Christ is not defeated, nor His church! Rather than fading out, God's true blood-washed believers are on the march. The increase amongst Pentecostals is a sign that Jesus is coming soon, and if Jesus is coming soon, then most Pentecostal believers feel a duty to tell others. The prophet Joel, referring to the last days, wrote: "And it shall come to pass afterward That I will pour out My Spirit upon all flesh, and your sons and your daughters shall prophesy, your old men shall dream dreams, your young men shall see visions" **Joel 2:28**

Joel's prophecy, however, pinpoints the "last days" as including both the fulfilment of the Holy Spirit being poured out on young and old (as happened on the day of Pentecost) and a future season of divine judgment and justice known among the prophets as the Day of the Lord.

"And I will show wonders in heaven above and signs on the earth below: blood, and fire, and vapour of smoke. The sun shall be turned into darkness, and the moon into blood, before that great and glorious day of the Lord comes" **Acts 2:19-20**

God is inviting those who are not right with Him to repent, allowing mercy to remain before the day of Judgment. Pentecostals like James McConnell don't just preach about heaven; they also believe in a literal hell. They believe in the Lord's Day but also accept there's the Day of the Lord.Many Christians view the 'Lord's Day' as referring to a Sunday, the first day in the week, which some early believers used as a day set aside for assembling for worship, prayers, teaching, and breaking of bread; notwithstanding, the Old and New Testaments also related the end times to a dreadful season of God's Judgment and wrath, known as the 'Day of the Lord'

Interestingly, both Joel in the Old Testament and Peter in the New Testament linked the lovely day of Pentecost with the awful "day of the Lord." How could this be? It appears we can't have one without the other! Yes, there is mercy with God, but also ultimately Judgment for those who reject God's Son Jesus and His offer of mercy. John, the beloved scribe of the "Revelation of Jesus Christ" (Rev. 1:1), said he was "in the Spirit on the Lord's Day" (Rev. 1:10), meaning he was not only hearing from God but in good standing with God if Judgment arrived.

As Christ's Second Coming approaches, a good question is: are we in good standing with God? To be so is to have experienced His great mercy and love.

Of all the signs that Christ is returning, Joel 2: 28 is one of the loveliest signs and immense comfort to many believers worldwide, but it also is a warning for those who reject Christ to receive His offer of mercy. The rapid growth of the Pentecostal movement and the church, in general, is a prophecy coming to pass. All the men I grew up with preached about this day and hour, and amazingly we are now living in it. I hung on to their every word and coattails because I believed what they were saying was right, and the signs are now appearing. These men preached about heaven and hell, which is the duty of every minister Pentecostal or otherwise. So while the gospel is good news, it is also God's warning to the world regarding the second coming of the Lord Jesus Christ and the need for people everywhere of all ages to repent and get right with God. Most Pentecostal churches understand this and preach a more balanced gospel. **James McConnell**

The Pastor certainly has fulfilled this commission throughout his life, preaching the gospel far and wide, in season and out of season, as the apostle Paul preached. On the second coming, he fashioned countless regular sermons at his Sunday evening gospel outreaches at Whitewell, where thousands of conversions took place. Many signs and wonders confirmed his Pentecostal roots. The proof of one's belief in Pentecost is the miracles that follow. The book of Mark speaks about the early church seeing miracles and supernatural manifestations as follows.

"And they went forth and preached everywhere, the Lord working with them, and confirming the word with signs following. Amen." **Mark 16:20**

Pentecostals believe that "signs and wonders" and spiritual gifts are well-grounded and should be "earnestly desired" to improve the church and spread the gospel.

The eminent Martyn Lloyd-Jones explained it like this in 1965: "It is clear that in New Testament times, the gospel was authenticated in this way by signs, wonders, and miracles of various characters and descriptions. Was it only meant to be true of the early church? The Scriptures never anywhere say that these things were only temporary – never! There is no such statement anywhere."

As impressive as the quote mentioned above is, again, the more significant proof we can have of the miraculous is experiencing supernatural incidents ourselves. Rather than an exception to the rule, these signs and wonders follow those who believe as day follows night.

One of the signs of the Holy Spirit's moving in the life of James McConnell was his extraordinary ability to win souls to Christ every week, and, like many of his predecessors, he could also prophesy of events to come with great accuracy. During the Troubles in Ulster, for example, he would predict impending disasters or incidents, and prophecy is still something he believes in passionately and sees as a vital part of any authentic Pentecostal church.

There is still a need for prophetic ministry in the church, but it will only come when leaders seek God and hear from Him. "Thus says the Lord" is just as relevant today as it was in the past; in some ways, it is even more important to experience a prophetic ministry because of the state of the world. However, one thing that leaves people feeling apprehensive is when false prophets emerge and predict stupid things that never happen. It is confusing and discouraging but shouldn't negate that genuine prophecy is still required and very much of God. False prophets only confirm what Jesus said: In the last days, many false prophets would arise. **James McConnell**

In September 1973, the Pastor received a genuine prophecy and a remarkable supernatural visitation of his own when the Angel of the Lord came and stood beside him on the balcony of his small church on the Whitewell Road, Belfast. It was not a vision, nor a dream, because he was fully conscious.

By his admission, the Pastor had seen this messenger many times previously, but always as a man. Nevertheless, there was a purpose in this personal visitation from the Angel of the Lord when he was informed that from that point on, every time he would preach the gospel, souls would be saved, a promise God has kept until this day. Stories, far too numerous to mention, abound in that small church. Indeed miracles and signs and wonders have always been part of the Whitewell ministry.

Proof that a Pentecostal church is Pentecostal is unmistakable when the power of God is in the midst of that church and ministry. Over the years, I have lost count of phenomenal incidents at Whitewell, but some are hard to forget. Like the time I held an Easter convention and preached to around 400 people in the Shankhill area of Belfast. It was a little billiard hall, but the Angel of the Lord entered the meeting. I had received Angel visitations before, but this time the people saw the Angel also. Afterwards, they said that when I moved, the Angel moved, and the Angel stayed for up to 45 minutes. Things like that can only happen in Pentecost. I recall another incredible experience when a lady fell sick and was admitted to the hospital. As she lay feeling very ill, she asked God to send His servant to help her. Immediately she saw me walking out of the wall singing, "Come to the water, stand by my side, I know you are thirsty, you won't be denied, I felt every teardrop when in the darkness you cried. And I strove to remind you; it's for those tears I died".I don't know how this happened because I was sitting at home and knew nothing about it. A similar event occurred when another ill person asked God to send his servant, and I again came and ministered to them. Notwithstanding, I was in America at that time, so I wasn't present. Furthermore, it is the power of the Spirit and the miracle of Pentecost. I can honestly say I have lost count of so many similar stories over the years. Let me put it like this: there's something supernatural about Pentecost! **James McConnell**

Although there is definite proof that the Pentecostal movement is increasing, particularly in non-western countries, supernatural events like these appear rare today in the West but more frequent in the Middle East, America, and Africa.

Why is this? Does the Pastor believe the western church is operating in the supernatural?

In some cases, yes, but I also don't believe the Pentecostal church has enough spirit-filled leaders, and that's why we don't see or hear of supernatural events like we used to, but it isn't the case everywhere. There seems to be more evidence of signs and wonders in many African-American Pentecostal churches today, where the Spirit of God seems to be moving. We hear of miracles in Africa and other countries that are exciting and should be the norm. Still, the church in the United Kingdom seems void of these experiences except for the occasional evidence, which should be the norm rather than the exception. This situation is concerning for mainstream western Pentecostals and must be addressed. **James McConnell**

So how do we return to the days of signs and wonders like Jesus and the apostles experienced?

After all, the book of Acts, known as the Acts of the Holy Spirit, records: "And through the hands of the apostle's many signs and wonders were done among the people. And they were all with one accord in Solomon's Porch." **Acts 5:12** while the book of Mark records "And they went forth and preached everywhere, the Lord working with them, and confirming the word with signs following. Amen." **Mark 16:20**

Any lack of supernatural evidence is concerning because every minister and church must demonstrate the Holy Spirit's power to ensure his credibility. There's a cry to preach the gospel again also and for evangelicals of all denominations to get on their knees and pray. My advice to young ministers seeking the power of the Holy Spirit is: God has not called you to be the keeper of an aquarium; instead, you are called to become a fisher of men. The signs of the times are all around us. The world has endured being locked down in homes during the Coronavirus pandemic. Instead of holding social events or entertaining people online, lock down your church and hold prayer meetings every night of the week until God moves. We frequently did this over the years and put up a sign that read: "Closed for repairs." Like Noah and his family on the ark, we didn't come out again until God had spoken, and the church returned to a healthy state. Men like Spurgeon and Parker did this, and we did it at Whitewell for over two years on one occasion. We would meet at 7 am on a Sunday when our church numbered fewer than 50 people, but God heard every one of those prayers, and later on, we had a record turnout of over 2,000 people to pray. People are trying everything to see growth in the church. How about trying prayer? How about producing prophetic ministry? I recall having ten days of prayer and nothing else until God showed up. There's no doubt prayer brings Pentecost, and the Holy Spirit brings deliverance quicker than any modern alternative. Take Joseph Parker, a great preacher, yet his prayers were even more impressive, and God answered them. People came to hear him pray, not just preach, and people were converted to Christ merely by listening to him pray. Prayer should be as essential as breakfast, lunch, and tea. Even when we don't know what to pray, pray anyway, and God will hear and answer. Or, as Spurgeon once said: "Groanings which cannot be uttered are often prayers which cannot be refused." Prayer brings the supernatural element and the prophetic to Pentecostal assemblies. **James McConnell**

Every week, seven prayer meetings seem to have left their mark with God for many years because the ministry at Whtewell has grown into a global one. Though it has declined considerably in numbers from the Pastor's peak, the church at Whitewell can still claim to be one of the healthier religious assemblies in the land. Pentecostals like James McConnell are and always have been convinced by the verse found in the book of Hebrews, which states, "Jesus Christ, the same yesterday, today, and forever." **Hebrews 13:5**

He believes miracles and great answers to prayer were not only for the early church but are as relevant today as ever. The Pentecostal movement is growing, but extra prayer can increase such growth.

He's in no doubt that the same Jesus who prayed for the disciples during the storm in the New Testament is the same Jesus who has prayed for him on many occasions, and this same Jesus will pray for and protect the church in the last days also. As organised religion fades, many new exciting and modern churches are springing up, led by people not necessarily qualified with a theology degree but people who have a sincere heart for the things of God and people anointed of the Holy Spirit.

Granted, some of the methods may not be conservative, but God is not worried; instead, He's raising an army of saints to combat the threat of apostasy.

Despite reports contrary, the church, particularly the Pentecostal movement, isn't closing anytime soon. It is still an army of men and women on the move, made continuously prosperous by their prayers and prophetic signs and wonders.

The Church and Pentecost are well and truly alive, and just as He promised, Jesus is building His church before His soon coming return.

Passion for Souls

A man who has found out what his true work is – winning souls to Christ – and does it, such is the happiest man.

DL Moody

25.

The Desire for Souls

It may seem surprising that I can recall the first converts so long ago, but preachers will tell you that winning their first soul to Christ is a great accomplishment in their life. I'm no exception. At 13, I was praying one day in my room when the Holy Spirit revealed a young man I knew who lived in Victor Street not far from my house. I got up from my knees, ran to his house, and led him to the Lord, where he went on to become an elder in the Presbyterian Church. The next convert was similar. I remember kneeling in the rain at a bus stop near Bloomfield in Belfast and leading my friend Harry to Christ, and he also became an elder in a local Presbyterian church for many years. From there on, I asked God to give me a soul every week. I would walk in the Castlereagh Hills, asking God to anoint me to win souls. I asked for this anointing and the maturity required to go with it. I quoted the apostle Paul's words in Corinthians' book to let my speech and message be not plausible words of wisdom but demonstrate the Spirit and power. It was here I heard the voice of God reassuring me with the words of John chapter 15 "You have not chosen me, but I have chosen you, and ordained you, that ye should go and bring forth fruit, and that your fruit should remain: that whatsoever ye shall ask of the Father in my name, he may give it *to you. You have not chosen me. I have chosen you".* **James McConnell**

There is much discussion in church circles these days about placing too much confidence in our education rather than in God's supernatural power to win souls.

It is a debate most justified, especially as the world and even religious organisations are becoming more and more secular in their thinking.

Numerous young ministers have been discouraged at bible schools for having the audacity to...wait for it, state things like "I believe the Bible."

How unusual is that?

Even some of the fundamental assignments that Jesus commissioned His "students" to fulfil are abrasively being replaced by what the modern world describes as "higher reasoning." It has produced churches overpopulated by preachers with a list of credentials the length of their arm but lacking the essential enablement, the Holy Spirit's supernatural power. "Educated devils" and "pulpit dolls", as the Pastor often called them during his tenure.

The apostle Paul gave a clear indication as to what every soul-winning preacher requires saying, "And my speech and my preaching was not with enticing words of man's wisdom, but in demonstration of the Spirit and of power" **1 Corinthians 2:4**

Too many well-meaning and sincere ministers seem to struggle to win souls. They are full of all the right cliches, doctrinally sound, and even display charismatic personalities, yet few listeners, if any, are encouraged or respond to their message in faith.

Over the years, a famous one-liner from Pastor McConnell is "Some preachers couldn't win a soul in a raffle."

It would often make his congregation chuckle and is an important observation of the Church today, if not a sad reflection. The most significant evidence of a God-inspired supernatural ministry is when people respond to the Word of God in faith and receive Jesus as their Saviour and Lord.

The great Kathryn Kuhlman said, "My purpose is to save souls, and my particular calling is to offer proof of the power of God."

Here is the supreme confirmation of men and women sent by God.

Is this a harsh standard or a fair assessment of a preacher?

Remember, Jesus said, "you will know them by their fruit" **Matthew 7:16** - not their suits or boots!

The most important fruit of preaching is converting men and women from darkness into light.

Today, too many churches appear like social clubs where winning a soul is as rare as a person winning the national lottery.

Was soul-winning high on Christ's list of priorities?

Jesus made that powerful statement: "For what shall it profit a man if he shall gain the whole world, and lose his soul?" **Mark 8:36**

Today, churches teach all sorts of stuff like self-improvement, prosperity, healing, faith, marriage, deliverance and the gifts of the Spirit. While there is nothing wrong with some of this, sadly, the winning souls to the Kingdom of God are viewed as not as necessary.

In its place, many pulpits in the land are have replaced the anointing of the Holy Spirit with counterfeit programmes and religious curriculums; while tellingly, those occupying high leadership positions are no longer the most anointed, but rather the ones with self-promotion ability, degrees and accolades and ironically no shortage of self-confidence.

By contrast, God's anointed servants are either put out of the Church as prophesied by the Lord **John 16:2** or similar to Jesus in the book of Revelation; they cannot gain access to it at all. **Revelation 3:20**

It is vastly different from the early Church in the New Testament.

A good reputation was necessary back then, but equally, the Holy Spirit and wisdom accompanied reputation in those days. **Acts 6:3** Bible schools and education is helpful, but the gift of winning souls is of greater significance than any theological training or degree.

Rarely do we hear the term "soul-winner" today, yet when the Pastor was growing up, a soul winner was not just a recognised term – it was seen as a great compliment and an honour.

Today, people are focused on sanctification, but there can be no sanctification without salvation.

The Pastor believes there's nothing wrong with making disciples but insists, "you have to catch a fish first before you clean it."

Even the Lord commanded his disciples to "go...and make disciples of all nations" **Matthew 28:19** In the New Testament, the apostle Paul makes no apology for using the exciting language of evangelism and consistently explains the concept of soul-winning.

He believed "sons" are, first of all, "*born*" before disciples can be "made."

No fewer than five times in 1 Corinthians 9:19-22, Paul used a Greek word (*kerdaino*) that means "to gain," "acquire," or "win (over)."

Paul says God sends His messengers to offer the world something more significant - a more extraordinary life and a greater Kingdom through the preaching of the gospel.

It has always been God's plan to take the gospel's message to the world.

The gospel offers people forgiveness and freedom, especially those trying to earn salvation by trying and failing miserably to make it themselves.

Instead, Paul preached the grace of the gospel, and he was even prepared to go to extraordinary lengths to win people to Christ, stating, "I have become all things to all people, so that I may by every possible means save some" **1 Corinthians 9:22**

Here was a man primarily focused on soul-winning.

Of course, by declaring he had "become all things to all people," Paul didn't mean that he was prepared to compromise his Christian character or conform to the things of this present world.

Instead, he was ready to try unorthodox methods to lead people to Jesus, albeit never deviating from the gospel's message.

Paul understood that new and creative methods are acceptable, even advantageous, but the gospel's message would never change.

Such an approach sums up the life and ministry of Pastor McConnell.

The Pastor spent a lifetime leading people to Jesus privately and winning souls from the pulpit. The desire to win souls has trumped all other things. In short, the Pastor's vocation was to win souls to Jesus, and according to the Bible, this is the more excellent form of wisdom.

The book of Proverbs declares: "The fruit of the righteous is a tree of life, And he who wins souls is wise.» **Proverbs 11:30**

One attention-grabbing translation of the word wise in this text is "cunning" or "street-wise". Those early days as an orphan boy running around Belfast were not without purpose in the young James McConnell's life. The Pastor gained excellent knowledge about life, pain, loneliness and even hopelessness. As a result, he became street-wise in every sense. In fact, despite the passing years, he can still recall one of the first tactics he employed to help influence people his age for Jesus. In his youth, and using the same approach as the apostle Paul, he would gladly speak to others about subjects he no longer had much interest in solely to win them to the Lord.

I remember buying the newspapers and going straight to the back pages to read the sports headlines. Of course, I had lost interest in sport with preaching so much, but I would find out which football teams had won at the weekend and which had failed. Like Paul, who addressed Athens's men in Acts 17 for what he described as being of "great superstition" and then appealed to that same superstition, so I would talk to my friends about their interest in football before sharing with them a gospel thought. I may not have had an education, but I was educated in the things of God. Soul winners need to be cunning and intelligent if they wish to succeed because they operate in areas where there are traps and hindering spirits. After all, Jesus told his followers as much, saying, "Behold, I send you forth as sheep among wolves. Be ye, therefore, wise as serpents and harmless as doves
James McConnell

Shortly afterwards, James became aware of just how true this would become. The winning of souls would become a life's work he has excelled in ever since. Even today, there's nothing more the Pastor loves than to witness a soul coming to Christ in his later years. As DL Moody wrote, "A man who has found out what his true work is – winning souls to Christ – and does it, such is the happiest man."

His focus and sacrifice regarding the conversion of souls can be summed up by recalling a story some years ago. One evening, he arrived at a church with his Bible under his arm, ready to preach the Word only to be greeted by the church caretaker preparing for the bowling club's arrival.

"Bowls?" said the caretaker, to which the Pastor replied, "Souls."

I have always had an insatiable desire to see souls saved. Even when I attend services where others are preaching and don't see souls saved, I become discouraged. After a life of soul-winning, you would think I would be content, but such is the passion for souls God has placed within me. I still have a burning desire to see men, women and children experiencing salvation. I have cried tears for souls on many occasions, and it has consumed me throughout my entire life. I particularly like what Spurgeon said: "winners of souls must first be weepers of souls." And such tears are required again between the porch and the altar from preachers if a revival of souls occurs. I do not see this as an old-fashioned view, or even a self-righteous one, but rather precisely what is required. **James McConnell**

Jack Hyles says, "Old fashioned, Spirit-filled, Christ-honouring, sin-hating, soul-winning, Bible-preaching. It is the hope of the Church, and it is the hope of the nation, and it is the hope of the world."

What else draws a soul to Christ no matter their origin, country or background? And is winning souls the absolute priority of the Church? Should a minister of God's Word be endowed with the gift for winning souls?

Who better to ask than someone who has invested a lifetime in fishing for the souls of men?

Souls can't be saved without the power and anointing of God. The unsaved only respond to the leading and drawing of Christ. Jesus said, "No man can come to me, except the Father which hath sent me draw him: and I will raise him at the last day. It is not the preacher, the worship, or the crowds, which saves a soul, although all these things are good; instead, it is the power of the Holy Spirit that wins men and women to Jesus. The most outstanding soul winner, therefore, is the Holy Spirit. Yes, a man must have a passion for souls. He must also study and possess a love for Christ; however, if he intends to win souls and succeed in his vocation, his message will always be Christ-centred, not political or necessarily theological. The power of the Holy Spirit will aid him. It is not more theology people require, but more of Christ. Some preachers can speak for the entire sermon and never mention the name of Jesus. How can this be? The power to win souls is in the name and person of the Lord Jesus, not in one's ability or theological insight. A man must also never be ashamed to say that he loves Jesus. Some of my most memorable conversions came after I openly confessed my love for the Lord during my message. Indeed, I have lost count of the people who told me that I had taught them to love Jesus on their deathbed. You can't make people love Jesus if you don't love him yourself. If a man is not winning souls, the question is who or what is his focus? Here is the key to soul winning and leading people to Christ. Fall in love with Jesus, and souls will result from this union. Understanding Jesus and His message is the key to winning souls. **James McConnell**

What we hear about God and religion in the Church is vital to understanding Christ and His purpose. It is crucial if souls are to be saved. It proves the difference between deliverance and defeat. It can draw people closer to God or scare them away from

His lovely presence. Simultaneously, the Bible tells us that "Faith comes by hearing", but so does fear come by hearing.

Nothing attracts souls faster, like the preaching of the cross and the love of God. Here is where the Pastor has excelled over the years. He has displayed the balance between revealing the truth with grace and deep confidence in God to see souls saved under his ministry. However, he insists it is due to God's promise and nothing to do with any personal ability and down to preaching about Christ and the person of Christ.

Here is one of his greatest preaching secrets revealed.

On the contrary, let's assume you have been exposed to a God who is primarily angry and waiting to trip you up for your sins; the question is obvious - where will you go when you need help and support? If this God you have heard about supposedly makes you ill and punishes you at every turn for your sins, how will you ever seek after Him for help and healing and prosperity?

Suppose you have been told that God wants you and your family to remain in poverty to teach you about humility. Yet, how can you ever hope to experience a financial breakthrough due to considerable debts? In fact, how can you believe anything positive about God if the sermons you've been listening to make you more and more condemned and exposed to judgement rather than mercy.

Yet sadly, many people and religions are hearing and learning about a God of anger, hatred and revenge, rather than a God of love, mercy and forgiveness through Christ and His accomplishment at the cross. No wonder many souls are scared to death of coming through the doors of a church!

On October 29th, 2020, a terrorist stormed into a church sanctuary in France and killed numerous people. After beheading one of them, he yelled out the words, "God is greatest."

Which God?

What sort of God would permit such evil behaviour?

It isn't the God of the Bible.

Nevertheless, somehow, this man learned and heard about God incorrectly, and the consequences proved devastating and highly fatal to innocent people. However, people don't have to be radical extremists to err in this way. There is danger in every religious environment, presenting God as some terrorist bent on having revenge against anyone who refuses to see things like Him.

Suppose we genuinely desire to properly understand who God is and experience victory over the enemy of the souls of men. In that case, we must hear the words of Christ in the new covenant and preach Christ as He is – a loving, merciful saviour.

The Word of Christ in Greek refers to the Word of His grace. So Paul told believers in the book of Colossians to "let the word of Christ dwell richly in you in all wisdom" **Colossians 3:16**. There's no doubt that many preachers and ministries are sincere today, but are they rooted in Jesus and His love?

When a person preaches about Jesus, a blessing is promised, and I always made it a habit to concentrate my messages on the life of Christ. It is the secret to winning souls. Having said this, I always knew souls would be saved when I preached, not due to arrogance, but because of the promise God had given me all those years before. God told me that if I preached Jesus, people would be converted. If this inner confidence seems conceited, the apostle, Peter, could sleep soundly in the prison even when he was in danger of being executed. Why? Because God had already told him, he would die as an older man and believed God rather than men. The Bible says the promises of God are "yea and amen", and nothing can stop Him blessing an individual if he so chooses. So when God promised me that no matter when or where I preached, souls would follow like Peter, I believed Him, and it happened. **James McConnell**

Aside from becoming a seasoned and skilful evangelist, the Pastor was also experienced and "in a league of his own" when holding funerals.

He certainly had more than enough practice having buried an entire congregation during his time as the Senior Pastor at Whitewell. Generations passed to glory during his ministry, and most of them were laid to rest by him. Anyone who witnessed these funerals or what he preferred to call "thanksgiving services" couldn't have failed to be impressed with the intimate way he knew the church members and how he often didn't use any sermon notes as he quoted many parts of the Bible concerning the death of the saints. "If I had a hundred people like this, I could do anything for God", he would often say as he encouraged grieving family and friends present.

The truth, however, was that back then, he did have a hundred people, maybe even a thousand, who were fully committed to the things of God and his ministry at Whitewell.

They say you shouldn't use a funeral to preach, but I always preached anyway. I never let a funeral or thanksgiving service pass without getting in a bit of gospel shot. There is no more fantastic opportunity to remind people of their mortality than at a funeral, and I witnessed many conversions take place afterwards that may not otherwise have happened. I've always had great liberty preaching the gospel, so I wouldn't know what else to do. ***James McConnell***

That's not to say every funeral goes according to plan, of course.

The Pastor said he could have written a book on funerals, and if he had, it would probably have become a best-seller.

Nevertheless, a soul winner of soul winners, few who know him, would argue against Pastor James McConnell as a man enormously gifted in reaching people for Jesus and His Kingdom, no matter the environment or circumstances. For him, soul-winning was never an option, a problem, or even a church growth idea. For him, it was a definite, unavoidable command of God. And it led to an abundance of souls being won into the Kingdom of God for well over half a century – a vintage period in the more modern history of evangelicalism.

ODYSSEY ARENA
ODYSSEY ARENA

HOPE
NOW AND FOREVER

It is not that the Church hasn't been trained in evangelism, it is not a lack of instruction or information. The fact is, if you don't love people through the eyes of Christ, the world will never be changed.

Reinhard Bonnke

26.

A Soul Winner of Soul Winners

In the early days, the standout event was probably at the Husband Memorial Hall at York Street when around 28 people came to Jesus when I was still a teenager. Thirty-three decisions at Devon Parade church followed it. Among those saved that night were Robert Gass, author of the Word for Today, my sister Lila, my brother in law Mervyn Foster and a man who would become a successful evangelist in his own right, Sydney Murray. Shortly afterwards, a meeting was held at the Ulster Hall, and another eight people surrendered their lives to Christ. I was young but on a roll. It gave me the confidence to continue evangelising the community, so it wasn't long before I began trying to emulate my boyhood hero George Jeffreys. He had preached at the King's Hall in Belfast many times, and I wanted to repeat that feat. With God's help, our single Church managed to fill the King's Hall and the Ulster Hall seven times each and thousands of souls came to know Christ. Our outreaches to the national soccer stadium, Winsdor Park, and other sports stadiums were highly successful ventures too. To repeat the accomplishment of my hero, however, was undoubtedly the icing on the cake. **James McConnell**

Many thousands of souls found Christ under Pastor James McConnell's ministry. From the earliest days in an old Orange Hall in North Belfast to the two churches which followed it on the Whitewell Road and the move in 1994 to the Metropolitan Tabernacle on the Shore Road, where it is estimated no fewer than 50,000 people have found Christ, Whitewell has been nothing short of a soul-winning factory.

Yet, it is not only within the Whitewell church where thousands of people of all ages have found God, but many have also trusted in the Lord through the Whitewell ministry in multiple venues throughout the entire island of Ireland and abroad. Countless evangelistic rallies in community centres and tent missions have also become part of Whitwell history, along with scores of events in local sports stadiums and invitations for the Pastor to speak at other churches.

In his early days, the Pastor travelled extensively and preached in various countries such as Estonia, Holland, Germany, Belgium, France, Russia, Romania, and the USA. He made trips to foreign countries to bring the gospel message even following his retirement in his late seventies and early eighties. His zeal has never diminished, and his desire is as strong as ever.

History will record James McConnell not only as one of the great preachers of his generation but one of the most prolific soul winners for Christ. He belongs alongside evangelical greats such as DL Moody, John Wesley, Charles Spurgeon, George Jeffries, Billy Graham, and Reinhard Bonnke, to name but a few.

However, it is essential to recall where this haul of souls began by identifying how many of the outreaches mentioned above helped change the lives of not just the individuals who came to know Jesus but calmed the temperature of a bitterly divided society.

Having witnessed thousands of converts give their lives to Christ, the Pastor need not worry about any lack of accomplishment in life. On the contrary, God graciously and carefully handpicked him for more extraordinary things - like preaching God's goodness, which brings all men to repentance.

Despite receiving an honorary doctorate for services to the United Kingdom from the California Graduate School of University, an establishment most impressed with his contribution to Christianity, he believes a greater reward is waiting for him in heaven. When it comes to his chosen soul-winning profession, a crown of righteousness awaits him and the many others he has subsequently led to the Lord.

And despite also being recognised by many fellow preachers and peers as "an outstanding preacher" and – "soul winner of soul winners"- he can rest in the knowledge that he has "fought a good fight" and "finished his course" with honours.

For 70 years, James McConnell has thought of nothing other than his primary calling of winning souls to Jesus; the number of people saved throughout his lifespan is impossible to calculate. Soul-winning is a business he takes so seriously he still recalls his first two conversions at the tender age of just 13 years old.

During the years which followed, winning souls became a weekly, even daily habit for the Pastor. Many books have been written highlighting his life's devotion to soul-winning and what many recall as 'the golden years' at Whitewell. Yet, thousands of more souls would come to know the Lord at the Tabernacle following that manuscript.

It was a remarkable season; it started with organising gospel tent missions in Mersey Street East Belfast. Initially holding 650 people, the tent became too small and was increased to over 1000, but still, it proved inadequate, so the event was moved to Ormeau Park, a place where the Pastor had played and sought God as a boy.

The giant tent erected at Ormeau had a capacity of over 3,000, and people flocked from every part of the province to hear the gospel preached. The missions, which lasted for nine nights and ran for eight successive years, were sheer "old-fashioned gospel preaching." There are no thrills, spills, or tricks; just a man behind a pulpit with an open Bible, preaching the gospel's good news to needy people experiencing the end of the Troubles and a fractured peace process. People were set free and delivered from all sorts of addictions, and remarkable healings took place in those tents as well. But, more importantly, hope and direction were offered as a way forward. Many who had the privilege of attending these vintage rallies recall them as incredibly unique. Even the Pastor appeared to have greater liberty on what was, after all, "home territory."

Today, people talk about these meetings as being extraordinary; I was highly motivated, of course, because I was preaching in a place where I grew up and had so many remarkable memories of it. Hundreds, probably even thousands, came to know the Lord in the tent missions. People from every religious background got saved, which proved when a man seeks God and has His Bible, the Word of God can do miracles. **James McConnell**

But it wasn't just the preaching and large gatherings people remember about those tent missions. Once the Pastor booked a tent in Enniskillen, there was a powerful smell of cows' dung. Everyone who sat through the service deserved medals; nevertheless, hundreds came, and people were saved. Those who attended the tent missions still talk about how their shoes were full of dung even when they arrived home, and the smell seemed to take days to clear.

There wasn't just the smell of cows dung lingering at that time, but also the smell of death. The Province of Ulster desperately required hope in a hopeless world due to the escalation of violence. The Pastor and his Church had provided it through the message of the gospel and unlikely tent missions. Even greater days followed, even though they would prove equally challenging.

As the decade of the 1990s drew to a close, the new Millennium emerged with blue skies and feelings of tremendous optimism, but hopes of a better period were quickly dashed, and it wasn't long before clouds of smoke and darkness quickly set in.

Then, a series of terrorist attacks by Al-Qaeda against the United States on Tuesday, September 11th 2001, changed the world as we knew it forever. Fear gripped the streets of many countries, and following the attacks, people ran for shelter to the House of God. The Whitewell Tabernacle in Belfast was no exception.

On reflection, if ever a house had been built to shelter and win souls, it was the Whitewell ministry in Belfast. Again, the Pastor took full advantage of the situation to lead men and women to the Lord. Never one to miss his moment, he began a series on the Second Coming of Jesus and a series of sermons offering hope at a precarious time and Whitewell exploded with conversions.

For about eight weeks, the Church was packed. I remember long queues to get into the Church, especially on Sunday evenings and bear in mind the Tabernacle already catered for over 3,000 people. I recall one particular night when it was snowing; people were still queued outside and overflowed the sanctuary. Our deacons ran out of chairs, and despite having a megachurch to house people, folk were spilling over into the minor hall where we had to erect extra screens. It was an incredible period and seemed to last for ages. It became clear that people were not just frightened, but perhaps they were considering faith matters for the first time. It led me to embark on an even more significant challenge, but one I have never regretted. **James McConnell**

With no real, lasting peace in Northern Ireland and other concerning world developments, it was a time when people believed the coming of the Lord was at hand, and this provoked another daring, primary outreach to the nation to win souls. Here again, was a street-wise, creative, and even astute Pastor at his work.

In September 2005, he decided to take another step of faith by booking one of Northern Ireland's most significant venues - the Odyssey Arena in Belfast. Seating nearly 9,000 people, the question was, could he and the Whitewell ministry fill such a place?

It was a huge commitment!

Many globally recognised evangelists had preached previously at the Odyssey. Still, none of them had previously managed to fill the venue, so how could a local man expect to do so?

A more critical question also remained; could it fill during some of the most frightening loyalist riots and civil disturbances seen in Ulster's province? Petrol and pipe bombs were being used, and at the height of the riots, gunmen opened fire on the police, cars were hijacked, and buildings were set alight. It was supposed to be "post Troubles," a time of the ceasefire, but some of the violence witnessed was even worse than when the Troubles were at their peak. Nevertheless, burning buses, protesting, and all-out anarchy failed to prevent what is still arguably the most miraculous night in the history of the Whitewell ministry.

On September 11th, 2005, the Odyssey Arena became too small a venue, with hundreds turned away at the doors and many more hundreds saved by God's grace.

Despite the obstacles, the Pastor, his congregation and those who bravely attended that night somehow found the strength to press on in Jesus' name. Good had prevailed over evil, and the light of God had defeated the works of darkness. Regardless of the miracle that had taken place, however, and against all the odds, the only preoccupation of the media the following day was one of the Whitewell buses carrying parishioners being burned as it entered an estate on the way home. Yet, it didn't detract from what is arguably one of the most memorable and extraordinary gospel missions ever held in the whole of Ireland.

The media may have missed the opportunity to report a genuinely "good news" story. Still, anyone privileged enough to be there witnessed what God had done - a genuine miracle had taken place before their eyes. The Holy Spirit had filled them and the venue with His power, which is unmistakable by the video footage that still exists today. Whitewell Church have produced many anniversary recordings celebrating 25 years at the Metropolitan Tabernacle. As the people of Whitewell watched this celebration video in 2019, and the events from that miraculous night at the Odyssey, it became clear to many of them that they had not just been part of a church but by God's grace, had also been associated with what can best be described as a "huge move of God."

I couldn't understand why the media wanted to focus on negative issues when God had produced a miracle and a most unlikely outcome right before our eyes. These were seasoned journalists who had covered the violence days before the event, yet they seemed to miss the transformation before their eyes at the Odyssey. No man or congregation could have done such a thing. Even allowing for those epic rallies at the King's Hall, Windsor Park, and many other places, I believe that night at the Odyssey was undoubtedly unique at Whitewell. I remember appealing for backsliders to come back to Jesus and one of our elders Alec Brown, who has since gone to be with the Lord, counted at least 40 people indicating their need of Jesus in one section. The Odyssey security staff had to close the doors early, leaving hundreds of people locked outside even before the event started. Some people were upset at not being allowed to enter the crusade, but the place was jam-packed. What took most people by surprise, especially the security staff, was that no one expected the crowd, which showed up in the province due to such a climate of fear. Nevertheless, it was a phenomenal evening in the presence of God and will live long in the annals of the history of our Church. **James McConnell**

People sometimes exaggerate when using the word miracle, but not on this occasion. God did a miraculous thing amid this local congregation and in the entire nation of Ireland. But further great outreaches followed, including a night to remember on September 11th, 2010, at Ravenhill rugby ground, now known as *The Kingspan Stadium* and home of Ulster Rugby. Again, many people came to Christ with several thousand people in attendance despite the pouring rain. The sight of the Pastor sprinting across the pitch in the lashing rain to find another hand in the crowd is still one of the most iconic pictures of his pastorate. If ever a sight depicted a dedicated and passionate servant of God, this was it – a man determined to reach souls for Jesus. Someone once remarked how the great evangelist John Wesley was "out of breath" chasing souls.

The same applied to the Pastor throughout his ministry but especially at Ravenhill, where he sprinted from one side of the pitch to the other to find responsive hands to his appeal.

Passion, persistence and the power of God were all in evidence that same evening.

A year later, the Whitewell ministry returned to the Odyssey Arena on April 23rd 2011. Huge crowds again descended on the Belfast venue to hear the gospel. It was just short of the previous turnout a few years previously, but with well over 7,000 people in attendance, still an incredible achievement allowing for the split at Whitewell just two years earlier.

As recorded in chapter six, another fantastic night of soul-winning in the Pastors' life and Whitewell came the same year when the Protestant evangelical church set up camp in the heart of Catholic West Belfast.

Whitewell was on a roll. The ministry would go from place to place, regardless of background, searching for souls for the Kingdom of God. It was a vintage period of soul-winning! Class or creed didn't matter; the colour of one's skin or previous religious convictions didn't enter the equation either. This gospel was for the "Whosoever", and it reached many souls.

Although Pastor McConnell conducted province-wide gospel rallies in nearly every town in Northern Ireland, he admitted how he loved preaching in Bangor. Over the years, he preached in the town many times. Bangor always had a special tug on Pastor McConnell's heart, and he seemed to have a divine affinity with the town. Whether it was because one of his childhood heroes, WP Nicholson, the great Presbyterian preacher and evangelist, was born there or whether it was his friendship with Mr Leeburn, one of his early spiritual mentors who owned the Redcliffe hotel where he visited on many occasions as a boy is unclear. Maybe it was a combination of both!!

From the early eighties and early nineties, through to 2019, at a series of gospel rallies in Bangor, Pastor James McConnell, the evangelist, preached a fiery gospel message with a burning zeal that was the chief characteristic of his whole life and ministry. The venues for the rallies were Hamilton House, The Kings Hall, Clandeboye Park, Bangor Leisure Centre and then venturing out to towns in the surrounding areas, Queens Hall Holywood, Queens Hall Newtownards and beyond. During this period, around twelve rallies were held in the different venues around the town, which yielded a harvest of souls for the Kingdom of God.

Pastor McConnell's other love was Sunday Schools and his unstinting spiritual, financial and moral support to the Whitewell Bangor Sunday School for over 30 years had an indirect influence on the attendance at the rallies as many of the Sunday School children, parents, and grandparents attended the rallies to hear him preach the gospel. Although all of the missions were full as Pastor McConnell's name was synonymous with soul-winning and his name on a poster always guaranteed to attract a large crowd, two gospel events deserve a special mention.

The rally at Bangor Football Ground Clandeboye Park, which took place on June 4th 1998, with the message "Eternity Where will you be?" was a fantastic night of soul winning. However, on a somewhat cool June summer evening that resembled October weather, his preaching was greatly hampered by problems with the sound system due to a robust bitter wind that swept across the pitch. Nevertheless, Pastor McConnell disposed of his notes and preached without a microphone, and over forty souls made decisions for Jesus despite the untimely hindrances.

Another memorable rally held in Bangor Leisure Centre on May 13th 2011, was part of the "Hope now and Forever" crusades. Nineteen people responded, and again, the Pastor used straightforward language, which he communicated to his audience and in biblical terminology - "the common people heard him gladly".

The anointing proved the secret ingredient no matter where he preached, and the result was souls saved. But his desire to see people won to Jesus spread much further than his homeland. During the middle years at Whitewell, overseas missions also sprouted throughout Europe and Africa as the gospel travelled even further afield. For example, the launch of the worldwide web and arrival of the information age has since seen the Whitewell ministry become a global one – the evidence of the fulfilment of that early prophecy in the first little hall in 1957 about how God would make Whitewell and the ministry into a worldwide outreach.

The timing of this was exemplified all the more following the outbreak of the national pandemic, Coronavirus, in early 2020, which for the first time in our lifetime saw places of worship closed, leaving only online churches in business. Thankfully, the online media ministry at Whitewell was already established to meet such a demand. Today, it reaches every corner of the globe, including places as far away as North Korea.

In this new and exciting generation, many quick-thinking Pastors and their staff have hit the ground running, embracing the online challenge of "going into all the world to preach the gospel." **Mark 16:15**

"It's Church, but not as we know it," and prompts the question: will we ever return to how things were previously? Winning souls is no longer confined to the local Church or a mission hall; souls are being reached for Jesus in their front livings rooms thanks to the power of the internet. (See Part Ten and chapter 29 - A Browser Window to the World.)

Notwithstanding, the Bible is clear that there should always be a gathering of God's people in a church building (Hebrews 10:25). Still, Church Online can now go well beyond the numbers found in a local assembly due to technology's power.

Isaiah said: "Enlarge the place of your tent and let the curtains of your habitations be stretched out; do not hold back; lengthen your cords and strengthen your stakes **Isaiah 54:2**

Has there ever been a more critical time or excellent platform to stretch forth and reach the fearful, bringing hope to their hearts and, most of all, introducing them to the love of God? That window of opportunity the Pastor exposed during nine eleven has opened again due to Covid-19 and all the uncertainty surrounding it.

Whether the communication with the lost is via technology or local teaching is irrelevant, and the important thing is to reach people where they are.

How serious are we as a nation and worldwide about the business of winning souls from the kingdom of darkness to the kingdom of God? If God has given the Church a mandate and the ability to take the gospel into the very living rooms of millions, will that same Church respond?

Online ministry is one form of soul-winning with huge potential, but there's still nothing like a preacher with a Bible and an audience in front of him. While souls cannot be saved without God's power and anointing, people who need God also require a local church with a passion for souls. They require a personal touch and one to one ministry. I believe some anointed ministries and churches are already meeting this demand and doing a good job, but many others are merely playing Church. Online Church is exciting in many ways, but it will never replace the fellowship of believers meeting inside the walls of God's ordained Church and fellowshipping together. Now is not the time to entertain, either online or inside a church. People need ministering to, and only when we preach Christ as the solution to our world's problems will this happen and more importantly, only then will souls be converted. **James McConnell**

Follow me, and I will make you to become fishers of men.

Matthew 4:19

27.

The Art of Soul Winning

The life of Jesus is proof that every sincere soul-winner must first learn to sacrifice and then prepare for God's assignment. The word discipline is derived from the word disciple", and Jesus said, "And whosoever doth not bear his cross, and come after me, cannot be my disciple.". People talk about men having "a burden for souls." They ask "how can I get this?! But a burden comes from time spent in God's presence, and then action follows. A real burden from God is the Spirit of the "great evangelist" coming upon a person to enable them and give them the desire to lead people to the Lord. We are supposed to excel in spiritual gifts. Many people have skills but haven't excelled in those gifts, while others don't possess the gifts as much as some have excelled even in the little they had. I would ask: if soul winning is a job, how many people would still be employed? The great commission is the greatest priority of the church. **James McConnell**

The Pastor makes no secret that he has based his entire life and ministry on his actual role model - the Lord Jesus Christ. From his earliest days in the church, time and again, he studied the life of Christ and His methods of converting men and women.

Therefore, when it comes to "winning souls," he's convinced that people can learn how to become great soul-winners. He not only believes soul winning is an art, but neither has there ever been a greater soul-winner than Christ Himself - exemplified when Christ met the Woman at the well in John chapter four.

In this same scene, one of the most potent examples of leading a soul to Christ, we see the master soul-winner of all at work.

In general, hallmarks of Christ's ministry are particularly evident in this extraordinary encounter, which includes showing great concern and interest for the individual (Luke fifteen being an example of his "concern for others" when He spoke about going after the lost sheep and the lost son.)

The mark of all great shepherds and servants of God is the desire to pursue lost causes and lost or straggling sheep.

Noticeable also is how Christ never shunned inconvenience to win one soul because the Bible records how he travelled through Samaria, a hostile place for Jews, to win this one sinful Woman to the Kingdom of God.

Would we have done this?

It's clear He also worked under a strong sense of urgency and constraint because we are informed: "He needs (must) to go through Samaria." A winsome personality is crucial in attracting people to God and His kingdom, something Jesus enormously possessed.

Jesus may not have been Charismatic in His theology, but he had charisma in abundance, a character trait all evangelists require. In addition, Christ was friendly, sympathetic, and engaging in his approach.

In short, he was a nice person. But He was also determined and persistent.

We can only learn from those we admire, and Christ was held in the highest esteem, even by His enemies.

Christ was not cold or self-important, although his authority was evident.

A master soul winner, Jesus played on ordinary circumstances in life to provide opportunities for soul winning to take place. True, He was Divine and the Son of God, but His methods are worthy of consideration.

He deliberately meant for His disciples to copy His excellent approach to evangelism so budding soul winners can benefit greatly by studying the life of Christ and, in particular, the story of the woman at the well.

For example, even when He sat down at the well due to tiredness, He used it as an opportunity to influence the woman beside him. Jesus also asked a favour of the woman that He would eventually win to the kingdom, requesting a drink of water.

Again, there was no pride or conceit apparent in Christ, just openness and humility.

Speaking to her alone, he dealt with any questions she had and overcame any religious obstacles.

Interestingly, however, Jesus refused to condemn the woman at the well. Yet, remarkably, she still accepted she was a sinner in need of a saviour. Instead, He discussed only things that could bless her life and meet her needs with her. Once she understood and announced Christ Himself as her Saviour, Jesus then moved on.

What can we learn from this tactful approach?

What stands out about the Masters' ministry is that He was continually willing to go the extra mile to win people to Himself and the kingdom. He travelled 30 miles on foot to win a single soul. He didn't have the luxury of public transport; He did whatever it took to reach the lost. He had power, authority, and knowledge in all things, but compassion. Every soul-winner must have this balance. Of course, His anointing didn't come cheap. Where was He, for example, between the ages of 12 in the temple and 30 when He began His earthly ministry? He was obviously in a place of preparation for his life's purpose, which we can all learn from today. People seem to assume they can set up a pulpit and preach, and souls will follow. It doesn't always work like this. Without preparation time spent in the presence of the Lord, souls will not be influenced in any way. For example, after I had received my life's calling to the ministry, I would rise early and seek God for the business of the day. I would then visit hospitals before 8 am and still make it back for a board meeting with my Pastors at 9 am. Focus and a selfless attitude are critical if a Pastor or minister wishes to see lots of fish caught in the net. **James McConnell**

Of course, as a young boy, Jesus was also prolific because the Bible records how the scribes and Pharisees were "astonished at his doctrine: for his word was with power" **Luke 4:32** One translation reads, "They were astounded at His understanding and the answers that he gave."

From that point on, the Bible says He "increased in knowledge and stature and the grace of God was upon him" **Luke 2:40**

While I recognised and understood the deity of Christ as a young man, but also His identification with humanity, I copied many of the Lord's soul-winning tactics and don't regret doing so because God's way is a perfect way. Don't forget, Jesus taught His disciples how to win souls, a teaching that is still available for many today. In the book of Matthew, Jesus told his disciples: "Follow me, and I will make you fishers of men" (Matthew 4:19). However, the original reads I will make you "to become" fishers of men. Therefore, it is possible to become a soul-winner. Soul-winning art can be learned, so I invested all my time in getting this trade, and it paid off. Of course, I studied other aspects of the character of Christ, which was my duty to do. Of course, a person needs the anointing to help attract souls, something we have already covered. Still, soul-winning is a trade like every other trade, and one needs to study it, learn how to do it, and follow the methods of the master soul-winner who, of course, is the Lord Jesus Christ. **James McConnell**

J I Packer wrote, "The preacher should work to convert his congregation; the wife should work to save her unbelieving husband. Christians are sent to convert, and they should not allow themselves, as Christ's representatives in the world, to aim at anything less. Therefore, evangelising is not simply teaching, instructing, and imparting information to the mind. There is more to it than that. Evangelising includes the endeavour to elicit a response to the truth taught."

Just as Christ demonstrated discipline and servanthood, the Pastor has also tried to live a life of sacrifice. To those who know him well, he is referred to as "servant" but can't recall when or where he received this endearing term. Nevertheless, it is an honest compliment given that his life has been dedicated to serving his church, people, and His Saviour, Jesus.

The life of Jesus is proof that every sincere soul-winner must first learn to sacrifice and then prepare for God's assignment. The word discipline is derived from the word disciple", and Jesus said, "And whosoever doth not bear his cross, and come after me, cannot be my disciple.". People talk about men having "a burden for souls." They ask "how can I get this?! But a burden comes from time spent in God's presence, and then action follows. A real burden from God is the Spirit of the "great evangelist" coming upon a person to enable them and give them the desire to lead people to the Lord. We are supposed to excel in spiritual gifts. Many people have skills but haven't excelled in those gifts, while others don't possess the gifts as much as some have excelled even in the little they had. I would ask: if soul winning is a job, how many people would still be employed? The great commission is the greatest priority of the church. **James McConnell**

Oswald J Smith said - "Any church that is not seriously involved in helping to fulfil the great commission has forfeited its right to exist."

The Pastor maintains to become a successful soul-winner requires more than preaching ability; it requires knowledge of the gospel. Paul stated in his letter to the Romans, "For I am not ashamed of the gospel of Christ: for it is the power of God unto salvation to every one that believeth; to the Jew first, and also to the Greek **Romans1:16**

Two things are vital in any would-be gospel exponent; firstly, a recognition that the power is in the person of Christ. Therefore, it is apparent that neither man's ability nor methods will make any difference if they are not preaching the gospel's good news. The gospel is the power to win souls, or like Jonah, the prophet said: "Salvation is of the Lord". Secondly, great gospel preachers understand that the message is for the entire world, not just a selected few. Paul brought the gospel to the children of Israel, but according to Romans, he was also called to preach to all the nations. **James McConnell**

One of the more controversial elements over the years of the soul-winning methods of Pastor McConnell was what was known at Whitewell as "the appeal."

For those not familiar with this method, once the gospel message has gone out, it is followed by a clear-cut invitation to allow people to give their lives to Christ. Thus, it is often referred to as 'throwing out the net' or, as some unkindly suggest.

This invitation has often felt prolonged at the end of the service, but most sincere evangelists like James McConnell believe it is essential. On many a hot, sticky summer evening and with the church bulging with people, the sight of the Tabernacle choir ladies using their Sunday bulletins as a cooling fan at the end of the service was a regular occurrence. Yet, it never distracted the Pastor from finishing his appeal. As far as he was concerned, the saving of some poor soul was more important than his congregation spending a few extra minutes in what definitely at times felt like a sauna.

For example, the Pastor believes the appeal is not only the most crucial point of the service but also impossible to leave out if one is serious about what the Bible describes as 'catching fish.'

Most previous soul-winning legends all used the method of appeal following their addresses. One illustration is the late Billy Graham's unforgettable sight searching for souls in a sea of faces at the end of his famous crusades. The Pastor also confesses to how he drew inspiration from John Wesley's approach to the appeal after Wesley became deeply impacted on life and death issues as a child following a rectory fire. In 1709, when Wesley was five years old, Wesley and others were caught in a fire, and while all the others managed to escape from the house, John remained stuck on the upper floor. Finally, a local parishioner helped the young man escape the place about to burn down, which Wesley would often later describe as being like "a brand plucked out of the fire," quoting Zechariah 3:2, to describe the incident. This childhood deliverance had a massive bearing on Wesley's spiritual perception and subsequently became part of the Wesley legend, attesting to his unique destiny and extraordinary work.

He hadn't just been privileged to peer into heavenly places but was also uniquely exposed to the location of burning called hell. Thus, he always vowed to give people an immediate opportunity to accept Christ through the appeal.

People have criticised the appeal at Whitewell and me for labouring through it. Still, we are talking about life and death issues, and tomorrow is not promised to anyone according to the Lord Jesus's words. So if you believe that and are serious about winning souls, how can you watch people leave your church without deciding? To use an old saying: a preacher needs to strike while the iron is hot. In the parable of the sower, Jesus talked about wayside ground and how when a man had sowed, some seeds fell by the wayside, and the fowls came and devoured them up. *It is similar when preaching God's word. The preacher plants the seed, but it must be responded to before the enemy can come and destroy it.* **James McConnell**

It's not just Wesley who inspired the Pastor to "get serious" about winning souls, however, through the appeal method. He admits to being significantly influenced by what he describes as legendary soul-winners such as CH Spurgeon, George Jeffreys, Reinhard Bonnke, and Billy Graham, the latter being one of the greatest soul-winners of any generation in Pastor McConnell's opinion.

Billy Graham was a man sent by God, totally anointed in fulfilling his life's purpose of winning souls. His voice, authority, and personality were heaven-sent and designed to reach the lost. I recall someone criticising him, finding fault with him, and even suggesting he was not of God. I responded that Billy Graham had touched millions' lives, and only heaven knows how many people he introduced to Jesus. How many people have you led to Christ? I asked. That was the end of the conversation. **James McConnell**

More locally, he believes men like Willie Mullen, the Rev Ian Paisley, Sam Workman, and Sandy Wilson were anointed soul winners.

Notwithstanding, as we conclude this section on soul-winning, two questions are arguably the most important when discerning what the Pastor has learned from a lifetime of soul-winning. Firstly, except for the Bible, which books should an inspiring young preacher read more than any other? Secondly, which theological point should remain uppermost in the mind of any budding preacher?

Without a doubt, I would encourage every young Bible student to read Spurgeon's lectures to his students. It is a prolific book and still incredibly relative and will help a ministry grow. It has that perfect balance of both grace and truth operating together, not to mention beautiful moments of humour. Regarding theology, without both grace and truth, considerable damage can be done in a preacher's life and in the life of those who hear him. A soul winner needs to have this equilibrium. John the Baptist announced the New Testament ministry of Jesus by saying He was a man "full of grace and truth." I have always tried to keep this balance because the truth is essential while grace is even more crucial. Remember, Paul said, "Where sin abounds, therefore doth grace abound even more. **James McConnell**

For those serious about winning souls to the Kingdom of God, the latter point is worth this book's price alone.

When a preacher receives a divine revelation of the grace of God, the floodgates of heaven will spring wide open to a whole host of people. So if preachers are keen to see an increase in their churches, the Pastor is adamant - preach God's grace and watch your ministry take off. When grace and truth replace law and legalism, expect people to come rushing back to God.

The Bible states, "For the law was given through Moses, but grace and truth came by Jesus Christ **John 1:17**

When a man was once asked to explain why the preaching of the Pastor seemed to be so effective, he replied, "many enthusiastic but legalistic evangelists preach you under the seat, but the Pastor leaves room for hope and lifts you back on top of the seat." It was a wise observation. Great soul winners do not ignore the subject of sin, but they also know how to offer people hope and introduce them to the solution to sin – the Lord Jesus Christ.

Every preacher and believer's job is to love others without stopping to inquire whether or not they are worthy.

That message hasn't changed.

As a new generation approaches, so does a revelation of God's great grace and hope-filled messages. God is still raising preachers, directors, producers, and scriptwriters who know how to present the gospel in all its purity, power, and balance.

Herein is the art form to the continual winning of souls.

Passion for the Last Generation

It is not by might nor by power, but by My Spirit,' saith the Lord of hosts.
Zechariah 4:6

28.

Come Hell or Corona

I believe we are the last generation, the seventh and final Church, just like Jesus said. He described it as the "amen church" or "the church of the last days." However, people are talking doom and gloom today due to the harmful and destructive patterns emerging in our world - something understandable - but we must remember before Jesus returns, the Bible promises a tremendous outpouring of His Spirit. Already we see this revival taking place around the world, but more in African countries than in Europe. Christ mentioned "buy of me gold" in Revelation; He allowed the churches to enjoy tremendous influence in the last days, despite the high apostasy level. This gold speaks of His spirit, but the eyesalve mentioned in Revelation, chapter 3, symbolises the anointing and the born-again mentality. Only the anointing will suffice if we are to be effective in the last generation. My advice to leaders and their people is to go into a room and ask God to anoint you to be a blessing to your church, community, and nation. This is far more important than holding services for no other reason than entertaining people or making a living. There's an invitation to every leader or clergyman, woman, and believer to seek the gold Christ has made available. For this reason, I do not see the future world as bleak as some are often keen to suggest. Similar to the Church of Laodicea, taking our faith for granted and putting earthly prosperity before our salvation could end up proving costly. In Revelation, Jesus warned that He would "spit out" lukewarm disciples. Instead, Christ is looking for followers who will continue to remain faithful to Him even after He has blessed them abundantly. He is looking for people willing to build things and leave a testimony of God's saving grace. **James McConnell**

Most ardent Bible scholars today believe that we live in the last generation.

The 21st-century generation is at serious risk due to many difficulties and dangers. Atrocities continue worldwide, and the global terrorist and extremist menace show no signs of abating. The failure to resolve the underlying causes of extremism and terrorism continues, and natural disasters and even pandemics threaten our civilisation.

Of course, we are witnessing none other than tomorrow's front page headlines already written in the Bible.

As Jesus foretold of the end times, there are wars, famines, natural disasters, and pandemics **Matthew 24**

No wonder the term "the last generation" produces uncomfortable and apprehensive thoughts in many people's minds. For some, the phrase creates the scary reality of earth's inability to sustain life infinitely; for others, the fear and threat of nuclear warfare; and for others still, an Armageddon-like ending with horrendous consequences.

Yet, for those looking forward to the soon return of the Lord Jesus Christ, these frightening prospects are strangely comforting and exciting in the light of His Second Coming, providing great hope to a seemingly hopeless generation.

Jesus encouraged His followers that when all these things would begin to take place, "then look up and lift your heads, for your redemption draws near." **Matthew 24.33**

Most people now agree that the world cannot continue to witness division and destruction on this scale in recent times, but Bible prophecy is also crucial in pinpointing where we are in history. This is because the Bible makes perfect sense of our current senselessness.

For example, the Book of Revelation deals with seven letters to seven churches in Asia Minor (modern-day Turkey) (Revelation 2-3)

Although Christ is the speaker, the message is delivered by John the Divine.

The latter highlights the successes and failures of the recipient churches and calls for repentance from each congregation. These letters are prophetic, showing modern-day Christians the traps and snares which can hinder believers, especially during the last generation of Laodicea.

In the first century A.D., John became exiled on the island of Patmos, a Roman penal colony near Asia Minor, for preaching about Jesus.

While in Patmos, John was visited by the Holy Spirit and received prophetic visions instructing him to: "Write on a scroll what you see and send it to the seven churches:" to Ephesus, Smyrna, Pergamum, Thyatira, Sardis, Philadelphia, and Laodicea" **Revelation1:1-2, 9-11**

John wrote about the last generation, Laodicea: "I know your works; you are neither cold nor hot. I wish that you were either cold or hot. So, because you are lukewarm, and neither cold nor hot, I am about to spit you out of my mouth."—**Revelation 3:15–16**

Why does the Book of Revelation author call the Church of Laodicea "lukewarm"? The Church of Laodicea is the last of seven churches addressed in Revelation, and many Bible experts agree it also represents the last generation. Revelation's seven churches were among several early Christian communities in Asia Minor. These seven churches have been deliberately selected to receive Christ's apocalyptic message due to their influential and highly populated location. The idea seems to have been to spread the gospel message to the Christian communities in the province.

Laodicea was a thriving industrial and commercial centre. Still, Christ uses it as a symbol of lack of spirituality rebuking it for its lukewarm faith and, of course, rather shockingly, threatening to "spit" the congregation out of His mouth. Strikingly, the Lord Jesus criticised this Church and generation for placing more importance on material things than spiritual things. Yet Jesus also gave this generation a lifeline and solution stating that regardless of their worldly prosperity, He could lead them to true riches, declaring;

"Because thou sayest, I am rich, and increased with goods, and need nothing; and knowest not that thou art wretched, and miserable, and poor, and blind, and naked: I counsel thee to buy of me gold tried in the fire, that thou mayest be rich; and white raiment, that thou mayest be clothed, and that the shame of thy nakedness do not appear; and anoint thine eyes with eyesalve, that thou mayest see" **Revelation 3:17-18**

In this latter thought, the Pastor finds hope for our present generation. No matter what takes place in the future, regardless of the unprecedented situation the world now finds itself in, he is convinced God is in control and has a positive plan for those living on earth today.

There is, of course, a difference between leaving a legacy and an inheritance. The former speaks of impact in a person's life, while the latter usually relates to material possessions being passed on to family members and friends.

While David left provisions for his son Solomon, his life and legacy were of considerably more incredible value. Even his words before he died in the book of Kings provided hope and a direction for those following after him. The opening paragraphs of the book of Kings state: "When David's time to die was near, he told his son, Solomon, "I am going the way of all the earth. So be strong. Show yourself to be a man. Do what the Lord your God tells you. Walk in His ways. Keep all His Laws and His Word by what is written in the Law of Moses. Then you will do well in all that you do and in every place you go. **1 Kings 2: 1-3**

An inheritance is good, but a legacy like this is of even greater value.

During his ministry, the Pastor made provision for the generation that would follow him by leaving substantial funds and building facilities to the current Senior Pastor, David Purse, for a rainy day - but the real legacy he has left is his undying passion for Christ.

His "one-liners" and "little pearls of wisdom" to his people (included in his book McConnellisms) will far outlast any preparation for a younger generation. Nevertheless, he became too aware of his mortality during his later years, especially following ill-health, causing him to save money and thoughtfully prepare for the future. Having been diagnosed with heart trouble, cancer, and diabetes, rather than retire, the Pastor redoubled his efforts to leave his Church and ministry in good shape by funding many projects, including building the McConnell Youth Complex - a purpose-built centre for youth activities.

So, how does the last generation face a future he knows he won't be a part of.

By continuing to preach the Word in season and out of season. Jesus said: "Occupy till I come," which means we are to serve the Lord and make provision as if He is coming any minute. One translation of this text reads: "engage in business till I come." Jesus also said: "I must be about my Father's business." Unfortunately, the reality of this is quite different. The Church in the British Isles, in particular, is fast asleep. So many distractions derail people from preaching the gospel and the Second Coming of the Lord Jesus Christ doctrine. The Bible says that "unless God builds the house, they labour in vain which build it." We must pray that God the Holy Spirit will raise men and women to reach a dying and hopeless world in the last days. Prayer has always been important to me and at Whitewell, but I don't recall it currently being as vital as now. Being retired helps you see things you might have missed otherwise. In other words, as discussed in the section about God's Word, we need to go back to the future. **James McConnell**

Again, it is essential to ask: is this realistic in such a fast-paced and forward-thinking generation? Can this seemingly backward suggestion of the Pastor succeed?

Aren't we living in a generation of progressive thinkers with a desire to forget the past and live in the present?

"Don't look back," "move forward," and "keep on going" is the cry of most positive thinkers, even evangelicals today.

It is realistic to go back and start again. For example, if I were back in the ministry, I would call prayer meetings weekly from Monday to Friday until God moves. Sunday would be a great day of worship and praise. I would start again from the bottom. I would teach young people to pray for an hour and a half every night and train them to seek God properly. No "happy-clappy stuff," just good old-fashioned seeking the Lord. I did it for over sixty years, and generations were blessed. I sowed the seed, and many reaped the harvest. It was an extraordinary, even vintage period, and if I had the chance, I would do it all again the same way. The old paths and ancient landmarks still apply. God is a spirit, and they who worship Him must worship him in spirit and truth. Call these methods old-fashioned if you like, but don't judge them until you try them. **James McConnell**

The Pastor's views of connecting with God in the last generation are perhaps not as oversimplified or antediluvian as they may first appear. Many church leaders face considerable challenges to reform their separate churches, which bring pressure to "move with the times" and embrace "new things."

People desire a "new thing," yet maybe it is the "old thing" that works. The odds may be stacked against the church, but that is always when the church has significantly shone.

When David went to fight Goliath, he too was facing an uphill battle, even an impossible task which could surely only end in inevitable defeat.

Yet having been handed Saul's mighty armour to help him bring down Goliath, the young David quickly realised the armour and the military equipment were insufficient for his quest to defeat Goliath and become King. So instead, David preferred to repeat a strategy that had always worked previously, especially when he slew a bear and a lion and triumphed due to his trust in the living God. In other words, he reverted to old tried and tested methods.

The Bible records, "David fastened his sword to his armour and tried to walk, for he had not tested them. And David said to Saul, "I cannot walk with these, for I have not tested them." So David took them off" **1 Samuel 17:39**

Before slaying Goliath, David revealed his determination to stick to "tried and tested" methods: "Then David said to the Philistine, "You come to me with a sword and with a spear and with a javelin, but I come to you in the name of the LORD of hosts, the God of the armies of Israel, whom you have defied **1 Samuel 17:45**

By all means, the Church should embrace the technology at its disposal and seek to use other methods to reach the unsaved. However, the words of Zechariah still apply - " it is not by might, nor by power, but by My Spirit,' saith the Lord of hosts" In this age of deadly pandemics, the former methods may not seem appropriate, even possible. Still, they've never failed before, and they can succeed again. **James McConnell**

Stepping back from his duties as a full-time minister in 2014 after he retired from the ministry was no easy task for Pastor McConnell. Especially during a time of immense opposition, indeed, he readily admits that it was "the hardest thing I have ever had to do."

When he retired, he perfectly understood that it was the end of his ministry at Whitewell, although not the end of his preaching by a long shot.

Preaching and being a Pastor is in his DNA and part of his passion for the things of God. He desperately wants to keep going, keep advancing, and moving forward for the Kingdom of God. Despite experiencing deteriorating health just before the publication of this book, come hell or corona; he's determined to "endure until the end," just like Jesus commanded.

Nevertheless, just as David made provision for Solomon and then took a back seat and watched from the sidelines, the Pastor has had to get used to remaining in the background at his local assembly at Whitewell, something he initially found extremely difficult.

The closing of churches worldwide due to Covid hasn't helped the local Church's growth, but it was for a short season. In other ways, the Church has reached many people through online ministry and risen to the challenge and even expanded, all in a different sense. More importantly, the pandemic has proved a real wake-up call for the Church. Before the virus outbreak, many churches were shallow in teaching and non-existent in power. Some were ticking over and holding their own. They had become far too comfortable, and a shock to the system has proved no bad thing. Notwithstanding, and extraordinarily, some churches seem to remain unaffected by everything, and what I have witnessed has been depressing, but like David, I have stood back from it. We are where we are, but the

Church should be advancing, not retreating in these last days. I pray this will continue to be the case. **James McConnell**

The question is not can the church survive, but will the Church overcome?

According to Jesus in Matthew chapter 16, the answer is yes, for He says, "I will build my Church, and the gates of hell shall not prevail against it **Matthew 16:18**

Come hell or Corona, Jesus has promised to build His Church!

Poor preaching, pitiable politics, and even unwelcome pandemics can't prevent the plan of God from coming to pass.

Remember, the Church has always provided hope into uncertainty and certainty into hopelessness. It is no different today, even in the face of Covid-19 and Coronavirus and a host of other obstacles and sinister developments in our world.

God is in control!

The light is still shinning in the darkness!

The Church has responded to these setbacks and the global pandemic with flexibility and unshakable hope.

But that's not to say that the changes are not challenging, and the plan is monumental. But unfortunately, too many churches and ministries remain unfocused on a generation in great need?

I do believe we are in a state similar to the Ichabod generation, which Jesus foretold in Revelation, chapter three with His disgust at the Laodicea generation, which, as mentioned, is the last generation. However, while the Church may be struggling to adapt to change, God has not left or abandoned us. He has promised never to leave or forsake us. Therefore, the Church must keep advancing no matter what. I have always said, 'If a church holds its own, then the devil is holding his'. Without a vision, the people perish, which happens in too many cases today. Ichabod has arrived because of a lack of vision. After one or two successes, Pastors sit back and admire what God has done, but the trick is to give God thanks and then keep pressing on. One battle won't win the war. The Church must endure until the end, and the Church must have a vision of the future. Asking people to attend each week without telling them where they are going is unacceptable and doomed to fail. **James McConnell**

Following Covid-19, church gatherings were closed down for the first time in living memory, leaving people to meet on Zoom and do Church online, and the landscape in these last days has changed even more since. Underground churches and house plants have emerged where necessary, and the pandemic has produced both positive and negative issues. Most people can point to the book of Joshua and relate entirely to the words "We have not passed this way before." , however, the Pastor and his generation have been here before, and he insists many survived to tell the tale.

As for the virus, I would encourage people to believe in God, according to Psalm 91. I can only speak for myself. I have always trusted God, and let's remember I came from a diseased home when half my family was wiped out due to T.B. It was an awful plague that caused many deaths. I can still remember drinking out of one cup, using one fork, and going to the doctor every six months for an x-ray. I wasn't affected, but that doesn't mean I am a more excellent spiritual than anyone else. I just trusted God. My generation also lived through the war and the Troubles in Ulster, yet God proved as faithful as ever. God is dependable no matter what is taking place. He hasn't gone away, you know! Jesus said, "According to your faith, be it unto you." **James McConnell**

In summary, the Church of the last generation will rise or fall, depending on the leaders' faith and wisdom. They are the ones who will set the bar and standard or miss their day of visitation. Times may indeed be bleak, but God is not weak. On the contrary, he is strong and can be trusted fully to finish what He started and build His church.

Behold, I will do a new thing; now it shall spring forth; shall ye not know it?
I will even make a way in the wilderness and rivers in the desert.
Isaiah 43:19

29.

A Browser Window to the World

When 9-11 happened in New York, people thought the end of the world was coming, yet that was precisely when the Church needed to be healthy. Many churches, including Whitewell, took advantage of the situation and went out to the community with the Gospel resulting in thousands of souls being saved. In the same way, following Coronavirus, I believe the Church was pushed out of its comfort zone to reach a scared and dying world by using online and other conventional methods. The book of Hebrews says, "Jesus Christ the same yesterday today and forever. No matter what Satan throws in the way of the Church, God always has an answer. **James McConnell**

Before Covid cruelly visited our world, the jury was still out concerning modern technology and many new methods introduced by revolutionary church leaders. For years, the contemporary Church has consistently clashed with the traditional Church on this issue, sparking, at times, some pretty heated exchanges and viewpoints.

Not anymore.

In this era of live streaming and social media, who would have imagined that online TV and a host of technological inventions would prove so vital, particularly during the national health pandemic?

Following the big "shut down" due to COVID-19 in March 2020, churches, big and small, rushed to use this technology to meet their parishioners' needs.

While phone calls and Facetimes proved essential in keeping in touch with people, it was the broadcasting of God's Word through these present-day channels which not only helped carry congregations through unprecedented times of uncertainty but also spoke into the lives of many apprehensive and frightened people who may never previously have attended a church.

Clergy, who might once have been sceptical of the online ministry's virtues, were all of a sudden grateful for the opportunity to stay in touch with people from their Church while also reaching many new converts with the Gospel.

A large window to the world sprung wide open – the Church Online.

HD cameras, Facebook Live, YouTube, Zoom, and Roku all came to the fore at the height of the pandemic, enabling the Church to broadcast songs, produce sermons and prayers and dare to go where it had never gone before.

"Must do" became a great master for many evangelically minded churches.

Yes, churches had previously used the online ministry, but just as many had not. The pandemic forced these assemblies to not only adapt but change their approach for the better. The result is lots of places of worship have doubled, even trebled in size, due to a new and vibrant online congregation. Suddenly long-standing church critics of these inventions are incredibly thankful for such a lifeline. Without them, after all, the Church would have had no voice, yet that voice was multiplied as the Gospel went forth to every nation just like Jesus intended. The result is millions of people worldwide are now watching national and local church services every week. They ask hard questions about life and death and find the answers via various online creative church ministries adapted to change at record speeds. People are concerned about jobs, food, family issues, and rightly so.

However, meeting this fear head-on is the Church. Online church ministries are now part of the "new normal," reaching homes of people who don't or can't go to Church ensuring their spiritual needs are met.

Hats off to numerous assemblies and their members to discover innovative ways to reach their communities and further afield during the pandemic, even at breakneck speed. Many quick-thinking pastors and their staff hit the ground running, embracing the online challenge of "going into all the world to preach the gospel." **Mark 16:15** Even churches with less technology at their disposal seemed to cope remarkably well. Post Coronavirus, many have been forced to stay at home, live local, and avoid contact with each other, yet paradoxically, many personal conversations about faith have taken place. At the most unlikely time, God birthed something new, something even the enemy didn't see coming, or indeed the Church!

Is this surprising?

"Behold, I will do a new thing; now it shall spring forth; shall ye not know it? I will even make a way in the wilderness and rivers in the desert." **Isaiah 43:19**

God is a God of new things.

He can make a way where there seems to be no way. Even in this last and apathetic generation, God can shock and surprise us with good things, yes, even during a global health emergency.

"Behold, I do a new thing", was the word spoken by God to deliver His people out of their seventy-year captivity into liberation and redemption. God was calling His people out from the old and into the new. He was calling things that were not as though they had already happened. As far as heaven was concerned, it was already a done deal. It is not the most robust or intelligent that survives in this harsh and unforgiving world, and it is often the most adaptable to change. Of course, morality doesn't change; neither does the Gospel's message, but God's methods do. He would announce hope for humanity through Jesus Christ and the Gospel's grace. During their darkest days, God offered a new and effective means of living and ministering without altering His central message.

Here is a question: Are we expecting God to do a new thing in our lives?

That may seem overwhelming when we consider our present circumstances but take courage – the Bible declares that God has made a way and created a path to lead us to better days, even when darkness has covered the earth. He has still managed to place rivers of provision to refresh in a time of sorrow.

A question is: will we accept His generous and life-saving invitation?

Will we drink from this well of new opportunities? Jesus said: If anyone thirsts, let him come to me and drink. Rivers of living water will brim and spill out of the depths of anyone who believes in me this way, just as the Scripture says. **John 7:38**

Despite the hostile and even alarming year 2020, there is much potential to be found right now in the Church of Jesus Christ if we continue to believe God and speak NEW things into the wilderness or your desert seasons. The Psalmist said: "Taste and see that the Lord is good, blessed is the man that trusts in him." **Psalm 34:8**

In many ways, Covid-19 created a necessary space to re-examine what God is doing to the Church and worldwide. For example, today, we may have a smaller gathering numerically in church assemblies, but a deeper, more connected church appears to have surfaced. Moreover, these spiritual leaders have managed to use the crisis as a genuine opportunity to establish more meaningful personal relationships.

According to prophesy, God does not require big crowds to move, although big groups will converge again to the Church in the latter days. Notwithstanding, if a revival is likely to happen, it will occur in the local Church where people are part of one vision. That's where many revivals have occurred in the past. Some revivals started with just a couple of people whose hearts were in touch with God. It is how Whitewell began with only a scattering of sheep. If a Pastor and his flock are of one mind, spirit, and unified, no matter what takes place, God can do miracles amongst the last generation, even beyond previous ones. Jesus said, "He that believeth on me, the works that I do shall he also do, and greater works than these shall he do; because I go unto my Father. The challenges and obstacles are no different for this last generation than the previous ones. Great church leaders know how to turn a negative situation into a positive one. **James McConnell**

Checking on the flock and their wellbeing has become more frequent.

Church leaders are finally serving their congregations in the manner Jesus commanded. Rather than continually asking for something, including more significant donations, the Church encourages them to participate actively. Mailing lists and weekly videos have become crucial in keeping congregations informed. Praying for individuals and encouraging them has also been a vital form of outreach in these last days. It's been a stressful yet fabulous time to Pastor and shepherd people through a storm. The Church has lived out the words of the book of Acts "Keep watch over yourselves and all the flock of which the Holy Spirit has made you overseers. Be shepherds of the church of God, which he bought with his blood" **Acts 20:28**

People are no longer focused on the wrong stuff like church programmes and laborious teachings. Instead, inside spirit-filled churches, people have felt the benefits of personal pastoring and attention, making them feel part of their church family.

Following a genuinely horrendous setback for the Church and society after Coronavirus's onset, remarkably, God has used this unlikely scenario to reach out and meet His people's needs. The Church may not look the same as before. It may appear less impressive in the eyes of the flesh. But this renewed Church is what Jesus wanted and meant when he encouraged it to come and buy from him gold in the book of Revelation. He promised it would be a more prosperous church in ways we could never have imagined before COVID-19. So revitalised, this Church can, in the last generation, witness to the rule and reign of Jesus Christ, the hope of the world. While the Pastor firmly believes the old paths are the best, he has long accepted that the Church does need to adapt to a changing and ever-demanding generation. Flexibility is the key to progress. The Pastor made a habit of interacting with and learning about the next generation during his sixty years in ministry. He survived decades of development within the Church and, for the most part, stuck to tried and tested methods, yet at the same time, the Pastor was always open to embracing new approaches. He became flexible and open to the moving of the Spirit.

When I was ministering, new things were continually emerging. I didn't understand them myself or how they worked, but I realised that good and evil are in everything, positive and negative, so I decided to use whatever methods I could to help spread the Gospel. Daniel said that knowledge would increase in the last days, so we should neither be surprised by this nor be afraid of it. As Paul said, 'I tried to be all things to all men that I might win them to Christ.' God gave me the people I needed, equipped in media and technology, which brought about an explosion in our ministry worldwide. This development has continued at a rapid speed. I don't think the Church will ever look the same again, especially post Coronavirus, but the thing to remember is that while methods constantly change, the message must never change. It has taken time to recover from Coronavirus, not just in evangelical circles, but in all walks of life, yet we can heal, and we are doing.
James McConnell

As stated earlier, despite the increase and popularity of the online Church, there should and will always be a gathering of God's people in a church building (Hebrews 10:25). Still, due to the power of technology, Church Online has shown the potential to go well beyond the numbers found in a local assembly. Therefore, it is worth quoting again the words found in the book of Isaiah: "Enlarge the place of your tent and let the curtains of your habitations be stretched out; do not hold back; lengthen your cords and strengthen your stakes **Isaiah 54:2**

For example, has there ever been a more critical time or excellent platform to stretch forth and reach the fearful, bringing hope to their hearts and, most of all, introducing them to the love of God? Young people don't care how the Church looks as long as it is on fire for God; it is a place of refuge and hope, saving souls for God's Kingdom and expanding every day. So long as it remains a light in the nation continues to be bold and fearless in reaching the lost, young people will want to be part of it.

If it continues to be a gospel-driven community of believers of all ages, who love, forgive and encourage one another; if it seeks the lost, helps restore the fallen, and carries out the great commission to make disciples of all nations, then the last generation church can and will overcome many of the challenges faced previously by the Pastor and his godly band of men and women.

God is not limited to seasons or people. The Bible states: "To everything, there is a season, and a time to every purpose under heaven A time to be born, and a time to die; a time to plant, and a time to pluck up that which is planted; A time to kill, and a time to heal; a time to break down, and a time to build up; A time to weep, and a time to laugh; a time to mourn, and a time to dance; A time to cast away stones, and a time to gather stones together; a time to embrace, and a time to refrain from embracing; A time to get, and a time to lose; a time to keep, and a time to cast away; A time to rend, and a time to sew; a time to keep silence, and a time to speak; A time to love, and a time to hate; a time of war, and a time of peace **Ecclesiastes 3:1-8**

Approaching the end of his days, the Pastor has come to appreciate those words' accuracy and profoundness. Referring to the many differing seasons he enjoyed, he is honest yet highly hopeful.

I have experienced all those seasons throughout my life, as has the Church of Jesus Christ. Sometimes things are for a season and are never repeated, which may prove the case at Whitewell, but only time will tell. If, however, God wants to repeat or better what God has done before, He can. He did it with Moses and Joshua and with Elijah and Elisha. One thing is sure, whether or not the methods change, the message of the Gospel will remain the same. It is never about the man but always about the message. Seasons change. Churches come and go. People pass away, but God remains and is still the same. He continues faithful during good times and bad. One of the enemy's key weapons is to keep people focused on a time of great success in their lives. It would help if you recognised when one season closes or dies and another arrives. Be brave enough to "move on" and trust God, Who will be faithful through every crisis and season. When Moses died, the people mourned him for only 30 days before God intervened and told them, "Moses my servant is dead; now, therefore, arise, go over this Jordan, thou, and all these people, unto the land which I do give to them, even to the children of Israel. *Don't be afraid of a new season or new things. If God is in the midst, we are in great hands.* **James McConnell**

As already highlighted, churches have seized a meaningful opportunity to connect with their local communities during the Coronavirus crisis and impact people globally. But many people are still suffering from the consequences of the pandemic.

They require genuine healing and hope, and even strength more than ever now. The world is confused and crying out for compassion and words of encouragement. People need to hear "good news," and they need it now.

Of course, where better to go than to the Church - a renowned and reliable hospital for sick souls. In the words of the apostle Peter, "To whom shall we go? thou hast the words of eternal life" **John 6:68** and "Casting all your care upon him; for he careth for you" **1 Peter 5:7**

The last generation's assignment is to take those words of life and comfort and the Kingdom's Gospel's message into the entire world. Due to the explosion of the online Church, never has this objective become more exciting or possible.

The great Methodist preacher John Wesley once said: "I look upon all the world as my parish." Yet neither he nor his generation could have imagined the unusual yet exhilarating situation the Church now finds itself and, at the very end of time. The doors of the Church may have been temporarily closed during the global pandemic, but a browser window swung wide open into every home across the world.

Fearful? Concerned? Frightened?

Not a bit of it. God is doing a new thing and moving in a meaningful and surprising way. Now is the most exciting time in Church history to be a Christian and be alive. It is not the time for the Church to retreat but advance and seize the day.

Did we make a difference in our generation? Did we create a better situation for our people and nation? Hand on the heart "Yes We Did" Can the next generation do something similar? Yes, they can! Can God move in miraculous ways? Yes, I genuinely believe He can! But it isn't going to be easy. Hard work and supernatural assistance will be required.

James McConnell

30.

Yes, We Can - And Yes, God Can Too!

"Those days when God moved mightily at Whitewell were both sovereign and wonderful, but without sounding boastful, such visits by the Holy Spirit don't grow on trees. Ours was unusual in that it lasted for years rather than months. I couldn't have endured without the help and loyalty of many of the great people God assigned to me. They were, and still are, the cream of the crop. Did we make a difference in our generation? Did we create a better situation for our people and nation? Hand on the heart "Yes We Did" Can the next generation do something similar? Yes, they can! Can God move in miraculous ways? Yes, I genuinely believe He can! But it isn't going to be easy. Hard work and supernatural assistance will be required. **James McConnell**

During his farewell speech in Chicago in 2017, President Barack Obama bookended his Presidency with the words, "Yes, we can. Yes, we did."

The Pastor believes those words aptly apply to Whitewell, the wider christian church, and the last generation as it navigates its way through unprecedented times and goes to battle before the return of the Lord Jesus Christ.

He neither takes for granted nor demands any glory from his years as a serving Pastor in Belfast and rejects any suggestion that the soul-saving phenomenon which has taken place at Whitewell and beyond from 1957 is anything other than a supernatural blessing from God. Instead, he quotes the words of a Psalm: "Not unto us, O Lord, not unto us, but unto thy name give glory, for thy mercy, and for thy truth's sake." **Psalm 115:1**

And, despite the doomsday forecasters, he believes the future is also bright for the last generation. However, whether lightning will strike twice, so to speak, or history repeats itself at Whitewell - a question many have asked -is up to God.

He makes an interesting point. I have rarely heard of any revival or outpouring of God for years, let alone months. Therefore, if ever the goodness of God towards the land of Ulster and to the people of Whitewell is evident, it is in this very disclosure. Thousands of souls were converted as week after week, month after month, and year after year, for generations, the Spirit of God brooded over the ministry at Whitewell. This phenomenon is not to be underestimated. The Whitewell ministry and the Pastor endured criticism and opposition during this prolific season, but God would have His way.

Long before technology, supernatural events were commonplace at Whitewell.

It was "a burning and a shining light."

People visited from all over the world, What made the difference? The anointing of God! Halcyon and holy days they were.

Many recall standing in the balcony on a Sunday evening in the Church on Whitewell Road, unable to leave the building because the anointing had been so heavy. Even the Pastor couldn't, on many occasions, bring the service to a conclusion; such was God's presence upon the worship at the close.

I need to close, but the Holy Spirit won't let me, the Pastor would say, before adding characteristically, Is there another one tonight who will surrender to Christ before we go home. Today people are running to the car park before the second last hymn! There's a chicken to turn or sports fixture to see. No wonder such people seem to miss God's best for their lives. When the authentic presence of God shows up, no born-again believer will wish to leave in a hurry the place of worship. **James McConnell**

But something else was present in those anointed services, which is still essential if the universal Church today hopes to rediscover blessing and success – the love of God. According to the apostle Paul, love is the greatest of all things, and this affection lasted for generations at Whitewell. As a result, the ministry at Whitewell became not just a house but a home for multitudes. It wasn't only a church; it was a family. Numerous neglected and rejected souls, who might otherwise have perished, found shelter at Whitewell while the so-called "great and good" also converged through its doors. The Pastor referred to his people often as a "motley crew" with "pickled vinegar faces." But, of course, it was just tongue-in-cheek stuff because he adored every one of them and would have given them his last cent.

A sweet-smelling fragrance from the presence of God permeated the place, and remarkably an ordinary man yet possessing a heaven-sent mantle managed to steer this godly ship through some of the choppiest waters imaginable, with love for God and his people being his stable compass.

Just as we succeeded in spreading the gospel in our generation, I believe the last age can do likewise, but there's a secret, and I will willingly share it. Although I haven't revealed this secret before, I must do so now. If the people of God love one another and trust in the Lord, and allow Him to build the house, success can be experienced. But if they prefer the arm of the flesh, and even self-promotion, and a competitive spirit, then nothing of any consequence is possible. Can the last generation conquer the forces of darkness in the same way our generation did? Can it overcome in some ways even more insurmountable obstacles? Yes, it can. The victories we saw in the past were not ours but God's. Without Him, nothing of any greatness can emerge. Suppose you ask what part James McConnell played in the development and even success of the Whitewell ministry. In that case, I will quote the words of the Lord Jesus in the book of Luke when he said, "So likewise ye, when ye shall have done all those things which are commanded you, say, We are unprofitable servants: we have done that which was our duty to do." Find this spirit of servanthood again, and anything is possible. Find fearless faith also, and supernatural breakthroughs will come. Find true love in your hearts, and miracles will appear before your eyes. Focus on God, and all things are possible. As Jesus said, "Seek ye first the Kingdom of God and His righteousness all these things shall be added unto you. Reach out again to society, and society will reach out to you. **James McConnell**

In many ways, the Pastor raises a vital point. Recalling what God did in the past is beneficial, even if we recollect the incredible things He has done, but this generation's question is similar to the last. Would God have us rely on the memory of past miracles he once performed while missing the blessing before our eyes? Would he leave us to rely on a system rather than the source of the system? Sometimes we are stuck in a season because we idolise what occurred then, rather than pressing on to even greater things. In this way, we miss God's supply.

As the Pastor has proved, the message never changes, but methods can alter and should be welcomed and re-examined.

Reengaging with society before the return of Christ is vital to reaching the nations.

So firmly believes the General Superintendent of the Elim Church in Ireland, Edwin Michael.

Edwin, himself a progressive leader who has embraced the future despite believing in what the Bible describes as "old paths."

A former Pastor, he stated in a 25th anniversary Whitewell documentary in 2019:

"In some ways, the church is almost back to where it was in the first century. I don't think anyone should expect God to reproduce the past, even the great revivals, though I do believe He can move in revival, yet somehow we want that to look like it did in the 1859 revival or whatever it may be. Coronavirus and other things have changed all this. In some ways, the Church is almost back to where it was in the first century. The Laodicean Church is again dealing with a society like the first-century Church, which is hostile and indifferent to God.That can, of course, be frightening, and it certainly is challenging, but it is not always a bad thing because the Church is then forced to discover how to reengage with and deliver the message of the gospel to today's society. In turn, it causes the Church into a place of prayer to call upon God.

In general, things may look bleak. I don't believe it is terrible at all. What has happened is a wake-up call for the Church, and if the Church responds to God in prayer and becomes more mission-like in its approach, amazing things can transpire. Remember, it is not just about what happens in the Church on a Sunday, but how the Church represents Jesus the other six days of the week out there in society, I believe we can still expect God to move. He is always working!

It was in January 2008 in New Hampshire. President Obama spoke those three powerful words, which are still hitting home today - "Yes, We Can."

These words have impacted political life and people from every background, colour, religion, and aspiration. The terms served as the backbone of his Presidency and have embodied his bedrock belief that all things are possible through hard work and a commitment to hope.

Words are essential, of course. Stories of hope are equally essential.

Who will ever forget that historic occasion when the President-elect spoke to the world from his home city of Chicago as he became the first black president of the United States?

The "Yes We Can" speech was so impactful it even inspired a song and celebrity-packed music video. However, the words and address "Yes, We Can" did more than remind us of his personal history of defying the odds — as the first black president of the Harvard Law Review and on issues such as death penalty reform and a parable about breaking down barriers. It moved a nation and even nations to believe that miracles still have a place in our world.

"Yes, We Can" speaks of an attitude and conviction and is more than a dazzling speechwriters' sentence and PR slogan.

It is who we are, not what we say.

It is important to note that when the Democratic candidate Barack Obama was elected in 2008, his rhetoric differed from his predecessor, George W Bush. Although Obama agreed that there were similar threats to be faced, he notably focused on the possibility of overcoming these challenges and managed to convince the voters that they could retake the path to prosperity and restore America's place as a superpower.

How would this be achieved?

Rather than focus on "I will," his genius used the phrase "Yes, we can."

He rarely, if ever, used the words "I" or "you." Instead, he preferred the power of "we."

He knew what the Bible has already told us, namely that there is power in two rather than one, and the word "we" resonated more with more voters than "I."

Obama's term "we" speaks of humility, excellent team building, and much more motivational and inclusive, and it reveals a heart for others rather than oneself.

Similarly, James McConnell may not have been a political icon like Barack Obama, but he was a spiritual heavyweight when getting people onside and uniting his troops for spiritual battle. PR gurus may not have surrounded him, but he has always known the importance of "we" rather than "you."

Here is the mark of every great leader and would-be preacher.

The secret of the Pastors' ministry involved many people, which bred team spirit and ultimately produced loyalty, camaraderie, and staying power.

James McConnell became a leading voice and figure in the spiritual world, not just in his nation but also throughout many countries worldwide. During his calling, he was very much a revolutionary, standing for many things, even breaking away from a church organisation he had grown up with to follow the voice of God and begin what became a sensational soul-saving ministry at Whitewell.

And he did it all through teamwork and great unity of purpose.

No one can build anything of any significance without courage and a sense of togetherness. Of course, the Pastor was far from perfect and has accepted making many mistakes. But he loved the Lord and, once established, continually fought for unity and harmony within his ranks. So as we push into what he firmly believes is the last generation, Pastor McConnell is optimistic. Asked if this generation of saints can triumph over the terrible tide of wickedness that currently exists, he insists, "Yes, we can."

Can God find a Spurgeon, a Wesley, a Wigglesworth, a Jeffreys, a Graham, or a McConnell?

The Pastor is optimistic -"Yes, He can."

I wish I could do it all over again, the ministry that is, but that's not how God works. It is someone else's turn. Every man has his day, and I had mine. Of course, had I known back when I started what I know now, I often wondered how different things might have been. But God was good to our Church and me, and anyway, there's no point reminiscing when there is an important job to be done by this generation. Like me, our current leaders will be required to take their stand if change comes. They must take the baton and run. My time is over. A new era has come, and a fresh opportunity has arrived, and it may be the last. **James McConnell**

Pastor David Purse, current Senior Pastor of the Whitewell Metropolitan Tabernacle agrees. He has overseen the Church during difficult times, mainly through the Covid-19 nightmare, but he too insists:

Can we win the city? Yes, an emphatic yes, we can, but not if we try to achieve this feat independently. Winning a city requires the supernatural enablement of Almighty God.

If you reach a town, you gain a province, and if you can impact a region, I believe you can touch a nation. The challenge is still there to win our land because all around, people are perishing. People are dying without Christ, and Christ is saying to me, our Church at Whitewell, and to His Church everywhere precisely what he said to the first-century church in the book of Acts "But you will receive power when the Holy Spirit comes on you, and you will be my witnesses in Jerusalem, and all Judea and Samaria, and to the ends of the earth". **David Purse**

There's no doubt that the congregation at Whitewell and the broader congregation of evangelicals worldwide are thankful not just for what has been but also for all that is to come. We may be living in a very different era to the one experienced by CH Spurgeon and his contemporaries during the nineteenth century and, of course, other great preachers of the gospel over the past number of centuries, but the hope is not extinguished; expectation has also arrived.

Fear still exists today on many fronts; however, fear of a lukewarm society, where perhaps great men of God like Spurgeon, like Joseph Parker, Billy Graham, and Pastor James McConnell, will not appear. But despite the changing times, the work of God will continue with the fearless faithful proclamation of the Word of God.

Can God replace the great preachers who have served us so well in the past?

Yes, He can!

Abraham told his son Isaac "And God will provide himself a lamb for a burnt offering **Genesis 22:8**

He must raise a new breed of preachers and believers. It is what God does and does well!

Remember, without the spiritual giants mentioned in this book, such as CH Spurgeon, Joseph Parker, Alexander McClaren, Alexander Whyte, George Jeffreys, Billy Graham, James McConnell, and the many not said, the future may have appeared bleak, but God has never been left without a witness.

As God said to Elijah: "I have reserved unto me seven thousand who have not bowed the knee to Baal," a statement Paul also quoted in the book of Romans.

In other words, God told Elijah that he had a reserved spot for sleeping giants ready to proclaim the glorious gospel of our Lord and Saviour Jesus Christ.

Similarly, God spoke to the children of Israel saying: "Moses, my servant, is dead, now therefore arise, go over this Jordan, thou and all this people, unto the land which I do give to them, even to the children of Israel **Joshua 1:2**

Elijah passed on his mantle to his successor Elijah while Paul passed his to Timothy.

God always has preachers in reserve despite the changing seasons or obstacles along the way.

Have no doubt, come hell or corona, Jesus will build His Church!

His servants die, but His work carries on. Generations change, methods change, but God's message of hope and victory remains.

God will always find a man for the hour and a preacher of preachers to expound His Word. Or, as John Wesley, another prolific exponent of the Word of God, once said: "God may bury his workmen, but the work will always carry on."

While men like James McConnell may be hard to replace, God can find others to carry on his work and expound His Word.

Yes, God can!

That's not to say we should either forget or be ungrateful for what has been. But, on the contrary, we must give God all the glory for this and, in the case of those who experienced it, count it a privilege to have been part of it.

So, in these last days, there is plenty to be optimistic about rather than focusing on the negative. Let's thank God not just for what has been but trust Him implicitly for all that is still to come.

God is on the Throne!

An army of anointed soul winners is on the march.

The future well may appear daunting; it even screams, "No, you can't," but God is saying, "Yes, I can – and Church, you can too!

WHITEWELL METROPOLIT

Epilogue

The Secret of His Success - the Life of David

By James McConnell

It would be remiss to conclude this book without mentioning a man I have revered throughout my Christian life. Besides the Lord Jesus Christ, no person has inspired me like King David in the Old Testament.

Many attributes about this man are appealing, from his humility and devotion to his strength and courage; King David provides us with an enormous encouragement source.

What is most remarkable is that despite experiencing one of the darkest and most terrible deeds committed by a child of God, when David committed adultery with Bathsheba and ordered the killing of her husband Uriah, God had once said of this king, "I have found a man after my own heart."

David was a boy when God spoke those words, but a man was inside him.

Even then, God observed what no one else saw in a Shepherd boy. Yes, David had flaws, but God noticed a King, a warrior, a poet, a leader, and a giant killer, prompting David to receive the greatest of all compliments from God – "a man after my own heart."

What, therefore, was the secret of David's success? How did he manage to impress Almighty God to such an extent? Indeed, why did God bless this man so much and appoint him King over Israel?

One of the reasons given in response to these questions has been because David was quick to repent of his sins, and he was. But this cannot be the real reason why God blessed him and singled him out for such unusual praise. After all, the Bible is full of men and women who were quick to repent, so this would not have made David stand out. It is also clear that God referred to David as "a man after my own heart" long before he committed his sin with Bathsheba, so again it cannot be anything to do with his speedy repentance. It is essential to establish the actual reason God highly favoured David because when we finally realise just why God said what He did about David, we begin to understand how this allows us, in turn, to feel the blessing of the Lord in our lives and experience victory.

Did you know that the secret of David's success is not a secret? It is found in **Psalm 132**

At the time of writing, David was being hunted by the jealous King Saul, who was paranoid that one day David would usurp him as king, causing Saul to track David into the wilderness. But David had a personal relationship with God. He knew who he was and even how much God loved him. In turn, this gave him the confidence to defeat a lion and a bear with his own hands and defeat Goliath with one stone and outlive and outlast the mighty King Saul.

In the first book of Chronicles, David says, "Howbeit the Lord God of Israel chose me before all the house of my Father to be King over Israel forever; for he hath chosen Judah to be the ruler, and of the house of Judah, the house of my Father, and among the sons of my Father he liked me to make me king over all Israel. (I Chronicles 28:4)

Notice how David said. "God liked him."

Now again, why did God like him?

Why was he so special?

I believe it is because David grasped something that many others before and after him have failed to get?

For example, while being hunted by Saul, David also wrote in Psalm 132, "Lord remember David and all his afflictions, 'how he swore to the Lord, and vowed to the mighty one of Jacob, "Surely I will not go into the chamber of my house, or go up to the comfort of my bed, I will not give sleep to my eyes or slumber to my eyelids until I find a place for the Lord, a dwelling place for the mighty one of Jacob out of Israel. **Psalm 132:1-5**

In short, David stated how his biggest priority, even more than sleep to his eyes, was bringing the Ark of the Covenant back to Jerusalem.

Here are two principal reasons why David was seen as "a man after God's heart."

Firstly, he knew deep in his heart that he was much liked and even loved by God.

And secondly, he was prepared to do everything in his power to serve the Lord in his generation. Finally, even as a teenager, David showed excellent character in the face of the frightening Goliath stating in **1 Samuel 17:29**, "Is there not a cause?"

While many others were fearful of the prolific Philistine, Goliath, the young David asked the most important question which can be addressed to the mystery of life. David was well aware of the giant's strength before him and his fellow citizens, and he observed their great fear. Despite his tender years, however, David had an interest in the things of God, and there was a destiny in his life when he was called forth by God to face the giant Goliath. Hence, David was not only called; he was chosen!

I once said, "Until a giant comes into your life, you will remain a shepherd boy," and I believe this is true. All great leaders and people have first faced their giants before experiencing their victories.

Interestingly, Eliab, David's elder brother, rebuked David for his faith; alas, the Church is still bugged by such critics. If Eliab's anger had been turned on Goliath instead of David, he might have been of some use to Israel. But, instead, Eliab talked loudly but vainly; he didn't see that there was a cause. Yet David didn't just see a reason; he noticed a cause even more incredible than himself. That cause turned a boy into a man, who would run through a troop and leap over a wall and tunnel through a mountain one day.

By contrast, King Saul offered gifts to anyone who would take on Goliath rather than repenting and turning to God.

Here were two Kings with two different natures and hearts. David loved a cause greater than himself, and, in return, God loved him."

Even at the end of his life, when a pestilence was in the land, he insisted on paying for the threshing floor to build an altar stating: "I will not offer burnt offerings unto the Lord my God of that which doth cost me nothing" **2 Samuel 24:24**

As we close this book, I have been asked many times for the secret of my success at Whitewell. I suppose it can only be explained in the same way as David.

God loved me, and I responded to His cause. It is as simple as that. Of course, there were better preachers than me, more gifted administrators, and even better-educated vessels, but God loved me, and I loved Him.

Like David, even as a young man, I always felt greatly loved by God and decided to dedicate my life to His calling. That cause was the preaching of the gospel of the Kingdom of God, and I never deviated from it.

In other words, I put God's cause before my aspirations, and God rewarded this faithfulness.

In Psalm 132, David adds the words "Arise, O Lord, to your resting place. You and the Ark of your strength."

Just as David had prioritised taking back the Ark of the Covenant, I can honestly say I have dedicated my life to prioritising the Kingdom of God and preaching about the love of God found in Jesus Christ.

But here is the question - is there not a similar cause remaining for the last generation, also?

Is it not time to unveil Jesus again in the same way David determined to serve the Lord and restore the Ark to its rightful place?

There is no greater satisfaction for any person or preacher than to feel the pleasure of leading men and women to the Saviour. I have had this privilege all my life, and nothing compares to it.

However, according to the scriptures, as we enter the last of the last days, if Jesus Christ is not the central part of a ministry, the fullness of His blessings cannot and will not flow inside or outside the Church.

Some grace exponents believe their priority is to preach the message of grace, and while this is good, the greatest need is to bring Jesus back into the forefront of the Church, and, of course, it naturally follows that His grace will follow.

Just as David was called in his generation to bring the Ark of the Covenant back to Jerusalem, it is time for this generation to get Jesus back to Mount Zion.

What does this mean?

It means bringing Him back to a central position in the Church, not relegating him to occasional sermons. Paul stated, "Preach Christ and Him Crucified," and without this focus, a minister's message is likely to lack power and the grace of God and be diminished.

So, if you would like to know and experience God's mantle in your life, two final tips for all aspiring preachers and believers of all backgrounds are: Understand and believe that God loves you with unconditional love and then give His cause all you've got.

It worked for an Old Testament King many centuries ago, and it worked for an everyday man centuries later.

There is only one thing that the Pastor really wants to be remembered for.

Nothing else!

"That I have taught my congregation to love the Lord Jesus Christ as I have loved him, from a boy. And even those that have died and been buried and those that are in hospital when I go and visit them, they say the same thing - Pastor McConnell you taught us how to love the Lord Jesus Christ. That's the only thing I want, that's the only thing I desire.

And if that is my epitaph, that's a great epitaph - that I taught people to love the Lord Jesus Christ. And you can't teach people to love the Lord Jesus, unless you love him yourself and I have loved him and loved him from a boy and still love him and He's a wonderful Saviour."

JAMES MCCONNELL

15th May 1937 - 17th July 2021

For further information: www.whitewell.church